This book is written to meet the needs of students following the syllabus requirements of BTEC, the HCIMA examinations and City and Guilds courses; and also to provide thoroughly up-to-date works of reference for all those engaged in the business of running hotels, catering establishments and tourist services.

GW00384478

General Editor
Dr Edwin Kerr
*Chief Officer, Council for National
Academic Awards*

Subject Editor
D. Ashen
*Head of Department of
Hotel and Catering Studies,
Plymouth College of Further Education*

To my long-suffering colleagues.

Housekeeping Supervision

JANE FELLOWS
MHCIMA
Lecturer, Huddersfield Polytechnic

Pitman

PITMAN PUBLISHING LIMITED
128 Long Acre, London WC2E 9AN

A Longman Group Company

© Pitman Publishing Limited 1984

First published in Great Britain 1984
Reprinted 1985, 1986

All rights reserved. No part of this publication may be reproduced,
stored in a retrieval system, or transmitted, in any form or by any
means, electronic, mechanical, photocopying, recording and/or
otherwise, without the prior written permission of the publishers.
This book may not be lent, resold, hired out or otherwise disposed of
by way of trade in any form of binding or cover other than that in
which it is published, without the prior consent of the publishers.

ISBN 0-273-02552-X

Printed and bound in Great Britain by
Richard Clay (The Chaucer Press) Ltd,
Bungay, Suffolk

Preface

In recent years housekeeping has become recognised as an area of work which, if carried out efficiently, can have a considerable influence on the profitability of an organisation. The introduction of the Health and Safety at Work Act has reinforced this attitude with the result that many college courses have been revised or re-written.

This book provides up-to-date information on practical housekeeping procedures and the appropriate theoretical knowledge to enable a housekeeping supervisor to maintain the standards of hygiene and comfort expected of establishments offering accommodation to the public. It begins by summarising the various sectors of the accommodation industry which require a housekeeping service. Chapters 2–6 provide detailed information on the equipment and chemicals used by housekeeping staff together with guidelines for when and how to use them on the variety of textiles and hard fabrics for which they are likely to be needed. Chapter 7 explains the responsibilities of supervisory staff and describes how the work of the housekeeping department is divided among its staff. A collection of job descriptions is included in Appendix II to re-inforce this information. The final chapter deals with the internal environment and describes how house-keeping staff can assist in the control of noise, light, pest infestation, fire and accidents. The book concludes with a series of case studies which it is hoped will help students to relate their theoretical knowledge to realistic situations and prompt discussion on a wide variety of topics.

This book should help housekeeping/cleaning supervisors to cope with all aspects of their work and provide students with the type of information they require for the following examinations:

BTEC Diploma and Certificate
HCIMA Part A
City and Guilds: 700/2 Specific Skill Scheme for Room
                  Attendants
               705 General Catering
               708 Accommodation Services
               764 Cleaning Science
MSC sponsored courses in hotel and catering subjects

I should like to acknowledge the kind assistance of the following people and organisations without whom I could not have completed this book:

Trust House Forte Hotels Ltd.;
Holiday Inns;
Huddersfield Polytechnic;
Rentokil Ltd;
Consumers' Association;
Lever Brothers;
P. L. G..Bateman;
Department of Health and Social Security.

1984 JF

Contents

CHAPTER ONE

The Accommodation Industry

CHAPTER OBJECTIVES

After studying this chapter you should be able to:
* outline the scope of the accommodation industry;
* define areas of potential custom;
* identify the aims of the various sectors of the industry;
* understand the role of housekeeping in each sector of the industry.

INTRODUCTION

The accommodation industry covers all those places that provide away-from-home sleeping and/or living accommodation. The general aim of all such establishments should be to provide their customers with clean, attractive, comfortable and welcoming surroundings which offer value for money.

Tables I and II indicate the scope of the industry. Each type of establishment has its own organisational structure, but in every case the housekeeping department plays a vital part in achieving the aims of the business:

Every type of establishment should aim at maximum utilisation of every facility it offers. If this is to be achieved, much reliance, is put on the housekeeping department to ensure that those

TABLE I. HOUSEKEEPING IN DIFFERENT TYPES OF ESTABLISHMENT.

Type of establishment	Aim of housekeeping department
Hotels Boarding houses Motels Holiday camps	To provide quick and thorough servicing of bedrooms and public areas to a consistently high standard and with as little inconvenience to the guest as possible.
Hospitals Nursing homes Convalescent homes Hospices	To operate a thorough, unobtrusive, regular cleaning programme aimed at reducing the dangers of cross-infection and meeting the need for the surroundings to be pleasant.
Hostels Local authority homes	To provide a regular if somewhat less frequent cleaning service which is sufficient to maintain acceptable standards of cleanliness within the confines of a budget.

TABLE II. CATERING FOR DIFFERENT CUSTOMERS.

Period away from home	Type of customer	Basic requirements	Establishments able to offer these requirements
1–24 hours	Businessmen/ women, VIPs travellers	Interview rooms Reception rooms Changing rooms Bedroom Business equipment, etc.	Hotels Motels Hostels Boarding houses
1–2 weeks	Conference delegates Holidaymakers The infirm The aged	Bedrooms Meeting rooms Lecture theatres Recreation areas Day rooms/ lounges Operating theatres and related areas Bars	Hotels Hostels Boarding houses Holiday camps Nursing homes Hospitals Local authority homes
Long term	Students The infirm The aged Seasonal staff Businessmen/ women School children	Bedroom/ dormitory Suites Utility rooms Laundry areas Leisure areas	Hostels Nursing homes Staff houses Hospitals Convalescent homes Local authority homes Flats Boarding schools
Permanent	Resident staff Handicapped Homeless Young offenders Chronically ill Nurses	Bedroom/ dormitory Kitchen Leisure areas Laundry areas Sun lounges	Hostels Hospitals Nursing homes Nurses homes Hospices Local authority homes Flats Staff houses

facilities are maintained throughout the twenty-four hour period to a standard which accords with management policy. If this is not achieved, the result may be substantial loss of custom and therefore revenue.

Facilities provided in the accommodation industry are extremely varied and are constantly changing. It is essential therefore that the housekeeping department is adaptable and able to cope with the introduction of more complicated work procedures such as those needed to maintain squash courts, computer rooms, Jacuzzi baths, saunas and certain medical facilities. The department should also be in touch with new developments regarding wall, floor and furniture finishes together with the cleaning materials needed to maintain them. Many businesses now feel that housekeeping is sufficiently complicated to warrant the services of an outside cleaning contractor to carry out the work, but even this system requires supervision by one of their own employees with knowledge of the work involved.

HOTELS

Hotels vary in shape, size and age, factors which together with the hotel's location dictate the work of the housekeeping department. The way in which the housekeeping is organised depends not only on the number of bedrooms but also on what the hotel believes the customer wants. As well as being a place to eat and sleep a hotel should be able to offer facilities for business meetings, special functions and exhibitions, and provide an atmosphere in which guests feel they are able to relax and perhaps pursue some leisure activity.

Modern marketing techniques require that hotel rooms are very flexible in their use. Bedrooms may therefore contain bed/settees or flip-up beds and have connecting doors or sliding partitions to allow for the provision of a suite or reception room. Ergonomically, the housekeeping department has benefited from the reduction in the size of the standard bedroom in order to provide all bedrooms with a private bathroom.

As commercial enterprises, hotels have had to modify many of the more labour-intensive traditions. In some cases this has led to the introduction of a less personal service (e.g. shoe shine machines), but in others there has been an increase in the services offered for which the housekeeping department is responsible such as the adoption of automatic morning call alarms and room status boards, and the provision of mini bars and gift packs. Consequently the work of the housekeeping staff is constantly changing with more of their time being spent on non-cleaning duties such as replenishing advertising material. Constant room usage throughout the day and night has also meant that cleaning of all areas has to be very closely monitored if standards are to be maintained. The important job of monitoring is usually the responsibility of the supervisor.

Housekeeping within the hotel organisation

In small hotels, that is those with less than sixty bedrooms, the assistant manager may undertake to organise the housekeeping duties (*see* Fig. 1). Much reliance may be put on part-time staff as the majority of the work can be completed in the morning. Many hotels of this size are open for only one season in the year. They employ a core of staff for the season who might be expected to work in all sections of the hotel as required. These staff are invariably untrained but capable.

Fig. 1. *Organisation structure of a small hotel (less than 60 rooms).*

As the number of bedrooms increases, so the housekeeping department warrants more supervisory and managerial staff. Figures 2 and 3 illustrate how the person responsible for housekeeping fits into the overall structure of a medium-sized and large hotel organisation.

Fig. 2. *Organisation structure of a medium-sized hotel (60–200 rooms).*

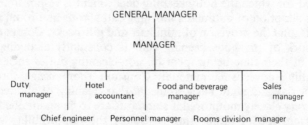

Fig. 3. *Organisation structure of a large hotel (over 200 rooms).*

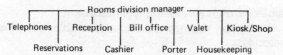

Fig. 4. *Organisation structure of rooms division in a large hotel.*

Figure 2 shows that in a medium-sized hotel the head house-keeper is a departmental head responsible directly to an assistant manager who most likely will have fairly scant knowledge of house-keeping, whereas in a large hotel the head housekeeper is responsible for one section only of the rooms division (*see* Fig. 4). The housekeeper in the smaller establishment will therefore probably have more responsibility than her counterpart in the larger one, and she will need to be able to co-operate with other departmental heads. This ability to work in harmony with other departments is vital because unlike any other departmental head, the housekeeper has responsibilities in all areas of the hotel from the provision of clean uniforms for chefs and cleaning materials for the kitchen to periodic cleaning of the restaurant and bars.

Role of supervisors
Like most departments in a hotel, housekeeping has a budget. It is the housekeeper's responsibility to organise her department in such a way that this budget is adhered to. To do this she has to rely a great deal on her supervisory team to monitor and train the semi-skilled staff in the performance of their duties, making sure that they work efficiently, using the correct cleaning materials, equip-ment and methods. The supervisory staff must therefore have a thorough knowledge of the cleaning materials used by the hotel as well as experience in the practical methods established by the housekeeper. The supervisors themselves should constantly update their knowledge in order that they may instruct and control with confidence.

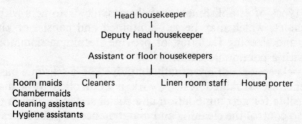

Fig. 5. *Organisation structure of housekeeping department in a large hotel.*

Responsibilities of housekeeping department

The housekeeping department is responsible for the daily maintenance of:

(a) bedrooms;
(b) corridors;
(c) public and private bathrooms;
(d) public cloakrooms;
(e) lifts,
(f) reception desk and related areas,
(g) offices;
(h) staff areas;
(i) ballrooms and conference rooms.

They will not, however, be required to maintain the kitchens, restaurants and bars except on a periodic basis when more thorough cleaning is necessary. All departments will be supplied with cleaning materials by the housekeeping department.

Figure 5 shows how the housekeeping department would be organised in a large hotel.

BOARDING HOUSES, PRIVATE HOTELS AND BED AND BREAKFAST

These establishments are similar to the continental *pension* offering lower-priced accommodation to families or businessmen requiring a homely, less formal atmosphere. As they have on average up to ten bedrooms, it is usually the owner or manager who is responsible for letting and servicing rooms, with the assistance of two or three staff, and the services and facilities offered are very limited. Such establishments form a substantial part of the tourist industry with many of them opening for eight months only each year (depending on the part of the country they are in).

HOLIDAY CAMPS

These types of establishment usually provide customers with their own chalet, which may be self-contained and consist of kitchen, dining and sleeping facilities, or provide sleeping accommodation only with a communal eating area.

Housekeeping staff are usually employed on a seasonal basis and are generally unskilled. Their work is controlled by a manager responsible for accommodation and social services. Such a person will also control the cleaning and maintenance of public areas, e.g. ballrooms, dining rooms, sports areas, bars, etc.

The work of the housekeeping staff, or chalet maids as they may be called, involves daily rubbish removal and thorough cleaning of all chalets, including the changing of linen, when guests leave. Linen will usually be washed on the camp site. Each maid will be allocated a group of chalets which will have its own set of cleaning equipment and materials. The type of service offered is a combination of hostel and hotel work, i.e. the minimum of cleaning in occupied chalets but thorough cleaning and extensive replacement of supplies such as rubbish sacks, soap, toilet paper, menu cards, camp notices, etc. at the end of each week.

Problems may arise during bad weather which can restrict the movement of staff and equipment between buildings.

HOSTELS

These are distinguished from hotels by the length of time their residents stay. This can vary from three weeks to three months to permanent. Many are provided by employers for their employees, e.g. nurses homes, or by universities and polytechnics for their students. Other organisations such as the YMCA, HM Forces and the Salvation Army also provide hostels. Room letting and allocation in a hostel is usually carried out by an administrator who may have one of a number of titles from hall manager to steward or bursar. This person takes overall responsibility for the financial control of the establishment. The day-to-day running is delegated to managers with specialist knowledge in individual areas such as catering and housekeeping (*see* Fig. 6).

In order to keep within a budget, labour costs are kept to a minimum. This can be done in the housekeeping department only by adopting simple work procedures and by asking the residents to perform certain tasks themselves such as making their own beds, changing their sheets and keeping their rooms reasonably tidy so that cleaning staff need only enter the bedrooms to empty the rubbish bins, carrying out a more thorough periodic clean when convenient to the resident, e.g. at the end of term or when the occupant is on leave. As a result cleaning staff may be part-time, with most of their work being concerned with maintaining the public areas

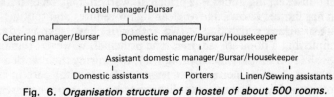

Fig. 6. *Organisation structure of a hostel of about 500 rooms.*

(games rooms, bars, TV lounges, etc.), dealing with linen and buffing or vacuuming corridors.

Student hostels are often used by the conference trade during vacations, which involves the upgrading of cleaning frequencies and standards—towels, soap, ashtrays and tea-making equipment may be provided and rooms will be cleaned daily. These conferences help to keep the cost of the rooms down for residents.

In order to cater for longer periods of stay, hostels must provide considerably more storage space than that found in hotels. The typical study bedroom will contain wardrobe, desk, shelves, washbasin, bed, drawers and either a pin board or walls designed and finished in such a way that the occupant can pin up posters, etc. without too much damage.

Hostels can be very friendly places to work in as staff get to know the residents more easily and may join in the life of the hostel, attending dances, discos, meetings, sports events, etc.

LOCAL AUTHORITY HOMES

Local authorities have to provide residential accommodation for a number of different categories of people in need including pensioners who are unable to cope on their own, children left without parents, the mentally and physically handicapped and young offenders. Such accommodation is usually longterm, although homes may offer one or two places on a short-term basis to give families a break from the routine care of dependent relations. Such establishments provide sleeping accommodation, which may be in a single or double room or a dormitory of several beds, washing facilities, storage space and appropriate recreational facilities. To cope with the special needs of residents, trained care staff work alongside the cleaning and catering staff to provide a clean, comfortable and homely atmosphere for the residents. The housekeeping duties in these establishments are fairly simple but must be performed frequently. The work demands that cleaning staff be tolerant and able to cope with some unpleasantness which is bound to arise on occasions.

Unlike a hotel manager who has most probably had some training in housekeeping duties, the principal, warden, matron or bursar often has limited knowledge of cleaning procedures and routines—a state of affairs which one or two authorities have acknowledged by employing a domestic adviser. The principal, however, remains responsible for employing cleaning staff, organising their work and purchasing cleaning materials. Cleaning plays a vital part in the smooth running of these establishments as the residents create problems which rarely occur in hotels and hostels, e.g. incontinency, clumsiness in the handicapped resulting in spillages and breakages, or vandalism in the case of young offenders, all of which could create costly maintenance bills.

HOSPITALS

The Health Service has long since recognised the importance of cleanliness and the part it plays in reducing the threat of cross-infection, with the result that housekeeping in hospitals is highly organised, often pioneering new methods and testing new products and equipment. Control of dust and germs are all important and to this end cleaning equipment has features which may not be found in other establishments; such as the following:

(*a*) electrical equipment is fitted with extra filters to reduce the risks of dust distribution;

(*b*) electrical equipment may be fitted with silencers to minimise irritation for patients;

(*c*) colours are used to identify equipment for certain jobs, e.g. green cloths, buckets, mops, gloves, etc. for toilet areas, pink for kitchen areas, etc.

Cleaning methods may also differ slightly, for example:

(*a*) dusting is carried out with damp cloths only so that dust is controlled;

(*b*) sweeping is carried out by using mops with heads which can be sterilised or disposed of after each session of cleaning;

(*c*) spray cleaning is carried out regularly using high-speed machinery which performs in such a way that highly resistant finishes are obtained on floorings.

Dust control mats are used extensively and surfaces tend to be non-absorbent, making them easy to clean and less likely to retain dust.

The scope of the hospital housekeeping department is enormous. It extends to operating theatres, lecture rooms, mortuaries, kitchens, dining areas, treatment rooms and waiting areas. Some areas require constant attention (e.g. geriatric wards) whereas others require hardly any. Many hospitals undertake to provide and maintain accommodation for doctors and nurses, and these may also be the responsibility of the housekeeping department. As in local authority homes, cleaning has to take place at times convenient to doctors, nurses and visitors.

Fig. 7. *Organisation structure of housekeeping department in a hospital.*

The structure of such a department inevitably varies according to the size and type of hospital, but generally the arrangement will be as in Fig. 7.

NURSING HOMES, CONVALESCENT HOMES AND HOSPICES

These establishments may be privately owned or run by the local authority. Some are run by HM Forces for war veterans and rely considerably on voluntary contributions. Hospices are homes for the terminally ill and may be adopted by health authorities once they have been set up by donations. All are organised in a similar way to that of a small hospital but, like many old people's homes, the staff in charge are usually trained nurses with only a limited knowledge of cleaning, and standards therefore depend very much on the common sense of cleaning staff.

CONTRACT CLEANING COMPANIES

Many organisations appreciate that their premises must be kept clean and in good repair but accept that they know little about how to organise such work satisfactorily. They therefore employ the services of a company which specialises in cleaning. Such firms are contracted for a specified period, e.g. three years, to carry out certain cleaning tasks to a pre-arranged standard and for an agreed sum of money. Cleaning contractors may be employed in many different situations such as hospitals, office blocks, schools, hotels, shops and hostels. Staff are usually employed on a part-time basis and may have very little training. Promotion to supervisor usually occurs with length of service and will probably be accompanied by some formal training. The type of work will vary according to the nature of the client but will usually involve daily cleaning tasks. Some companies specialise in one type of cleaning such as carpet cleaning, high-level cleaning or floor sealing.

SELF-ASSESSMENT QUESTIONS

1. How does the type of customer affect the work of the housekeeping department of an accommodation establishment?

2. In what ways can the work of the housekeeping department affect the profitability of an accommodation establishment?

3. Describe how the size of an accommodation establishment can affect the work carried out by the head housekeeper.

4. Outline the work-load of the housekeeping department in each sector of the accommodation industry.

CHAPTER TWO

The Tools of the Trade

CHAPTER OBJECTIVES

After studying this chapter you should be able to:
* outline the variety of equipment used by cleaning staff;
* appreciate the importance of controlling the use and storage of cleaning equipment;
* understand when to use cleaning equipment and how to look after it.

INTRODUCTION

Cleaning equipment may be purchased outright, hired or possibly leased, but in all cases it should be selected by someone with a thorough knowledge and experience of cleaning. This should be the domestic manager or housekeeper depending on the type of establishment. (Contract cleaning companies may supply their own equipment.) No cleaning equipment, however, is effective unless it is kept in good working order and used correctly. Considerable costs may be incurred through inadequate control of cleaning equipment and supplies and it is up to the supervisors to ensure that what is purchased is used correctly.

STORAGE

A cleaning store will have to provide space for:

(a) machinery;
(b) tools and containers;
(c) chemicals (see Chapter 3).

It must be kept clean and well ordered otherwise items will become damaged and may be mislaid—a state of affairs which will encourage pilfering and lead to a loss of efficiency.

The housekeeper/manager is responsible for instituting a system of control but it is up to the supervisors to ensure the system is adhered to. It may mean that certain items are allocated special storage positions, e.g. vacuum cleaners and trolleys kept on certain floors or blocks, in which case a weekly inspection of such an arrangement must take place to ensure the items are being stored and maintained correctly. Wherever equipment is stored, it must be possible to lock it away.

MAINTENANCE

Daily maintenance of cleaning equipment is the responsibility of individual operatives. It is very easy to assume that certain simple maintenance tasks will be carried out without telling staff to do them, e.g. emptying dust bags or washing out cloths. However, it is very often these basic if somewhat unpleasant tasks which get neglected resulting in quite serious problems—machine motors become damaged and standards of cleanliness fall.

All new staff should undergo a period of induction during which they are informed about:

(a) when to use equipment;
(b) how to use equipment;
(c) how to clean each item;
(d) where to clean equipment;
(e) how often to attend to equipment;
(f) how to obtain assistance if required;
(g) where to obtain supplies of brushes, dust bags, rubber gloves, etc.

It is the job of the supervisor to inform new staff of these matters and to check their work regularly. They should also stress the importance of safety procedures especially when using machinery, e.g. use of warning signs, (*see also* Chapter 7, Induction). Whenever new equipment is issued, information about its correct use should be passed on to existing staff.

During the course of her duties, a supervisor may discover valid reasons for staff failing to perform these simple maintenance tasks, for example:

(a) lack of space in which to do them;
(b) absence of staff;
(c) poor facilities for drying cloths, brushes, etc.;
(d) increased workloads resulting in lack of time.

All these situations should be investigated and reported to the departmental manager immediately.

MACHINERY

Most machinery is powered by electricity but some may be powered by gas, steam or air pressure; the last of these has the advantage of being very quiet. The machinery for which a supervisor is most often responsible on a day-to-day basis is that used for floor maintenance. Other items are used in the laundry or linen room.

TABLE III. USE AND MAINTENANCE OF MACHINERY.

Equipment	Types	Uses	Attachments	Storage	Care
Dry suction machines	Electric broom Dustette Back pack vacuum Upright vacuum Cylinder vacuum Built-in vacuum	Removing surface dust and small pieces of debris from walls, floors, ceilings, soft furnishings and furniture	Flexible hose Extension tubes Power head Hard/soft floor head Dusting head Crevice head Upholstery head (*See also* Fig. 8)	Hang hoses on hooks. Place tubes in boxes. Place heads in boxes, drawers or on shelves.	Check dust bags after use. Wipe casing daily and check flex and hose. Clean head after use. Oil wheels when necessary. Check filter after use.
Wet suction machines	May be combined with a scrubbing machine	Removing waste liquids or solutions from floors or containers	Bucket or tank Squeegee Hose	On machine, exposed to air and off ground if possible.	Empty, wash, rinse and dry bucket. Wipe squeegee and replace when necessary. Rinse out hose. Wipe casing and wheels after use. Check filter after use.
Wet/dry suction machines	Dry suction only Wet suction only Wet/Dry simultaneously	(As wet and dry suction machines)			

Machine	Types	Use	Parts	Storage	Care
General purpose floor machine	Single, double, triple brush. With or without suction	Buffing, polishing, stripping polishes and seals, scrubbing, shampooing; usually on floors but may be adapted for use on upholstery	Brushes Drive discs Pads Tank Shampoo tank Spray	Place discs and pads on hooks or shelves. Fit tops of tanks loosely.	*Brushes.* Remove fluff, etc. Wash, rinse and dry wet ones after use and dry ones occasionally. *Pads.* As above. Empty, wash, rinse and dry tanks. Wipe wheels and casing after use. Check flex, etc.
Shampooers	Rotary brush Cylindrical brush Steam extraction Sonic	Removing ingrained dirt from soft floor surfaces and upholstered furniture	Hoses Extension tubes Tanks Brushes Plates	Hang hoses on hooks. Place tubes in boxes. Tanks with lids loosely attached. Brushes with bristles horizontal. Plates on shelves.	As general purpose machine

Table Continued

TABLE III. (*Continued*).

Equipment	Types	Uses	Care
Irons	Hand, dry Hand, steam Press Rotary Specialised irons	Small shaped items Small flat items Flat items Overalls, shirts	*Hand irons.* Use distilled water only and empty after use. Allow iron to cool before winding flex around it. Store upright. Occasionally rub sole plate over coarse fabric while warm, to remove any stickiness. Clean plate with a solvent, mild abrasive or fine steel wool. *Mechanical irons.* Keep covered when not in use. Never leave unattended when on. Place buttons, zips, etc. away from plate.
Washing machines	Automatic: top loading front loading Twin tub: pulsator agitator	Soft fabrics as specified by the Codes (*see* Chapter 4)	Do not overload—weigh items first. Ensure water is turned on and off at appropriate times for automatics. Keep soap dispensers clear and clean. Do not bang doors. Leave doors and lids open slightly until thoroughly dry inside. Wipe outer casing after use. Clean filters after use. Store hoses correctly after use. Use rubber guard in twin tub spinners.

Spin dryers	Varying sizes May be combined with a washer	Removing excess water from soft fabrics	Load evenly. Do not overload. Keep lid open until thoroughly dry. Do not attempt to remove items before completely still.
Tumble dryers	Manual control Electronic control Reverse tumble Intermittent tumble	Reduces ironing requirements Dries fabrics as required	Do not overload. Load correctly (shake items out). Clean filters after use. Do not bang door.
Sewing machines	Hand Electric Electronic Industrial	Repair work Making up uniforms and soft furnishings Applying labels and tapes, etc.	Keep covered when not in use. Remove fluff, etc. frequently. Use correct needles, thread, etc. Oil occasionally.

Table III summarises the most popular equipment and indicates how each should be maintained.

Some machines can be adapted to perform several tasks. It is the supervisor's responsibility to ensure that each set of tools is maintained in a clean state, with all items kept together, and is fitted on to the machine correctly when required, otherwise the machine will not perform efficiently.

General care of electrical cleaning equipment

(*a*) Check flex and plug frequently.

(*b*) Use only with dry hands.

(*c*) Report damage or unusual noises immediately.

(*d*) Machines using water have a float valve which automatically cuts off the motor when the water level inside the machine reaches a certain level. This valve must be kept in working order.

(*e*) Rubber plugs withstand use better.

(*f*) Always use the nearest available socket and take care with trailing flexes.

TOOLS AND CONTAINERS

Figures 8–13 illustrate some of the many different items of cleaning equipment.

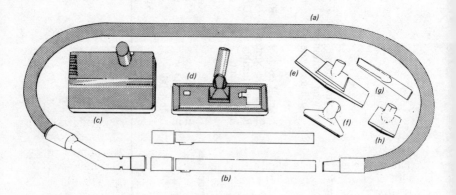

Fig. 8. *Dry suction machine attachments.*
(a) *Hose;* (b) *hose extensions;* (c) *power brush;* (d) *carpet and floor tool;* (e) *floor and wall brush;* (f) *upholstery nozzle;* (g) *crevice tool;* (h) *dusting brush.*

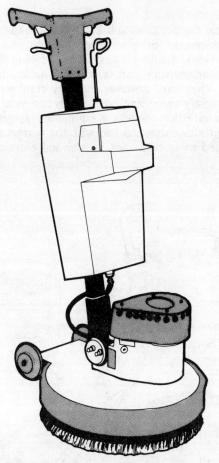

Fig. 9. *Scrubbing machine with tank.*

Cleaners' boxes

Cleaning staff find work a lot less tiring if they have a container, such as a bucket, basket or box, in which to carry their basic equipment from room to room. Some manufacturers now supply specially designed containers for use with their own products so that staff can see at a glance that they have everything they need with them and have not left anything behind in a room. (The shape of the box is obviously designed for the manufacturer's own products.) These must be kept clean and be labelled according to the area in which they are to be used. They must be kept topped up with the appropriate items so that they are always ready for use.

Trolleys

These are ideal for use in establishments where there is a need for constant replacement of a variety of items, e.g. linen, soap, beverage portions, laundry bags, shoe cleaning cloths, tissues, shower caps, advertising leaflets, rubbish sacks, toilet rolls and menu cards. They can, however, be very cumbersome and look extremely unsightly unless stacked correctly and neatly. A supervisor should make sure that trolleys are not used as general dumping areas but kept adequately stocked with the correct items. Trolleys must be locked away when not in use, and emptied and cleaned once a week.

Fig. 10. *Floor cleaning equipment.*
(a) *Step-on roller bucket;* (b) *bucket on castors;* (c) *janitorial trolley;* (d) *double bucket;* (e) *polish applicators;* (f) *floor squeegees;* (g) *mop holders;* (h) *edging tool;* (i) *magistrip;* (j) *dish;* (k) *floor scraper;* (l) *Kentucky mop;* (m) *mop wringer.*

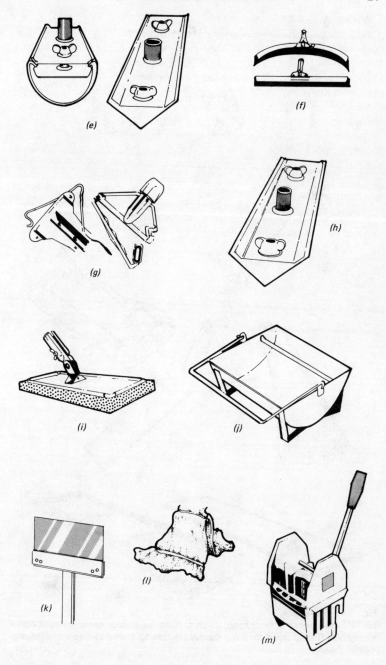

(e)

(f)

(g)

(h)

(i)

(j)

(k)

(l)

(m)

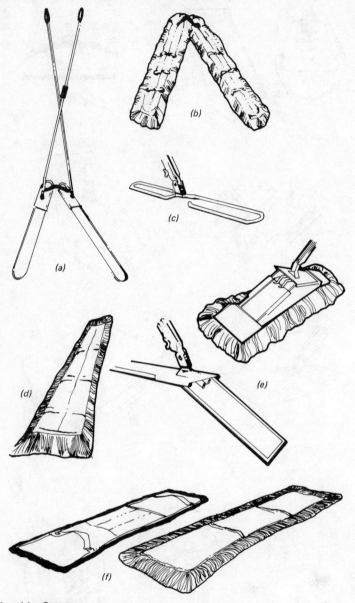

Fig. 11. *Sweepers.*
(a) *"V" sweeper or scissor mop; (b) mop head for scissor mop; (c) fixed frame sweeper; (d) mop head for fixed frame; (e) folding frame sweepers; (f) damp-sweep heads.*

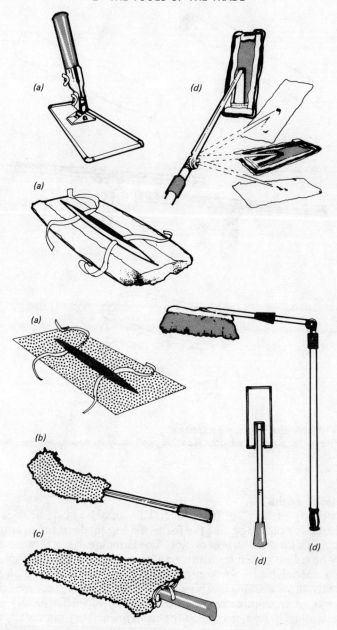

Fig. 12. *Special purpose tools.*
(a) *Wall/window washers;* (b) *pipe duster;* (c) *wall duster;* (d) *wall mops.*

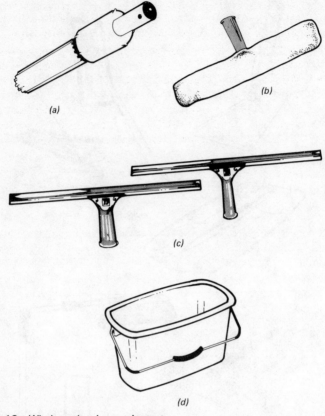

Fig. 13. *Window cleaning equipment.*
(a) *Telescopic pole;* (b) *window washing applicator;* (c) *squeegees;* (d) *plastic bucket.*

Laundry sacks

These may or may not be mobile. They may be made of wicker, fibreglass or plastic or take the form of a bag made of tough cotton or nylon with draw strings or zips. The latter are easier to store and may be colour coded to identify different types of linen. Hospitals use a special fabric for contaminated linen which can be placed directly into a washing machine where it will dissolve, thus reducing the risk of cross-infection. Baskets must be wiped frequently and bags washed before being used for clean linen. They are usually the property of the laundry but any losses or damage may be charged to the establishment.

Laundry carts

These are necessary in large complexes which have several buildings, e.g. hospitals, holiday camps and university campuses, as linen may have to be transferred to a central collection point in all weathers. They are often made of aluminium, which is light but may get damaged easily, so supervisors should ensure that they are kept clean, their wheels oiled and that they are kept in a dry, well-ordered storage area.

Buckets

These may be metal or plastic. Those used with mops may have one or two sections and usually have a wringer device of some sort which should be detachable for easy cleaning. The larger buckets have castors which must be kept clean and free from dust and dirt. Coloured buckets can be identified easily for use in certain areas or for special tasks, e.g. toilets or in operating theatres. All buckets should have labels indicating where they belong. To prevent them becoming a source of contamination they should be thoroughly washed and rinsed inside and out every time they have been used and stored dry.

Waste bins

These are used at three different stages during cleaning.

(a) *In individual rooms.* Such bins should be emptied daily and wiped or washed once a week.

(b) *On cleaners' trolleys.* Here they are used to collect waste from individual rooms. There should be two, one made of metal for waste found in ashtrays to prevent the risks of fire, and the other of paper or plastic which will incinerate easily.

Some large establishments have a waste chute built into the structure of the building. These must be kept clear and should not be used for ashes or cigarette ends.

Cleaners should have an ample supply of waste sacks and should be told to seal them when full and store them in a safe place for collection by porters.

(c) *In waste collection areas.* These are usually outside the building, hidden from view. Bins should be kept covered and be swilled out weekly if possible. If this is not done pests are likely to appear and may find their way into the building. An untidy bin area is often an indication of a poor standard of hygiene inside the building.

Dustpans

These are used in conjunction with a brush for removing superficial dust and dirt and may be metal or plastic. They should always be emptied after use and occasionally washed. They should be labelled clearly as to where they are to be used, and stored either suspended from a hook or on the wide edge to avoid damaging the flat edge. Some have long handles and a lid for ease of use and to prevent dust distribution. These should be checked for cleanliness regularly.

Polish trays

These are use when applying liquid polish to floors with a polish applicator mop. Both items must be clearly labelled as to the type of polish they are used with, e.g. spirit or water based. Cleaning them after use is difficult. The best way is to pour any excess polish back into the container and soak the tray in a little of the solution used to remove the polish, finishing off by wiping round with a dry cloth.

Sanibins

These are used in female toilets for storing soiled sanitary dressings. They should be emptied and wiped daily—a task made more pleasant by providing staff with rubber gloves and by placing paper bags in the toilets. Care of sanibins is frequently undertaken by specialist firms. The efficiency of such a service must be closely monitored by supervisors.

Cloths

These may be used for wet or dry work and controlling their use can be difficult. Different cloths are designed for specific purposes, but generally speaking the fewer available for staff to choose from the better. Hospitals use damp cloths only, to avoid dust distribution. They also use a colour code system, e.g. green for toilets and sluices, pink for kitchens. It is important that such a system is well supervised. Many cloths nowadays are disposable, in which case care should be taken to ensure that they are disposed of immediately after use. Tables IV and V summarise the most frequently found cleaning cloths and indicate when they should be used.

Brushes

These are used to remove ingrained dust from hard or soft surfaces. It would be impossible to identify every kind of brush or broom likely to be found in a cleaning store, but all of them are made up of three basic parts: bristles, stock and handle.

TABLE IV. CLOTHS USED FOR CLEANING.

Cloth	Uses	Care
Duster	(a) Collecting dust (b) Rubbing surfaces up to a shine	Wash, rinse and dry after use (wash yellow dusters separately)
Dusting mitten	As for duster	May be impregnated with oil or polish after washing, in which case the head should be kept covered when not in use
Rag	Applying polish or strong cleaning agent	Dispose of after use (storage of strong smelling polish cloths is a fire hazard)
All-purpose damp cloth	(a) Damp dusting all surfaces above floor (b) Removing sticky marks from surfaces above floor (c) Daily cleaning of sanitary fittings	Wash, rinse and dry after use; if used on toilets disinfect after washing
Floor cloth (Do not confuse with all-purpose damp cloths as floors harbour many germs; they are bigger and thicker)	(a) Used to wipe up spills from floors (b) Placed under buckets to protect floors	Wash, rinse and dry after use; disinfect if used in toilet areas
Scrim (looks like fine sackcloth but made from varying qualities of linen; cheaper than chamois leather)	Windows, mirrors, etc.	Wash, rinse, dry after use

Table Continued

TABLE IV. (*Continued*).

Cloth	Uses	Care
Chamois leather	(*a*) When wet, used on windows and mirrors (*b*) When dry, used to polish up metals	Easily damaged; wash in warm water (no detergent), rinse and either store damp or dry flat and rub up to soften; to avoid excessive dirt on leather, remove dirt initially from surface with newspaper or by washing

TABLE V. CLOTHS USED FOR PROTECTION WHILE CLEANING.

Cloth	Uses	Care
Dust sheets (usually made from discarded linen or soft furnishings)	(*a*) Protecting stored items from dust and pests (*b*) Placed over furniture or floor during decorating or special cleaning	Wash, rinse and dry when necessary; fold neatly while in store
Druggets	Placed on floor in door-ways where dirt is excessive, e.g. in bad weather, while decorating or special cleaning, or between a kitchen and dining area	Change frequently; wash, rinse and dry canvas or cotton ones; plastic ones can be wiped

(*a*) *Bristles.* Generally speaking the harder these are the softer the surface on which the brush should be used. The exceptions are yard brooms, toilet brushes and brushes found on all-purpose floor machines. Bristles have a tendency to fall out or become irretrievably bent. To prevent this they should be cleaned of all fluff and cotton threads before washing and rinsing, then left to dry in such a way that the excess water is allowed to drip off to the side of the brush or via the tops of the bristles. If the brush is left resting on the bristles they will splay out, and if left resting on the stock, the water will rot the stock causing leakage of bristles. Nylon bristles tend to go soft with washing and are best rinsed in a saline solution.

(*b*) *The stock*. This is the part of the brush into which the bristles are placed. It should be kept clean and dry at all times.

(*c*) *Handle*. This may be detachable but must be held firmly in place when in use with the head. It must be kept clean, dry and grease free. Long-handled brooms should be stored in spring clips attached to a wall, or suspended by string.

A brush is not a very efficient item of cleaning equipment as it tends to distribute dust. However, when used in conjunction with suction it is very effective.

Mops

Despite the variety of sophisticated machinery used for cleaning today, the mop is still extremely popular and has itself undergone development. Mops can, however, be extremely unpleasant items of equipment unless their use and care are closely monitored.

(*a*) *Dry mops*. These may be used on floors, walls or ceilings. However, unless a dry mop is impregnated with oil or polish, the surface must first be dusted. An impregnated mop must be used correctly if it is to be effective—long, even strokes or a continual movement leaving the mop in contact with the surface all the time, ensuring the minimum of dust distribution and the maximum of dust collection. The mop head should be easily detachable so that it can frequently be washed, rinsed and dried, preferably in a machine, then re-impregnated. This is a service which may be carried out by a contractor. The more traditional floor polishing mop is only used where a machine cannot operate, e.g. a carpet surround. This type of mop must be shaken frequently, but washing may be less frequent as the floor should be cleaned before the mop is used to give a shine.

(*b*) *Disposable dry mops*. Although very expensive these are extremely hygienic. They consist of a handle with a soft pad at the end on to which is placed a piece of synthetic material which has properties enabling it to attract and hold dust. The fabric is held in place by clips, poppers or special tape and is usually purchased in large rolls from which the desired amount can be cut. It is disposed of immediately after use. If this does not happen, the advantages of such a system are lost.

(*c*) *Damp mops*. These are used for the removal of light soiling from floors or for the application of polish. The heads are made of cotton, sponge or any fibre capable of absorbing moisture well. It should be possible to detach the heads easily for regular and thorough washing, preferably in a machine, followed by drying. The drying is the most important part of mop care as bacteria require moisture in which to multiply. Disinfectant is only effective for a short period of time. Damp mops should be renewed as soon as there are signs of wear, and should be stored in spring clips or in such a way that air is allowed to get to the head.

Polish applicator mops are oblong in shape to make the application of the polish more efficient. The heads should slide out from a metal or plastic casing when replacement is necessary. Washing the head should not be necessary. Applicator mops must always be labelled with the type of polish for which they are to be used.

SELF-ASSESSMENT QUESTIONS

1. What responsibilities does a cleaner have with regard to cleaning equipment?

2. What responsibilities does a supervisor have with regard to cleaning equipment?

3. Why is it essential to maintain a well-ordered cleaning store?

4. Why should cleaning staff have to undergo a period of induction relating to equipment?

5. What safety factors should be borne in mind when using the items of equipment mentioned?

6. How can colour-coded equipment be used to assist the work of a domestic department?

7. Suggest suitable equipment for use in three of the establishments mentioned in Chapter 1.

8. What is the most important stage of cloth and mop care?

CHAPTER THREE

Cleaning Agents

CHAPTER OBJECTIVES

After studying this chapter you should be able to:
* explain why cleaning agents are needed for cleaning;
* identify different types of soiling that cleaning agents might be expected to remove;
* describe the chemical make-up of the most commonly used cleaning agents and polishes;
* understand the importance of using the correct cleaning agents for specific cleaning tasks;
* appreciate the importance of correct dilution;
* explain where and how often to use the most frequently used cleaning agents and polishes;
* show how cleaning agents should be stored and controlled in order to achieve economical and safe usage.

IMPORTANCE OF CLEANING

Cleaning always has been and is always likely to be considered a chore. Many companies now realise, however, that good cleaning organisation can be cost effective, for the following reasons.

(*a*) It creates a pleasant and hygienic environment in which to work with the result that staff morale remains high and work output is increased.

(*b*) It reduces labour costs through the use of mechanical cleaning methods and chemicals which speed up the cleaning process.

Before beginning to clean it is necessary for staff to understand what the process is trying to achieve.

THE NATURE OF SOILING

Soiling occurs on both hard and soft surfaces in all except absolutely sterile areas. It can occur in four forms:

(*a*) dust;
(*b*) dirt;
(*c*) staining;
(*d*) tarnishing.

Dust

This is found floating in the air and on all surfaces exposed to the air. If it is not removed regularly it will remain on both horizontal and vertical surfaces, particularly if these are textured, causing them to look dull and unattractive and to smell stale. Such conditions will attract pests, e.g. moths, mites, beetles, etc.

Dust consists of some or all of the following: ash, hairs, fluff, skin particles, fur, germs and grit. Grit is much heavier than most dust particles and causes considerable damage to floorings. However, it should be removed in a similar way to other constituents.

No cleaning agent should be required to remove dust, although the use of spray polish will help to reduce the static on certain surfaces and therefore repel dust for a short period.

As long as moisture is kept away from dust, it can be removed quickly and simply with very little effort. However, as soon as dust comes into contact with liquid, steam or grease, it becomes attached to the surface and requires more effort and expense to remove it. Damp cloths and suction equipment are used in hospitals to remove dust, as this reduces dust distribution and therefore the dangers of cross-infection. Surfaces in hospitals are also of a type which will reduce the attraction of dust, e.g. gloss paint, ceramic tiles, and vinyl furnishings and floorings.

Dirt

This is either grease-based or water-based and can be removed by mechanical or chemical means or both.

Mechanical

There is a wide variety of equipment available to remove dirt, ranging from steel wool and abrasive pads to scarifying and sanding machines (*see* Chapter 2). All, however, require storage space, sometimes a disproportionate amount for the size of building, and in most cases staff require a period of training in order to use them. Their effectiveness depends on how ingrained the dirt has become. In some cases this is so deep that the equipment cannot reach it without considerable physical effort on the part of staff.

Chemical

Chemicals when used in conjuction with suitable equipment can remove dirt quickly and efficiently. The variety of chemicals available is extensive and great care should be taken to ensure money is not wasted by under-dilution or incorrect usage. One incorrect application of cleaning agent could result in considerable damage being caused to a surface so that costly repair work has to take place.

Manufacturers produce a vast number of cleaning agents, all with their individual trade names, which can be very confusing to cleaning staff. Time should therefore be spent on staff training in this area, together with frequent checking of their work and their stores requisitions.

Cleaning agents likely to be found in most establishments fall into the following categories:

    (a) detergents;
    (b) acid cleaners;
    (c) alkaline cleaners;
    (d) solvent cleaners;
    (e) disinfectants;
    (f) deodorants;
    (g) laundry aids;
    (h) polishes;
    (i) floor seals.

These are analysed in detail later in the chapter.

Staining

A stain is a discoloration often caused by unwanted proteins, acids, alkalis, dyes and in some cases accidental or careless use of heat. A stain differs from dirt in that it cannot be removed during routine cleaning. It is not always possible to remove old stains, but if the nature of a fresh stain is known, it should be possible to remove it by using one of the following:

    (a) a powder (to absorb it);
    (b) a solvent (to dissolve it);
    (c) an acid or alkaline cleaner (to neutralise it).

Staining may occur on hard and soft surfaces. (*See* Appendix I for further details on stain removal.)

Tarnishing

This is a discoloration caused by chemical reaction between a metal and substances found in water, food and the atmosphere. The type of tarnish depends on the type of metal, e.g. rust on iron (brown), verdigris on copper (green), and darkening of silver, gold and aluminium. If not removed regularly, the metal will eventually corrode. Acid is the most effective tarnish remover and is often combined with an abrasive detergent. Tarnish can also be removed using a hot solution of soda and aluminium (Polivit). None of these methods produces a shiny surface and so a polish may be applied after cleaning. Metals may be protected from tarnishing by being galvanised, enamelled, anodised, lacquered or coated with chromium, nylon, plastic or paint.

WATER

Water was not mentioned in the list of cleaning agents given above as it is not purchased and stored in the same way, nor is it specific in its use. When softened, water is used extensively for making up cleaning solutions and is an extremely effective sterilising agent when used at a high temperature. However, unless used sparingly, water can do considerable harm to surfaces such as wood, cork and textiles, softening them and causing colours to bleed and run. It is also heavy, a characteristic which can cause fabrics to become distorted during laundering and puts strain on staff who may have to lift or carry buckets and tanks of water.

Hard water occurs naturally in many parts of the country. It contains either calcium bicarbonate (temporary hardness) or calcium and magnesium sulphates (permanent hardness). Temporary hardness can be removed by heating the water to over 60°C, but this creates fur or scale in the pipes or equipment in which it is heated. Permanently hard water cannot be softened by heat. The hardness can be removed, however, by dissolving one of the following alkalis in the water:

(a) sodium hexametaphosphate ("Calgon");
(b) sodium carbonate (washing soda);
(c) ammonia.

Many soap products and disinfectants are prevented from working properly when mixed with hard water and so wherever possible water should be softened before adding a cleaning agent to it.

CHEMICAL MAKE-UP OF CLEANING AGENTS

Before using any chemical cleaning agent operatives must know its strength. This knowledge should be acquired during training and not through trial and error. A supervisor needs to be aware of the chemical group to which each cleaning agent belongs so that she can counteract its effectiveness if a mistake occurs, and can adapt quickly to any new cleaning tasks which may arise. Incorrect use could result in:

(*a*) discoloration of a surface;
(*b*) slippery and therefore dangerous flooring;
(*c*) loosening of adhesives used for tiles, panels, etc.;
(*d*) removal of special finishing treatments, e.g. flameproofing, anti-static or non-slip surfaces, etc.;
(*e*) time-consuming and unnecessary corrective treatments.

A cleaning agent may be classed as: Acidic; Neutral; Alkaline; or Caustic. Any solution can be tested by using litmus-paper or Universal Indicator Paper. Litmus-paper will turn blue if the solution is alkaline or caustic, or red if it is acidic. It will remain unchanged in neutral solutions. Universal Indicator Paper is graded to show the degree of strength and so provides a much more accurate measure. The colour of this type of paper relates to the pH number of the solution. The pH scale is only used in connection with solutions which are near neutrality such as those used for cleaning.

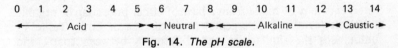

Fig. 14. *The pH scale.*

Solutions with a pH of 7 are chemically neutral, e.g. distilled water. However, commercially, a measurement of 6–9 on the scale may be considered neutral. Each point on the scale is 10 times that of the previous point and so testing of an unknown solution is advisable. Solutions at the extreme ends of the scale are very strong and should be used with caution. Rubber gloves should be worn when using these cleaning agents. Storing acid and alkaline agents also involves care as they are poisonous and corrosive.

DETERGENTS

How a detergent works
If a detergent is to be effective it must be able to do the following:

(*a*) reduce the surface tension of water sufficiently to enable it to wet thoroughly;
(*b*) dissolve in water;
(*c*) loosen and lift out dirt from a surface;
(*d*) suspend dirt in solution sufficiently to prevent it being redeposited;

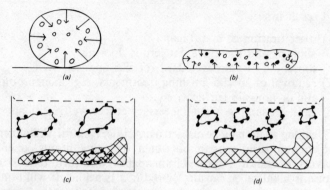

Fig. 15. *How a detergent works.*
(a) *Water droplet;* (b) *water droplet with added detergent — reduced surface tension;* (c) *loosening and lifting out dirt;* (d) *suspending dirt in solution.*

(*e*) rinse away easily;
(*f*) perform the above without harming surfaces or users.

Detergents may be made from a base of either pure soap or organic chemicals (synthetic detergents) or a mixture of both. Table VI summarises the similarities and differences between soapy and synthetic detergents.

TABLE VI. COMPARISON BETWEEN SOAPY AND SYNTHETIC DETERGENTS.

Soapy detergents	Synthetic detergents
pH 8.5	pH 6–7
Creates a scum in hard water	Unaffected by hard water
Emulsifies grease well	As soap
Acts well on non-greasy dirt	Not very good at removing non-greasy dirt
Suspends dirt well	Fairly good at suspending dirt
Will not dissolve in cold water	Dissolves in water of any temperature
Good lather occurs naturally in soft water	Slight lather occurs unless stabilisers are added to give more
Does not remove stains easily	As soap
Does not counteract yellowing in old fabrics	As soap

Additives

Both types of detergents can be improved by the addition of some or all of the following.

(*a*) *Washing soda* (sodium carbonate). This softens water and emulsifies fats, but may cause cotton to shrink and can damage wool and silk.

(*b*) *Bleach* (sodium perborate). When dissolved in water above 40 °C, oxygen is given off which reacts with many stains and turns them into colourless substances. The hotter the solution the more effective the bleach becomes. When used with coloured items, however, the fabric will gradually fade. Fabrics which cannot be washed at high temperatures are unaffected by this additive.

(*c*) *SCMC* (sodium carboxymethyl cellulose). This is added to synthetic detergents to help the suspension of dirt in the solution and thus prevent it from being redeposited on the fabric.

(*d*) *Fluorescent whiteners*. These help to counteract the yellowing of fabrics which occurs with age. They are dyes which absorb ultraviolet light and reflect it as blue light, creating an illusion of whiteness.

(*e*) *Sodium silicate*. This has two purposes. It prevents the corrosion of aluminium found in washing machines and solution tanks and it assists with the suspension of dirt.

(*f*) *Bulk fillers*. These are chemicals which are added to keep powders dry and free flowing while increasing their bulk and giving the appearance of better value for money. One example of a filler is salt which is added to liquid detergents to create a thicker liquid and therefore a more controlled flow.

(*g*) *Lather improvers*. These assist synthetic detergents to retain lather so that it can be used to indicate the strength of the detergent solution. They are not needed in soapy detergents.

(*h*) *Enzymes*. These occur in biological washing powders. They assist in the removal of protein stains, e.g. milk and egg. The enzymes are heat sensitive, working best at temperatures between 30°C and 50°C. Below 30°C they are inactive and above 50°C they are likely to be destroyed. They also need time to work and so fabrics should be allowed to soak in a solution for two to three hours depending on how dirty they are. Care should be taken with wool and silk fabrics as these also contain protein which could be damaged by enzymes. It is recommended that gloves be worn when hand washing with a biological detergent to protect sensitive skin.

(*i*) *Perfumes*. These are added to cover up the unpleasant smell of synthetic detergents, created during their manufacture.

(*j*) *Dyes.* These are usually blue or green. They colour powder particles and have the effect of making a product look more attractive.

(*k*) *Ground pumice.* This is added to detergents to create a rough texture which will help remove stubborn dirt. Detergents containing pumice may be grouped as abrasives and are sold as powders, creams or pastes.

Additives are found in most powder detergents. Liquid detergents, such as those used for dish washing or for washing delicate fabrics, will not usually contain soda, SCMC or bleach. They will not therefore wash very dirty fabrics efficiently, but will remove grease well and may have lanolin or glycerin added for skin care.

Figure 16 illustrates the composition of the various forms of detergents, which are discussed in more detail below.

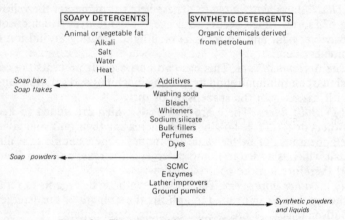

Fig. 16. *The composition of detergents (neutral).*

Soapy detergents

These may be used as a solid block, for washing skin and clothes, as flakes for washing delicate fabrics, or as a powder, for general purpose washing of soft fabrics.

Soap is made by boiling fat with a strong alkali. The characteristics of a soap depend on the type of fat used, e.g. coconut oil provides a soap which is quick to lather, excellent at cleaning but hard on the skin; olive oil provides a soap which has plentiful and persistent lathering, is mild on the skin but is less efficient at cleaning.

Many people are confused by the effects of lather on the cleaning power of a detergent. Lather found in soapy detergents has two advantages. When used to wash skin, it forms a concentrated solution of soap which does not run off the skin so that cleaning is efficient. When used for washing fabrics, the amount of lather indicates the amount of soap present in the solution, and as the lather reduces so the efficiency of the solution is reduced. The amount of lather found in a synthetic detergent solution is no indication of its washing power unless the detergent has been specially formulated for a specific use such as a non-automatic washing powder.

Synthetic detergents

These are used extensively in housekeeping. They can be formulated to suit practically any cleaning task from washing-up to degreasing a factory floor. They may be in the form of a powder, liquid, gel or crystals, and can be broadly grouped into the following categories according to their chemical composition (*see also* Table VII).

Anionics (pH 7–9)

These account for over 80 per cent of all synthetic detergents, i.e. washing powders, washing-up liquids, hard floor cleaning products and carpet shampoos. They are used in solution, at strengths

TABLE VII. SUMMARY OF SYNTHETIC DETERGENTS.

Type	*Uses*
NEUTRAL	
(*a*) Anionic	Washing powders
	Washing-up liquids
	Floor care detergents
(*b*) Non-ionic	Added to anionic detergents to improve lather
	General purpose industrial cleaner
(*c*) Cationic	Blended with non-ionics to give anti-static properties
	General purpose detergent for hard surfaces where hygiene is essential
(*d*) Amphoterics	Speciality detergents for use on hard surfaces
ALKALINE	Cleaning of badly soiled hard surfaces
	Removal of water-based floor polish
SOLVENT-BASED	Removal of solvent/spirit based polish
	Cleaning of oily and greasy floors
	Removal of oil and grease from equipment and machinery

recommended by the manufacturer, followed by thorough rinsing and drying. Anionics will remove only light soiling and are therefore very safe to use. They have a tendency to produce considerable lather and so under-dilution should be avoided.

Non-ionics (pH 7)
These have excellent detergent properties and are particularly effective at removing oil and grease. They are, however, expensive to produce and are therefore usually added to the cheaper anionics. When used alone the solution produces very little lather and that which is produced does not last very long. This characteristic can be used to advantage in detergents required for use with scrubbing machines, where an excess of foam can cause damage to the motor. Non-ionics are used in solution, at strengths recommended by the manufacturer, followed by thorough rinsing and drying. Rinsing is much easier than with anionic detergents as there is less lather to remove.

Cationics (pH below 7)
These detergents are never used alone as they have very little cleaning power. They are often combined with non-ionic detergents to form what are known as quaternary ammonium compounds (QUATS). The chemical nature of cationic materials enables a surface which has been wiped with such a solution to repel dust for a longer period than surfaces treated with other detergents. They are therefore usually regarded as sanitising agents rather than detergents, and are used extensively in hospitals and food preparation areas for wiping floors, walls, furniture and dishes. They are applied in the same way as anionics and non-ionics, are very safe to use and have no apparent taste or smell.

Amphoterics
These detergents are expensive and are found in speciality formulations such as those used in metal cleaners, steam cleaners and oven cleaners. They may also be found in shampoos and medical detergents as they have germicidal properties. Unlike anionics, non-ionics and cationics their performance will alter according to the acidic or alkaline nature of the liquid to which they are added. In acidic solutions an amphoteric detergent will perform like a cationic detergent, in a neutral solution it will perform like a non-ionic detergent and in an alkaline solution it will perform like an anionic detergent. All amphoterics are non-toxic and non-irritant.

Alkaline detergents (pH 9–12.5)

Anionic, non-ionic, cationic and amphoteric detergents are all suitable for light duty cleaning and are most likely to be used on a daily basis. Alkaline detergents are much stronger and are very useful to the housekeeper for removing grease. They have low foaming properties but require thorough rinsing. They are used for cleaning badly soiled surfaces and for removing water-based floor polishes. With such a high pH these detergents can be very damaging and gloves should be worn by staff when using them. They may be used undiluted or in solution. In the latter case the correct dilution for the task in hand is essential. Thorough rinsing should be carried out, preferably with a mild acid such as vinegar added to the final rinsing water. Inadequate rinsing means that when the surface dries a white alkaline powder remains which not only looks unsightly but in the case of floors will begin to break down any fresh application of polish, leaving the floor looking dull and patchy.

Solvent-based detergents

These are neutral detergents containing a solvent which will soften heavy deposits of wax and oil. The detergent solution suspends the dissolved wax so that it can be rinsed away easily. Solvents will damage many synthetic materials and so these detergents are only recommended for use on surfaces such as wood, wood composition, cork, magnesite, linoleum, concrete or stone. Solvent-based detergents are non-flammable.

Points to consider when using detergents

(*a*) Use the correct type of detergent for the task to be performed.

(*b*) Dilute accurately in water of a suitable temperature.

(*c*) Dissolve detergent thoroughly before use.

(*d*) Apply detergent methodically to avoid patchiness.

(*e*) Use clean equipment and wash away all traces of detergent after use.

(*f*) Rinse thoroughly when necessary.

(*g*) Store containers on stable shelving in a dry, well-ventilated store.

(*h*) Label containers clearly and renew when necessary.

(*i*) Use dispensers and measures where possible.

(*j*) Wipe up spillages immediately to avoid wastage and accidents.

ACID CLEANERS

These will vary in strength from acetic acid found in vinegar to the highly corrosive dilute hydrochloric acid with a pH of 1. They should always be used in solution followed by thorough rinsing. All, except perhaps citric and acetic acid, should be used under supervision, with extreme caution and with the protection of rubber gloves. Strong acids are poisonous and corrosive. Some acid cleaners have special formulas, e.g. crystalline toilet cleaners which contain an acid resistant synthetic detergent. Table VIII summarises the types and uses of acid cleaners.

TABLE VIII. SUMMARY OF ACID CLEANERS

Types of acid used in cleaning	Uses
Citric acid ⎫ (Liquids, pH 3) Acetic acid ⎬	Metal cleaning (tarnish removal) Neutralising alkaline cleaners Removing light soiling and stickiness from unvarnished wood Preventing colours from running during washing/shampooing
Dilute hydrochloric acid (HCl, liquid, pH 1)	Removing limescale particularly from sanitaryware Removing cement and plaster from newly applied tile areas
Sodium acid sulphate (pH 5)	Removing water stains and scale from toilets
Oxalic acid (pH 2) Concentrated hydrochloric acid ⎫ (HCl, "spirits of salt", pH 1) ⎬	Removing stubborn water stains

ALKALINE CLEANERS

Alkaline-based cleaning agents are used a great deal in laundering and are particularly good at removing grease. Very strong alkalis are known as caustic materials and are extremely corrosive as well as being poisonous. They must be used under strict supervision with the protection of rubber gloves. The types and uses of alkaline cleaners are summarised in Table IX.

Bleach and ammonia may be added to abrasive detergents. Bleach may also be added to powdered toilet cleaners, but sodium hypochlorite bleach should never be used in conjuction with an acid toilet cleaner as chlorine gas will be produced which is poisonous.

TABLE IX. SUMMARY OF ALKALINE CLEANERS.

Types of alkali used in cleaning	Uses
Sodium bicarbonate (baking soda ⎫ pH 8, powder, fine abrasive) ⎬ Sodium pyroborate (borax, pH 8, ⎪ powder) ⎭	Removing acid-based stains, e.g. tea and coffee, and stubborn grease from smooth surfaces, such as enamel, porcelain and plastic, and textile fabrics Excellent for cleaning refrigerators, etc.
Sodium carbonate (washing soda, pH 10, powder or crystals)	Added to soapy and synthetic detergent powders to soften water and remove light grease marks Cleaning drains
Sodium hydroxide (caustic soda, pH 14, liquid, flakes, aerosols)	Removing congealed grease such as that found in ovens, grills and blocked drains
Ammonia (pH 11, liquid)	Removing stubborn grease stains; frequently added to carpet shampoos Very strong fumes
Sodium hypochlorite (bleach, pH 8–9, liquid, powder)	Whitening and removing stains from hard and soft surfaces Disinfectant Should not be used on silk, wool, drip-dry or crease-resistant fabrics May be labelled "Household Bleach"
Sodium perborate (bleach, pH 10, powder)	Whitening and removing stains from hard and soft surfaces Inactive in solutions below 40 °C Action increases as the temperature of the solution increases
Hydrogen peroxide (bleach, pH 4, liquid, 20 vol; pH 3, liquid, 100 vol.)	Whitening and removing stains from any hard or soft surface
Sodium thiosulphite (hypo, pH 7)	Removing iodine stains

SOLVENT CLEANERS

These cleaning agents are used extensively for dry cleaning and for stain removal. They all have strong fumes and should be used in a well-ventilated room. Solvents are useful for cleaning grease or polish from surfaces which might be damaged by water-based solutions, e.g. silk fabrics and porous floorings. Solvents will evaporate and so are ideal for cleaning windows, mirrors and pictures. They are present in window and glass polishes and solvent-based floor polishes. As solvents are flammable, poisonous and possibly addictive, only small amounts should be kept in stock. Solvent cleaners may damage skin, and a barrier cream should therefore be applied to the hands before using them. The following are the main types of solvent used for cleaning:

Perchlorethylene
Trichlorethylene   } poisonous fumes

Methylated spirits
Turpentine
White spirit   } flammable
Amyl acetate
Acetone

DISINFECTANTS

Disinfectants should only be used in areas where harmful germs are likely to exist. Many germs are removed by normal cleaning so that if this occurs regularly, the use of a disinfectant should be unnecessary.

Types of disinfectant

The types of disinfectant most likely to be used by the housekeeper are as follows.

(a) *Halogens* (Domestos, Diversol CX). May be added to anionic detergents. Good general purpose disinfectants.

(b) *Phenolics* (Dettol, Izal, Stericol, Hycolin). Must be used in high concentration for effectiveness.

(c) *Pine fluids*. Not very efficient as easily inactivated but have a pleasing smell.

Each group has its own characteristics and the supervisor should assume that a suitable one has been purchased for use in her establishment.

Correct use of disinfectants

Disinfectants are very sensitive to external conditions. They will be ineffective if any of the following are present:

(*a*) organic matter (blood, vomit, urine, faeces);
(*b*) certain foods (e.g. milk);
(*c*) hard water;
(*d*) cork, wood, cotton, paper, rubber, certain plastics.

A considerable amount of money can be wasted by the incorrect use of disinfectants. To ensure correct use, the following rules should be observed:

(*a*) Rinse away detergent solutions thoroughly before disinfecting.
(*b*) Wash, rinse and dry all equipment after use with detergents and disinfectants. (Germs cannot breed in dry conditions.)
(*c*) Remove all unwanted organic matter before using a disinfectant.
(*d*) Use softened water.
(*e*) Do not use inactivating materials where disinfection may need to take place. If necessary seal an inactivating surface.
(*f*) The effectiveness of a disinfectant may depend on the types of germs present. This is of particular importance in hospitals, but here laboratories are able to advise on the best disinfectants to use.
(*g*) Dilute disinfectants accurately for effectiveness.
(*h*) Allow time for a disinfectant to work. The time needed will depend on the number and type of germs present and the strength of the solution.

TABLE X. SUMMARY OF TERMS USED FOR DISINFECTION.

Term	Definition
Sterilisation 121 °C for 15 minutes (moist) 160 °C for 45 minutes (dry)	Will kill *all* germs/bacteria and their spores (Not used extensively in housekeeping)
Disinfectant Bactericide	Will kill *most* germs/bacteria, but not their spores
Antiseptic Bacteriostat	Provide unsuitable conditions for the growth of germs/bacteria
Sanitiser Detergent/steriliser Detergent/sterilant	Will reduce the number of germs/bacteria to an acceptable level

(*i*) Never "top up" a disinfectant solution. Bacteria which survive a disinfectant may multiply in a solution which has deteriorated. If a solution is kept and used again it may spread germs rather than kill them.

Many containers are confusingly labelled. Table X summarises the more familiar terms used.

Many people believe that the smell of disinfectant is an indication of cleanliness. It could also be said that a smell of disinfectant is an indication that there are germs to be killed and that the establishment is not as clean as it might be. They should therefore be used with discretion.

DEODORANTS

These are agents for disguising bad smells. They are expensive and may need to be so strong that they are unpleasantly sweet. Good ventilation and thorough cleaning should make the use of deodorants unnecessary unless it is policy to use one.

LAUNDRY AIDS

Not every residential establishment undertakes the regular washing of bed and table linen. However, cleaning materials stores may contain stiffening agents and fabric conditioners.

Stiffening agents

These aim to improve the appearance of a fabric and to provide a smooth surface which will remain clean longer than an unstarched fabric. Starch is only effective when used on cotton or linen fabrics and is applied to clean items. The following are the main types of stiffening agent.

(*a*) *Boiling water starch*. The starch used is that from rice or maize. When the starch grains are mixed with boiling water, they burst and then gelatinise. This thick solution coats the fabric causing the yarn fibres to stick together. This type is suitable for bed linen.

(*b*) *Cold water starch*. The rice and maize grains swell by soaking in cold water. After soaking in the solution for about ten minutes, depending on the stiffness required, the fabric is dried until only slightly damp and then ironed. The heat from the iron causes the grains to burst and thus fill the gaps in the woven fabric. Cold water starch gives a very long-lasting result and is ideal for chefs' uniforms and table linen.

(c) *Instant starch.* In this case the starch grains are pre-cooked giving a finish like boiling water starch.

(d) *Spray starch.* This method of applying starch is very expensive as in order to obtain a reasonable result, a large amount must be used. It is, however, ideal for short-term and emergency use on waitress aprons and personal items of clothing.

(e) *Cotton crispers.* This method of stiffening does not use starch grains. The fabric is coated with a fine layer of plastic emulsion. It gives a long-lasting but slightly less efficient result.

Fabric conditioners

These solutions should be used sparingly as they are expensive. Like stiffening agents, they coat the yarn fibres with a substance which makes them smooth. This prevents them from becoming tangled and reduces shrinkage. They also help to reduce static in synthetic fabrics. Unfortunately this coating has an adverse effect on towels as it reduces the absorbency of the pile. Towels are best washed without conditioner and tumble dried.

POLISHES

Polishes are not cleaning agents but are usually stored in the same area and used after cleaning has taken place. Polishes are applied to a surface to form a hard, protective layer and thus guard against finger marks, stains and scratches. They also create a pleasant sheen on a hard surface. Polishes are used on metal surfaces, furniture and floors.

Metal polishes

The aim of a metal polish is to remove superficial tarnish and scratching. Metal polishes therefore contain a very mild abrasive, fatty acid, solvent and water. Long-life metal polishes also contain an ingredient which coats the surface of the metal and slows down the formation of tarnish considerably.

Metal polish may be in the form of a milky liquid, a powder, a clear liquid or a fabric or wadding which is impregnated with polish solution. Metal polishes are formulated for either hard or soft metals. It is important to use the correct type as the hard metal polish is harsher and will eventually damage soft metal. Stainless steel tends to scratch and become dull with constant use and so will require polishing eventually. Stainless steel polishes are more abrasive than those designed for silver, gold, brass, copper, pewter, etc.

Metal polishes smell very strong and should be used and stored in a well-ventilated area. They should be stored with the tops well secured, otherwise the solvent content will evaporate and the solution become too dry to use. Metal items which require regular polishing if they are to look attractive include:

(a) cutlery;
(b) serving dishes, salvers, etc.;
(c) tableware such as jugs and vases;
(d) door handles and plates;
(e) ornaments, shields, etc.;
(f) foot rails in bars;
(g) banisters;
(h) ashtrays;
(i) bathroom fittings;
(j) chair and table legs.

Points to remember when using metal polishes

(a) Protect yourself with an overall and the surroundings with paper, etc. (metal polishing can be very messy).
(b) Work in a ventilated area.
(c) Polish clean metals only.
(d) Apply polish with a rag or applicator provided.
(e) Use a soft silver brush or a cocktail stick for ornate inaccessible areas.
(f) Remove polish with a soft dry cloth.
(g) Rub up to a shine with a duster.
(h) After polishing, wash any item to be used with food in warm synthetic detergent solution.
(i) Constant use of a clear liquid tarnish remover (e.g. Silver Dip) will eventually damage silver plating (EPNS).
(j) Dispose of used rags after use to prevent a build-up of fumes and reduce the risk of fire.

Furniture polishes

Furniture polish should only be used occasionally. "Rubbing up" while dusting should keep furniture looking clean and attractive. Unvarnished or unpainted wooden furniture, however, may require "feeding" with a polish fairly frequently. Furniture polish is applied to clean surfaces only and may be in the form of a paste, a cream (thick or thin), a liquid, an oil or a spray. They all contain:

(a) wax, to enrich porous surfaces;
(b) solvent, to remove grease;
(c) water, to remove water soluble stains;

(*d*) silicone, to lubricate the polish and ease its application, to increase gloss and to improve resistance to water, heat, dust and smears.

Pastes (high percentage wax)

These are suitable for use on antique wooden surfaces. Care should be taken to remove all traces of polish from carved surfaces. A paste may also be used on wood which is in poor condition, as the high percentage of wax will "feed" it and help to create a sheen rather than a brilliant gloss. Pastes are applied with a rag then rubbed up with a duster. They require considerable effort to obtain a good result.

Creams (high percentage solvent)

Cream polishes should be used on satin or gloss finishes only, as they increase the shine on a surface with continual use. Their cleaning power is greater than the pastes but they have a much stronger smell. They are applied with a dry or damp rag and polished up immediately with a dry cloth or duster.

Liquids (high percentage solvent)

Liquid polishes may also contain a dye, which is useful for covering up scratches in a varnished surface. Used on glossy surfaces they will help remove food and drink stains and light grease marks. After application with a dry rag, they should be rubbed up with a soft dry cloth while still wet to produce a good shine.

Sprays/aerosols (high percentage silicone)

The high silicone content of these polishes means that they clean as well as polish. This saves time as pre-dusting is unnecessary. They are ideal for use on non-porous surfaces such as glass, chromium, plastic, varnished or gloss painted wood where the surface may become dull and fingermarked. They are particularly effective at reducing static so that dust does not settle on the surface so readily. Unlike other furniture polishes, spray polish is applied and rubbed up with a duster. It is advisable to apply the polish to the duster and then rub this on to the surface otherwise there can be unnecessary waste.

Points to remember when using furniture polish

(*a*) Apply to clean surfaces only.

(*b*) Use a little and rub up well with a duster. (Too much polish will create a sticky surface which is likely to attract dust.)

(c) Apply with a rag (except spray polish).

(d) Replace the top of the polish container firmly after use to prevent the evaporation of the solvent and consequent drying-up.

(e) All furniture polishes are used undiluted.

(f) Polishes containing a high percentage of solvent are flammable.

Floor polishes

Like furniture polishes, these should be applied only when buffing up no longer creates the desired effect. There are two types of floor polish:

(a) spirit or solvent-based;

(b) water-based (sometimes referred to as an emulsion polish).

Both types of polish deposit a layer of wax on to floors, and may therefore be referred to as floor waxes.

It is very important that the correct polish is used for specific types of floor and that the equipment used for applying one type is kept separate from that used to apply the other. If a mistake is made, not only will the surface look unsightly, but the floor will become damaged and dangerous.

Spirit or solvent-based polish

This may be in the form of a liquid or paste and consists of a blend of waxes dispersed in a solvent. After it has been applied, the solvent evaporates, leaving a layer of wax which is rubbed or buffed up to a shine. The spirit ingredient gives the polish a small amount of cleaning power. Silicone may also be added to assist in the application of the polish and create a more resistant finish, but it may cause the surface to become slippery. Floors treated with a solvent-based floor polish may dull quickly but will withstand frequent buffing-up to restore the shine. It is used on porous floors (wood, wood composition, cork, magnesite and linoleum).

Water-based polish

This type of polish takes the form of a creamy liquid and consists of a blend of waxes or polymer resins (glues), suspended in water by means of an emulsifying agent. (An emulsifying agent such as a synthetic detergent or ammonia helps to blend the wax and water.) When applied to a floor surface, the water will evaporate leaving a hard film. Silicones are rarely added but some emulsion floor polishes contain an anti-slip ingredient (colloidal silicon). Most polishes of this nature dry to a shine and require only occasional buffing. Because of this they may be referred to as "dri-bright" polish. They are used on semi-porous and plastic floors such as rubber, asphalt, thermoplastic, PVC (vinyl), asbestos, flexible PVC, linoleum, terrazzo and marble.

The water content of this type of polish prevents it from being used on porous floors unless they are well sealed. In order to streamline what can be a very costly and time-consuming area of work, porous floors are frequently sealed and water-based polishes used throughout the establishment.

One disadvantage of water-based polish is that, having a low solvent content, its cleaning power is limited. To overcome this the formula of the polish may be altered to give a high percentage of emulsifying agent. The polish then becomes thinner and can be dispensed through a spray, The floor is then buffed up immediately. The results achieved by this "spray cleaning" system are not as good as the original method of polish stripping followed by reapplication, but it does enable a floor to retain a reasonable appearance for some considerable time, and has been adopted on a regular basis by many areas of the industry.

High-speed emulsion polish

This type of polish is formulated especially for use with high-speed machines. It is applied in the same way as ordinary emulsion polish but contains a high percentage of polymers which are heat sensitive. When a high-speed machine is used to buff up the polish, the friction causes considerable heat which melts the polymer resins. When these dry they leave a very tough finish and one which will remain in good condition for a long period.

Points to consider when using floor polish

(*a*) Apply to a clean floor.

(*b*) Apply to a dry floor.

(*c*) Rinse floor thoroughly after stripping off old polish using a neutralising agent, e.g. vineger in the final rinsing water.

(*d*) Apply several thin coats of polish rather than one thick coat and work methodically to ensure all areas are covered.

(*e*) Allow each coat of polish to dry before applying the next.

(*f*) Ventilate the area in which polishing is to take place.

(*g*) Use warning signs to block off the area to be polished.

(*h*) Buff up thoroughly to prevent slippiness.

(*i*) Do not use water-based polish on an unsealed porous floor or one where the seal is damaged. Linoleum will not be damaged by either type of polish.

(*j*) Do not use solvent-based polish on plastic or semi-porous floors.

(*k*) Remove any build-up of polish with a suitable polish remover and an abrasive pad or disc.

(*l*) Damp mop floors after spray cleaning to remove any residue.

(*m*) Clean all equipment immediately and thoroughly after use and store correctly and safely.

FLOOR SEALS

A floor seal can be either solvent or water based. It is applied to a floor surface to form a semi-permanent protective barrier which will prevent the entry of dirt, liquids, grease, stains and bacteria. Depending on the traffic they receive and whether they are covered with a floor wax, they may last for up to five years before replacement is necessary, but those used in busy corridors and entrances will require renewal about every year. The added protection of a floor wax can increase the life-span of a seal considerably.

There are six main groups of floor seals:

(*a*) oleo-resinous;
(*b*) one-pot plastic; } clear } solvent-based
(*c*) two-pot plastic;
(*d*) pigmented;
(*e*) water-based;
(*f*) silicate dressing.

It is important that the correct type is used if the floor surface is to remain safe and attractive. Their main characteristics are analysed below and summarised in Table XI.

Oleo-resinous
(Wood, wood composition, cork and magnesite floors.) This is a frequently used type of seal. It is fairly cheap and is easy to apply and renew. It consists of oils, resins, solvents and driers and penetrates the floor as well as depositing a glossy layer on the surface. Although this type of seal is sold as a clear seal it tends to darken the floor but at the same time highlight the colour and grain. For this reason, it should not be applied to linoleum floors.

One-pot plastic
(Wood, wood composition, cork and magnesite floors.) These seals are described as "one-pot" or "one-can" to distinguish them from the "two-pot" variety (*see* below). They are composed entirely of

TABLE XI. CHARACTERISTICS OF FLOOR SEALS.

Seal	Shelf life	Recommended number coats	Solvent odour	Resistance to chemicals	Durability	Dry time per coat (hours)	Hardening time (hours)	Suitable floor wax	Cleaning solvent
OLEO-RESINOUS	Good	2–3	Mild	Fair	Good	8–10	12–16	Solvent or water	White spirit
ONE-POT PLASTIC									
Urea-formaldehyde	Poor	2–3	Moderate	Fair	Good	6–8	12–16	Solvent or water	Special solvent
Polyurethane	Very good	2–3	Mild	Very good	Very good	3–4	12–16	Solvent or water	White spirit or special solvent
TWO-POT PLASTIC									
Urea-formaldehyde	Base and accelerator very good	2–3	Strong	Very good	Very good	3–4	12–16	Solvent or water	Special solvent
Polyurethane	Base, very good; accelerator, poor	3	Strong	Excellent	Excellent	2	12–16 (min. 4)	Solvent or water	Special solvent
PIGMENTED									
Synthetic rubber	Good	2	Mild	Good	Good	3–4	12–16	Water	Special solvent
Polyurethane	Base, very good; accelerator, poor	3	Fair	Excellent	Excellent	2	12–16 (min. 4)	Solvent or water	Special solvent
WATER-BASED	Very good	1–2	None	Fair	Needs protecting	20–30 minutes	1 (min. 30 minutes)	Water	Water
SILICATE DRESSING	Very good	2–3	None	Poor	Fair	12–14	12–16	Water (if used)	Water

synthetic materials and so contain no natural drying oil. There are several types of one-pot plastic seal, the main ones being:

(*a*) urea-formaldehyde;
(*b*) oil-modified polyurethane;
(*c*) moisture-cured polyurethane.

Types (*b*) and (*c*) may also be used on concrete. All three give improved performance over the oleo-resinous seals.

Two-pot plastic
(Wood, wood composition, cork and magnesite floors.) This type of seal consists of a base and a hardener. The two are kept separate until required, because when mixed a chemical reaction begins which continues until the mixture is hard. The advantage of such a system is that a high quality seal can be used which has a long shelf life. It is essential, however, that the correct proportions are used, otherwise the seal will be soft, slow to dry and patchy. Two-pot plastic seals smell strongly of solvent and should be used in a well-ventilated room. There are two main types:

(*a*) urea-formaldehyde;
(*b*) polyurethane (can also be used on concrete, asphalt and linoleum).

Pigmented
(Concrete, magnesite, asphalt and stone floors.) These seals contain a colour which gives added strength to the seal. There are two types:

(*a*) one-pot synthetic rubber;
(*b*) two-pot polyurethane (stronger but less simple to apply).

Water-based
(Thermoplastic tiles, PVC, rubber, asphalt, terrazzo, marble, linoleum, magnesite, concrete, stone and quarry tile floors.) This type of seal is less durable than the solvent-based ones and should therefore be protected with a water-based floor wax. On the other hand, they are easily "touched-up" or removed and renewed. They consist of acrylic polymer resins and a plasticiser. The particles of resin are larger than those found in the water-based floor wax and so are able to fill the open pores of the floor surface and provide a "plastic" skin. The seal is resistant to neutral and alkaline detergents and is therefore unaffected by these when used to remove water-based floor wax.

Silicate dressing

(Concrete and stone floors.) This does not strictly seal a floor but reinforces the surface and prevents the creation of dust. It is much cheaper than a seal, and consists of a base of sodium silicate dissolved in water. The sodium silicate reacts with the lime content of the concrete to form insoluble calcium silicate. The water acts as a carrier and when it has evaporated, silicate glass is formed.

STORAGE OF CLEANING AGENTS

On delivery, cleaning agents are received into a central store, which should always be kept locked when not manned. From this store, cleaning agents will be issued to all departments, e.g. restaurant, kitchen, porters and, of course, the housekeeping department itself. Once they have been issued they will be taken to peripheral storage areas throughout the establishment. These should be kept locked when not in use.

Responsibilities of supervisor

A cleaning supervisor is usually responsible for the following.

(a) Issuing cleaning agents according to the system adopted by the establishment.

(b) Ensuring they are stored safely and tidily in the peripheral storage areas.

(c) Informing staff of how and where they should be used.

(d) Reporting to the housekeeper any problems encountered with the use or performance of any cleaning agent.

(e) Assisting in stock control.

Issuing of cleaning agents

This may be a time-consuming task depending on the method used. Cleaning agents should be issued at pre-arranged intervals so that access to the main store cannot occur without the knowledge of the supervisor, housekeeper or storekeeper. Stores may be issued by one of the following methods.

Requisition

Each peripheral storage area will have a requisition book with forms in triplicate (*see* Fig. 17). Every time goods are required, the person responsible for the store area will complete the form and sign it. The top copy of this form will then be taken or sent to the central store prior to the collection time, where it will be checked by the supervisor and the items put together for collection by the

STORES REQUISITION		No. 259
Department/Section	ANNEX	

Quantity	Unit	Description
6	500 ml	CREAM CLEANSER

Signed *S. Green*   Date *19/ 3/ 6*

Fig. 17. *Sample requisition form.*

cleaner (alternatively, the porters may distribute cleaning agents). The second copy will be sent to the housekeeper or whoever may be responsible for cleaning expenditure. The third copy will remain in the book which is returned with the fresh supplies. This system is expensive to operate but very efficient. It is suitable for large establishments where control of cleaning agents is difficult.

Full-for-empty/new-for-old
This system is used extensively in smaller establishments. Individual cleaners will take empty containers or old dusters, etc. to the central store and will be given a replacement in return. This system, however, requires that the store be open indefinitely as staff may run out of supplies while working. It therefore creates a lot of work for the supervisor. An improvement on this method is the topping-up system (*see* below).

Topping-up
At a fixed time each day or week, the cleaners will take their containers to the main store to be "topped-up". This avoids the danger of running out of supplies while cleaning. Alternatively, a supervisor or porter will visit each peripheral store and top-up the containers. In some establishments cleaners will deposit their bucket of cleaning agents in the main store at the end of each day or at regular intervals. These will be replenished ready for collection at the start of the next shift. While this saves the supervisor time, a regular visit to each storage area enables her to check on its cleanliness and tidiness and to check that the cleaner has no problems.

Points to consider when storing cleaning agents

(*a*) Label all containers clearly and with waterproof pens or labels.

(*b*) Indicate the dilution rate if necessary.

(*c*) Ensure all tops are secure and containers kept clean.

(*d*) Store containers neatly to avoid damage and spillage.

(*e*) Keep aerosol containers away from hot pipes and radiators.

(*f*) Ensure shelves are strong enough to bear the weight of the cleaning agents.

(*g*) Keep the store locked when not in use.

(*h*) Keep bin cards up to date.

(*i*) Rotate stock.

(*j*) Use funnels for dispensing and pre-diluting.

(*k*) Keep the store well ventilated.

(*l*) Do not store heavy items on high shelves.

(*m*) Use dispensers where possible.

(*n*) Clean the store regularly.

(*o*) Check stock regularly. Consider the use of a computer.

SELF-ASSESSMENT QUESTIONS

1. What are the advantages of having an efficiently run housekeeping department?

2. What is meant by soiling?

3. Define the terms "staining" and "tarnishing".

4. What are the disadvantages of using water-based cleaning solutions?

5. Why is it necessary for a supervisor to know the chemical nature of cleaning agents?

6. Why are liquid detergents inefficient for washing badly soiled fabrics?

7. List the various types of detergents and suggest two areas of use for each.

8. What measures should be taken to ensure effective use of disinfectants?

9. Why are fabrics starched? Where would you use each type?

10. What are the basic ingredients of metal, furniture and floor polishes? Why is each ingredient necessary?

11. What care should be taken when using and storing powders, liquids, pastes, creams and aerosols?

12. What might be the result of using a floor polish incorrectly?

Textiles

CHAPTER OBJECTIVES

After studying this chapter you should be able to:
* describe which fibres are used in the construction of textiles;
* appreciate how a knowledge of the characteristics of these fibres is useful to the housekeeper;
* understand how fabrics are constructed;
* appreciate how fabric construction can affect the performance and maintenance of a textile fabric;
* describe the variety of finishes which might be applied to textile fabrics and how these may be retained while cleaning;
* identify which textile items are likely to need maintaining by a housekeeping department;
* explain how to control the storage, issue and despatch of these items.
* show how to maintain textile fabrics and remove any stains from them.

INTRODUCTION

Textiles differ from hard fabrics in that they are maintained by either laundering or dry cleaning. Well-cared for textiles look extremely attractive and will last for many years, depending on their quality and the use to which they are subjected. Ignorance as to the nature of a textile fabric can result in the incorrect cleaning procedure being adopted and the fabric being damaged beyond repair or ending up with unsightly creases, stains, discoloration, etc. The fibres used for textile fabrics fall into three main categories: natural, man-made and mineral.

NATURAL FIBRES

Cotton, linen and wool are the most frequently used natural textile fibres in hotels and institutions. Silk is occasionally found, together with jute, kapok, hemp and sisal, the last of these often being used for wall coverings and carpeting.

Natural fibres usually have one or two very good characteristics and one or two very poor ones. They are therefore frequently combined with man-made fibres which help to offset the weaker points. They vary in quality and so may be used for an expensive item such as a loose cover, or for an inexpensive item such as a duster or mop head. Natural fibres are generally costly to maintain requiring dry cleaning or high washing temperatures and extensive drying periods, unlike the synthetic group of fibres which in most cases can be maintained by laundering which will involve very little if any drying and ironing.

Cotton
A photograph of a cotton fibre is shown in Fig. 18, while Fig. 19 illustrates the international cotton symbol.

Characteristics

(*a*) Twenty-five per cent stronger when wet, therefore washes very well.

(*b*) Non-elastic, therefore creases and pile fabrics tend to flatten easily (non-resilient).

(*c*) Conducts heat well, therefore comfortable to wear as a uniform.

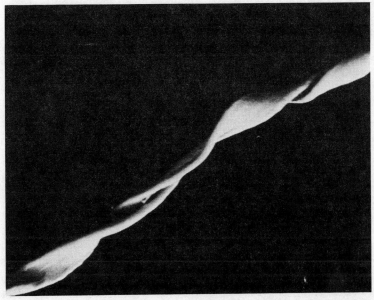

Courtesy Huddersfield Polytechnic

Fig. 18. *Cotton fibre.*

cotton

Fig. 19. *International cotton symbol.*

(*d*) Absorbs water well, therefore can be dyed easily, but this means it will not dry very quickly.

(*e*) Soils easily as the fibre is short (1–6 cm) and when spun, creates a rough yarn.

(*f*) Tends to shrink when washed, particularly when strong alkalis such as bleach are used.

(*g*) Undiluted bleaches will cause damage but this can be avoided by thorough rinsing.

(*h*) Flammable, especially when brushed (flannelette).

(*i*) Easily damaged by mildew, therefore must be stored in dry conditions.

(*j*) Weakens and turns yellow after constant exposure to sunlight.

(*k*) Easily damaged by acids.

Uses
Cotton is very versatile. It is used on its own or in blends, e.g. polyester and cotton, the polyester being added to reduce shrinkage and shorten the drying time. It is used for bed and table linen; uniforms, particularly for people working in a hot environment; hospital blankets and bedspreads which may require boiling; soft furnishings; upholstery; cloths; dusters and wet mop heads, etc.

Examples of fabrics made from cotton
Damask. Sometimes blended with rayon to improve sheen. Used for table linen and curtaining.
Denim Tough, closely woven. Used for uniforms.
Flannelette. Brushed, to increase warmth. Used for sheets and pillowslips.
Winceyette. Blended with wool then brushed to increase warmth. Used for sheets.

Repp. Firm fabric, woven with a distinct rib effect. Used for soft furnishings.

Gingham. Lightweight fabric woven with a white and a coloured yarn to create a checked pattern. Used for table linen and curtains.

Huckaback. A type of towel with a closely woven textured appearance. Used for continuous roller towels.

Towelling. Terry towelling has a pile which creates an absorbent fabric suitable for bathroom towels and robes.

Corduroy. A cut pile fabric used for soft furnishings and upholstery.

Drill. Similar to denim but heavier and very strong. Ideal for uniforms.

Chintz. This has a glazed finish and traditionally has a floral pattern. Used for soft furnishings.

Cretonne. Hard-wearing, coarse fabric used for soft furnishings.

Folkweave. Loosely woven fabric, usually with a textured appearance. Used for bedspreads.

Ticking. A closely woven fabric with a stripe. Traditionally it is black and white stripe but it may also be blue and white or plain white with a striped effect. Used for mattress and pillow casings.

Candlewick. A tufted pile fabric used for bedspreads and bathmats.

Velour/velvet. A close cut pile fabric used for soft furnishings and upholstery.

Sateen. A smooth lightweight fabric used to line curtains.

Special treatments applied to cotton fabrics
To overcome the shortcomings of cotton, many fabrics are treated during manufacture. These "finishes" may be unstable and so care should be taken during cleaning.

Mercerising. This makes the fabric stronger and more lustrous. It can create a very smooth or a puckered fabric (seersucker).

Shrink-resistance. Fabrics with this finish have been pre-shrunk before being sold by the metre or as an item such as a loose cover.

Crease-resistance. This treatment impregnates the cotton fabric with a type of plastic which prevents creases from forming. The process also makes the fabric shrink proof.

Flameproofing. Cotton burns very easily with a flame. It is a legal requirement for all furnishings in establishments used by the public to have this treatment. Professionally flameproofed cotton fabric is permanent as long as the manufacturer's washing instructions are followed. Temporary flameproofing (which will be destroyed by washing) can be applied by soaking clean, detergent-free fabric in one of the following solutions:

(*a*) 320 g borax, 250 g boracic acid, 5 litres water;

(*b*) 330 g ammonium phosphate, 650 g ammonium chloride, 5 litres water.

Maintenance of cotton fabrics

(*a*) If very dirty, soak in a lukewarm detergent solution.

(*b*) Boil to improve whiteness. This also sterilises the fabric. White cotton is therefore very useful for hospitals.

(*c*) Bleach if necessary (*see* Appendix I).

(*d*) Starch if necessary.

(*e*) Wash according, to appropriate wash code (*see* Fig. 41):

white cotton—Code 1;
fast coloureds—Code 2;
non-fast coloureds—Code 5;
treated fabrics—Code 4.

(*f*) Better results are obtained from ironing fabric when slightly damp.

(*g*) Cotton upholstery should be lightly sponged or brushed with upholstery shampoo. Do not over-wet and allow to dry naturally.

Removing stains from cotton fabrics

Do not use acids as they rot cotton fibres. If bleach is used, rinse thoroughly. If this is not done, the fabric will gradually weaken with repeated washing. As cotton is very absorbent, it will attract liquid staining, but most of these stains can be removed from white cotton by washing at high temperatures, when the sodium perborate (bleach) content of the detergent will be activated.

Linen

Characteristics

(*a*) Fibre is very long, therefore fabrics are less "fluffy" than cotton and will remain clean longer. Soiling is easily removed.

(*b*) Poor elasticity, therefore creases very badly and shrinks (non-resilient).

(*c*) Good conductor of heat, therefore used for uniforms, sheets, etc.

(*d*) Very absorbent.

(*e*) Very strong especially when wet, therefore will withstand tough wear (upholstery) and constant washing (sheets, bedspreads, uniforms).

(*f*) Damaged by bleach, mildew, acids.

(g) Flammable.
(h) Resists moths, sunlight and most alkalis (except bleach).
(i) Does not take dyes easily.
(j) Expensive.

Uses

Like cotton, linen is very versatile. To reduce the cost of linen items the fibres may be blended with cotton (union) but they are rarely blended with man-made fibres. Its strength makes it ideal for use as sheets, bedspreads, soft furnishing fabrics and upholstery. Cotton and synthetic blends, however, are equally strong; they are also cheaper, dry quicker and are lighter—a fact which should be considered when staff have to distribute and store sheets. As linen fibres are very long (0.5–1 m) there are fewer "ends" in linen yarn, with the result that linen fabrics leave less "fluff" when used as cloths for wiping glass, mirrors, cutlery, etc. Linen is used extensively for soft furnishing fabrics.

Linen fabrics

Fabrics made from linen are usually described by referring to the uses to which they are put, for example sheeting, table linen. Canvas is traditionally woven from linen yarn, and is used for bedstead underlays and protective mats, e.g. druggets. The word "linen" is also used collectively to describe washable items stored and maintained by the housekeeping department. The following is a list of typical linen room stock.

Bed linen. Sheets, pillowslips, towels, bathmats, bathrobes, etc.
Restaurant linen. Table-cloths, slip cloths, waiters' cloths, glass cloths, tray cloths, sideboard covers, etc.
Kitchen linen. Tea towels, oven gloves, etc.
Uniforms. For kitchen, restaurant, housekeeping, reception, porters, etc.
Soft furnishings. Curtains, loose covers, cushions, blinds.
Miscellaneous. Continuous roller towels, mattress covers, dust sheets, ironing board covers, etc.

Special treatments applied to linen fabrics

Beetling. This gives the fabric an extra lustre.
Crease-resistance. Similar to cotton (*see* above).

Maintenance of linen fabrics

This is similar to that for cotton. However, some cream linen fabrics may have been manufactured and sold as "unbleached", in which case wash Code 1 should be avoided. A particularly hot iron is recommended on a damp fabric.

Removing stains from linen fabrics
Similar to cotton.

Wool

Figure 20 is a photograph of a wool fibre, while the international Woolmark is shown in Fig. 21.

Woollen fabric is noted for being very warm. This is because the short crimped fibres trap a considerable amount of air and air is a poor conductor of heat. Items made from 100 per cent wool are now used less frequently in housekeeping as they are expensive and difficult to maintain. Wool is, however, frequently blended with synthetic fibres.

Characteristics
(*a*) Weak. This weakness increases when the fibres are wet.
(*b*) Very elastic, therefore does not crease and is very resilient.
(*c*) Bad conductor of heat, therefore warm.

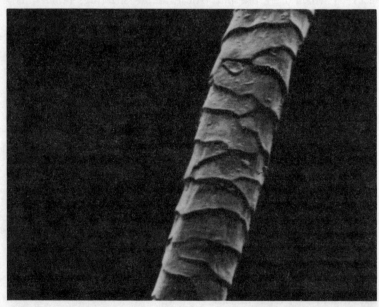

Courtesy Huddersfield Polytechnic

Fig. 20. *Wool fibre.*

PURE NEW
wool

Fig. 21. *The woolmark.*

(*d*) Very absorbent, therefore takes a long time to dry. It will hold up to 30 per cent of its weight in water without feeling wet.

(*e*) Does not soil easily but retains smells.

(*f*) Felts and therefore shrinkage occurs if washed incorrectly.

(*g*) Damaged by alkalis, especially chlorine bleach.

(*h*) Scorches easily.

(*i*) Damaged by moth larvae (*see* Fig. 22), mildew and bacteria.

(*j*) Yellows with exposure to sun.

(*k*) Not damaged by acid solutions.

(*l*) Can be dyed easily.

(*m*) Expensive.

(*n*) Inherently flameproof.

Uses

The main uses are blankets, upholstery, carpets and uniforms. Wool is used extensively in carpeting, usually blended with nylon, as its resilience reduces flattening of the pile.

Woollen fabrics

Worsted. Fibres are combed to create a smooth, strong fabric. Used mainly for clothing.

Barathea. Worsted yarns woven with a twill effect. Used for uniforms.

Gaberdine. Similar to barathea but using normal woollen yarn. Used for lightweight uniforms.

Jersey. Woollen yarn which is knitted. Used for uniforms.

Serge. A heavy, hard-wearing fabric with a twill weave. Used for uniforms. (May now contain cotton and man-made fibres.)

Tweed. A heavy fabric woven in a twill or plain weave. Used for upholstery.

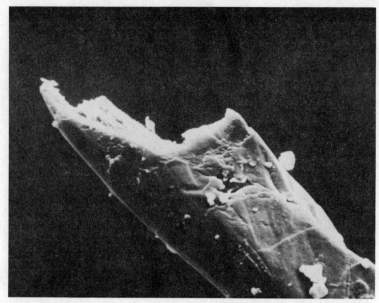

Courtesy Huddersfield Polytechnic

Fig. 22. *Moth-damaged wool fibre.*

Moquette. A cut or uncut pile fabric or a mixture of both. Used for upholstery. (May now contain cotton and rayon.)

Tapestry. Closely woven patterned fabric with coloured weft threads. Used for curtains and upholstery. (May now contain cotton and rayon.)

Felt. Densely matted woollen fibres. Used to line cutlery drawers and for placing under table-cloths. Thick qualities are used as carpet underlays (underfelt).

Baize. Plain woven with a short, raised surface. Traditionally green and used for billiard, snooker and card tables. It is also used as a backing for blotters and place mats and may be found on display screens.

Special treatments applied to woollen fabrics

Non-felting. Wool fibres may be coated with a synthetic film such as nylon to reduce tangling, or they may be treated with chemicals to reduce the scaly part of the fibre which causes the fibres to interlock. This treatment also renders the fabric shrinkproof.

Mothproofing. Woollen fabrics are treated with a substance which is poisonous to moth maggots.

Maintenance of woollen fabrics

(*a*) Do not soak unless very badly soiled or the item is new. In the latter case soaking for ten minutes in a mild ammonia solution will neutralise the acids which may be left after manufacture (the acid would react with the soap).

(*b*) Use warm water and pure soap or neutral synthetic detergent.

(*c*) Wash in water 40 °C and below.

(*d*) Never boil.

(*e*) Rinse well.

(*f*) Spin dry then dry flat away from direct sun.

(*g*) Use warm iron, covering the fabric with a damp cloth.

(*h*) Do not tumble dry.

(*i*) Dry clean large items to avoid damaging equipment.

(*j*) Wool mixtures and blends—Code 6.

(*k*) 100 per cent wool—Code 7 or hand wash.

Removing stains from woollen fabrics

Wool contains a protein, keratin, which will be damaged by the enzymes in biological detergents, and so these should be avoided. Alkalis should also be avoided, with the exception of hydrogen peroxide (bleach) which can be used on scorch marks. Great care should be taken when removing stains from woollen fabrics as excessive rubbing could result in felting of the fibres.

Silk

A photograph of a silk fibre is shown in Fig. 23. Silk is rarely used now in hotels and institutions for furnishings. It may, however, be used for decorative wall hangings and guests may require a valeting service for their silk clothing.

Characteristics

(*a*) The silk fibre is extremely long and produces fabrics with a lustrous appearance.

(*b*) Strong but becomes weaker when wet.

(*c*) Elastic but fabrics tend to crease. These creases will disappear with hanging.

(*d*) Poor conductor of heat, therefore warm.

(*e*) Absorbent but dries fairly quickly.

(*f*) Will not shrink.

(*g*) Will not soil easily as very smooth.

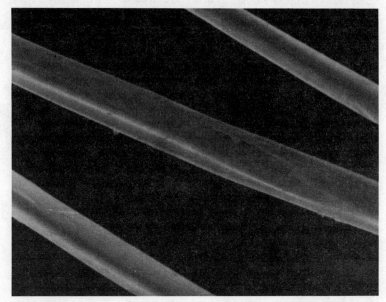

Courtesy Huddersfield Polytechnic
Fig. 23. *Cultivated silk (degummed).*

(*h*) Harmed by strong acids and alkalis especially chlorine bleach.

(*i*) Scorches easily.

(*j*) Non-flammable.

(*k*) Tendency to mildew attack.

(*l*) Will absorb dyes but these tend to bleed.

(*m*) Expensive.

Uses
Decorative panels, nets, velvet curtaining and clothing. (Nets and velvet fabrics are now usually made from cotton or synthetic fibres.)

Fabrics made from silk fibres
These include chiffon, foulard, net, poult and velvet.

Special treatments applied to silk fabrics
Silk fabrics are so delicate that most special treatments would spoil their appearance. Their lightness, however, tends to make them blow about and they may be chemically treated to assist draping. This process is called "weighting".

Maintenance of silk fabrics

(*a*) Soak only if very badly soiled.

(*b*) Use warm water and pure soap or neutral synthetic detergent. Rinse well.

(*c*) Do not boil.

(*d*) Use hydrogen peroxide bleach only if such treatment is necessary.

(*e*) If stiffening is required (for wall hangings, lampshades, etc.) use gum arabic only.

(*f*) Iron on the right side for a glossy finish and the wrong side for a dull finish.

(*g*) Colour fast fabric—Code 7.

(*h*) Non colour fast fabric or heavily embroidered fabric—Code 8 or hand wash.

(*i*) Dry cleaning is recommended for silk fabrics which may water mark.

Removing stains from silk fabrics

Never allow silk to become too dirty. Attend to stains on wall hangings *in situ*. Avoid hanging silk curtaining and hangings in direct sunlight, where they will fade, or in a damp environment, where they may suffer from mildew. Avoid acids, alkalis and bleach (except hydrogen peroxide). Rub very gently when attempting to remove stains.

MAN-MADE FIBRES

Man-made fibres may be 100 per cent synthetic, with a base of coal or petrol, or they may have a base of cellulose (cotton linters and wood). The latter are referred to as regenerated cellulose fibres or rayons. All man-made fibres are marketed under trade names. These vary from country to country which is confusing when trying to identify a fabric for maintenance purposes. Below are listed the chemical names of some of the most commonly found man-made fibres.

(*a*) *Regenerated cellulose*:
    cuprammonium rayon;
    viscose rayon (*see* Fig. 24);
    acetate rayon;
    triacetate rayon;
    polynosic rayon;

(*b*) *Synthetic*:
    acrylic;
    modacrylic;
    polyamide;

Courtesy Huddersfield Polytechnic

Fig. 24. *Viscose rayon.*

polyester;
polyethylene;
polypropylene;
polyvinylidene.

Regenerated cellulose fibres

Characteristics

(*a*) Lustrous and soft.

(*b*) Drape well, particularly acetate and triacetate.

(*c*) Weak. Strength decreases when wet (50–70 per cent weaker).

(*d*) Cuprammonium and viscose are not very elastic, therefore crease badly and are usually given special crease-resistant finishes.

(*e*) Acetate and triacetate are sufficiently elastic to make treatment unnecessary.

(*f*) Moderately good conductors of heat.

(*g*) Cuprammonium and viscose are very absorbent but as a result do not dry quickly.

(*h*) Acetate and triacetate are not very absorbent and therefore dry quickly.

(*i*) Will withstand mild alkalis and solutions of oxidising bleach which must be rinsed away thoroughly.

(*j*) Damaged by weak acids.

(*k*) Resist attack by moths, mildew and bacteria.

(*l*) Cheap, particularly cuprammonium and viscose.

(*m*) Do not soil easily, shrink or lose their shape.

(*n*) Weakened by prolonged exposure to sunlight but are not discoloured by it.

(*o*) Acetate fibres dissolve in acetone. Triacetate is softened by acetone.

(*p*) Cuprammonium and viscose burn like cotton with a dangerous flame, whereas acetate and triacetate give off strong fumes and are left with a black beaded texture after smouldering.

(*q*) All rayons are thermoplastic, which means that the fibres melt when they become warm or hot and set hard on cooling. This is useful for making permanent pleats but a problem when laundering—if the washing solution is too hot, the fabric will dry with an irreversible creased appearance.

Uses

Fabrics made of 100 per cent rayon are not generally used in hotels and institutions as they are too weak to withstand hard wear and constant laundering. However, the weakness of rayon fibres can be used to advantage in the field of disposables. Many cleaning cloths, restaurant linen and hygienic wipes are made from rayon fibres which are bonded together, sometimes dyed and in some cases impregnated with detergent, germicide, etc. Rayons are frequently blended with natural or synthetic fibres, and they then resemble cotton, wool or silk fabrics, suitable for uniforms.

Trade names used for regenerated cellulose fabrics

Cuprammonium rayon. Bemberg Rayon: resembles silk.

Viscose rayon. Delustra ⎫
Fibro   ⎬ resemble cotton;
Evlan: crimped and used in carpeting;
Sarille: crimped to resemble wool.

Acetate rayon. Dicel ⎫
Celanese   ⎬
Celafibre   ⎬ lightweight clothing and accessories.
Fibroceta ⎭

Triacetate rayon. Tricel ⎫
Arnel   ⎬ frequently permanently pleated and
Trilan ⎭ suitable for uniforms.

Polynosic rayon. Vincel ⎫
Zantrel ⎬ lightweight clothing and curtaining.

Fabrics made from rayon fibres

Brocade. A thick fabric with a predominance of weft threads giving a rich, patterned appearance. Used for upholstery, curtaining and bedspreads.

Dupion. Plain fabric with slub yarns giving a textured appearance. Used for soft furnishings and upholstery.

Gaberdine. Strong fabric with a twill weave. Used for uniforms.

Tapestry.
Velvet.
Velveteen. } Soft furnishings.
Damask.

Finishes applied to rayon fabrics

Crease-resistance.
Flameproofing. } Applied to cuprammonium and viscose rayons only in a similar way to cotton fabrics.

Permanent pleating. The fibres are softened with heat and pleated while soft. On cooling the pleats remain.

Trubenising. The thermoplastic nature of rayons allows two pieces of rayon fabric to be bonded together. This is used for stiffening fabrics needed for collars and cuffs in uniforms.

Maintenance of rayon fabrics

(*a*) Do not soak.

(*b*) Wash frequently but with care.

(*c*) Do not boil.

(*d*) Rinse well with final rinse in cold water.

(*e*) Do not twist or wring.

(*f*) Iron when evenly damp on the wrong side with a warm iron.

(*g*) Cuprammonium, viscose and polynosic rayons with special finishes—Code 4; and where colours are not fast—Code 5.

(*h*) Acetate, triacetate and rayon mixtures—Codes 6, 7, 8.

Removing stains from rayon fabrics

Do not boil or soak in biological detergent (although washing with it should do no damage). Do not use acids and use only a weak solution of bleach if necessary. Acetone will damage acetate rayon.

Synthetic fibres

It is very difficult to distinguish between the many synthetic fabrics likely to be found in hotels and institutions where they are used extensively for furnishings as well as for uniforms. They are frequently blended with other fibres to add strength, e.g. carpets where polyamide fibres are combined with wool, and sheeting where polyester fibres are combined with cotton. Polyamide, polyester and acrylic fibres have many uses, whereas the modacrylics, polyethylene and polypropylene are more specific.

Characteristics

(*a*) Non-absorbent which makes them very easy to launder as they dry easily.

(*b*) Elastic; they keep their shape and require little or no ironing.

(*c*) Smooth which means they resist soiling.

(*d*) Electro-static; this means they will tend to attract dust but as this is only surface dust it is easily removed with frequent washing.

(*e*) Very strong and hard-wearing and therefore frequently blended with other fibres to lengthen the life of a fabric, e.g. carpeting.

(*f*) Resistant to acids and most alkalis, mildew, bacteria and moths. Polyester is particularly resistant to the effects of sunlight.

(*g*) Low-melting point which means that care is needed in laundering to ensure washing and ironing temperatures are not too high. Many synthetic fabrics are damaged by cigarette burns. In the event of a fire, fabrics will melt rather than burn with a flame, but they may create highly poisonous fumes.

Trade names and uses
See Table XII.

TABLE XII. IDENTIFICATION MARKS AND USES OF SYNTHETIC FIBRES.

Type of synthetic fibre	Trade names	Uses
Polyamide	Bri-nylon	Sheets
	Nylon 66	Blankets
	Nylon Type 91	Carpets
	Enkalon	Curtains
	Perlon/Nylon 6	Uniforms
	Celon	
	Monsanto Nylon	
	Banlon	
	Helanca	
Polyester (*see also* Fig. 25)	Terylene	Bed linen
	Dacron	Table linen
	Kodel	Uniforms
	Crimplene	Nets
	Terlenka	Pillow fillings
	Trevira	Quilt fillings
	Lirelle	

Table Continued

TABLE XII. (*Continued*).

Type of synthetic fibre	Trade names	Uses
Acrylic (*see also* Fig. 26)	Orlon Dralon Acrilan Courtelle	Blankets Upholstery Carpets Uniforms
Modacrylic	Teklan Dynel Verel	Curtains Overalls Blankets Upholstery Rugs
Polyethylene (Polythene)	Courlene	Upholstery
Polypropylene	Cournova Nufil Spunstron Cotlon	Carpets

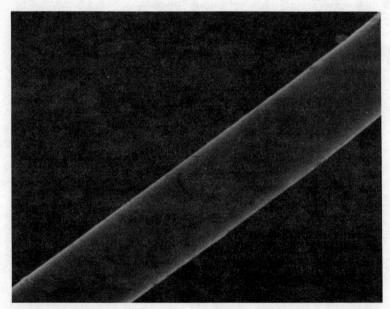

Courtesy Huddersfield Polytechnic

Fig. 25. *Polyester.*

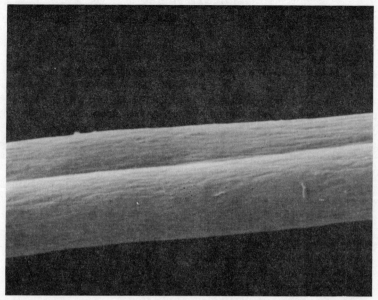

Courtesy Huddersfield Polytechnic

Fig. 26. *Acrylic.*

Special treatment applied to synthetic fabrics

Bulking. The yarns are heat set into a crimped state. Fabrics made with crimped yarns are stretchy, warm, fairly absorbent and less likely to "pull".

Maintenance of synthetic fabrics

(*a*) Launder frequently.
(*b*) Wash whites separately.
(*c*) Do not boil.
(*d*) Avoid squeezing and creasing in hot water, therefore rinse finally in cold water.
(*e*) Care is necessary when ironing to avoid melting the fibres.
(*f*) Whites—Code 3; coloureds—Code 4.

Removing stains from synthetic fabrics

Do not use bleach except on polyester fibres. Do not boil. Polyamide is weakened by acids.

MINERAL FIBRES

Fibres made from silver or gold may be found in very old tapestries, wall hangings and upholstery fabrics. However, aluminium (Lurex) is now more frequently found blended with polyester as this allows the fibre to be coloured and makes the fabric easier to clean. Aluminium, however, is sensitive to alkalis and so these should not be used. As most upholstery shampoos contain some alkali, dry-cleaning with a solvent is recommended. Aluminium fibres have excellent insulating properties and are used as a backing for curtaining and for ironing board covers (Milium).

Glass can be manufactured as a textile fibre (Fibreglass, Fiberglas, Marglass) and is used for curtaining as it is not damaged in any way by exposure to the sun or air. It is also easily laundered. On the other hand, the rather brittle fibres are sensitive to abrasion and glass fibre curtains are best hung inside a window recess. Glass fibres are inherently fireproof and are therefore suitable for fire blankets and pipe lagging.

SPECIAL FINISHES

Many of the finishes that can be applied to fabrics have been discussed in the preceding sections. Below is a summary of the different types of finish.

Brushing. Increases bulk and therefore warmth, e.g. flannelette, winceyette, sheeting.

Mercerising. Improves lustre. Can create a rough texture.

Shrink-resistance. Fibres are pre-shrunk before the fabric is constructed or chemically treated ("Rigmel", "Sanforized", "Superwash", "Dylan").

Crease-resistance. Improves resilience ("Permalose").

Trubenising. (Stable.) Stiffens fabric, eliminating the need for starching.

Glazing/embossing. (Stable.) Creates a shine, e.g. chintz ("Everglaze").

Flame-resistance. (Unstable.) Fabrics are impregnated with chemicals to prevent a flame forming when they reach flash point.

Waterproofing. (Stable.) Makes a fabric non-absorbent.

Water-repellent. (Unstable.) Reduces absorbency ("Scotchgard").

Mothproofing. Fabric treated with chemicals which are poisonous to moth larvae ("Dielmoth", "Mitin", "Eulan").

Weighting. Silk fabrics are impregnated with tin salts to improve draping.

Beetling. Improves lustre of linen fabrics.

Bacteria proof. Fabrics are treated with an anti-bacteria fluid ("Sanitized", "Durafresh", "Actifresh").

Maintenance of fabrics with special finishes

Great care should be taken when laundering fabrics with special treatments. Laundering and dry cleaning contractors should always be informed of any unstable finishes applied to articles so that they can take this into account during the cleaning process, or re-apply the finish if necessary. Manufacturers usually supply labels to sew on to articles made from fabrics treated with fire-retardant finishes. The following specific points should be noted.

(*a*) Do not boil, bleach or starch glazed or embossed cotton.

(*b*) Rinse water-repellent finished fabrics very well as any detergent left in the fabric will weaken the finish.

(*c*) Water-repellent finishes are damaged by dry cleaning.

(*d*) Soap may impair flameproofing, therefore use a synthetic detergent.

(*e*) Crease-resistant finishes weaken with repeated laundering.

FABRIC CONSTRUCTION

Figure 27 illustrates how fibres are turned into fabrics. The following sections discuss the four main categories of fabric construction: knitting, felting, bonding and weaving.

FABRIC CONSTRUCTION

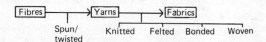

Fig. 27. *The progression of fibres to fabrics.*

Knitting

This uses one yarn which is interlocked with loops (*see* Figs. 28 and 29). It is used for stockinette cleaning cloths, loose covers and

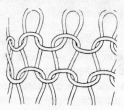

Fig. 28. *Knitting.*

Courtesy Huddersfield Polytechnic

Fig. 29. *Weft knit.*

jumpers, etc. worn as uniforms. These fabrics pull out of shape easily if washed incorrectly and may also ladder. They are, however, stretchy and if this can be kept under control knitting can be a versatile method of fabric construction.

Felting

A very cheap fabric is created by moistening and rubbing together short animal fibres, usually wool, so that they interlock. Felts are not very strong nor will they withstand much laundering. They are used under table cloths to protect the surface of the table and reduce noise. They are used extensively as a carpet underfelt, in varying thicknesses. Felts will pull apart fairly easily and eventually flatten. They are best dry-cleaned.

Bonded felt

(*See* Fig. 30.) Man-made fibres as well as natural ones can be mixed with plastic resin and pressed into sheets of varying thicknesses. When this mixture is heated a bonded fabric is created which is extremely cheap and may be impregnated with detergents, polish, etc. Bonded felts do not crease, shrink or fray. They are used as

Courtesy Huddersfield Polytechnic

Fig. 30. *Bonded felt.*

interlining fabrics, but their main use is in the field of disposables—cleaning cloths and table linen, including banqueting rolls which can be cut to size. In hospitals they are used for dry mop heads, sheets, laundry bags and protective clothing.

Weaving

Two yarns, a warp running vertically and a weft running horizontally, are interlocked to give a firmly constructed fabric. The warp and weft yarns may both be spun from one type of fibre or blend. If they are not then the fabric is described as a mixture of fibres.

Weaving is a very adaptable method of fabric construction. The simplest method of weaving is a *plain* weave when identical warp and weft yarns interlock evenly (*see* Figs. 31 and 32). Plain weaves can be adapted to create a very regular pattern by using different coloured yarns (gingham); and texture can be created by using yarns of varying thicknesses (repp, *see* Fig. 33). Plain woven fabrics may be used for all items used in housekeeping, especially sheets. They will, however, tear quite easily once snagged, although repair is quite simple.

A plain weave forms the base of many pile fabrics such as terry

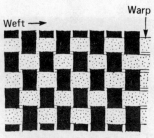

Fig. 31. *Plain weave.*

Courtesy Huddersfield Polytechnic

Fig. 32. *Plain weave.*

towelling, velvet, candlewick and carpeting. These fabrics have a pile which is created by looping or knotting a short piece of yarn or tufts of yarn on to a plain woven base (*see* Fig. 34). A pile is introduced into a fabric to increase absorbency (towels), to improve insulation (curtaining) or to create a more interesting and rich fabric (upholstered chairs). All pile fabrics, however, attract dust and smells and need constant vacuuming and frequent dry cleaning or laundering.

Some methods of weaving create extremely strong fabrics. A

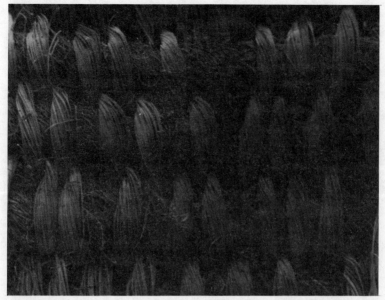

Courtesy Huddersfield Polytechnic

Fig. 33. *Repp.*

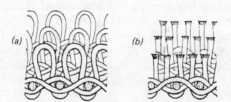

Fig. 34. (a) *Pile weave, uncut;* (b) *pile weave, cut.*

Fig. 35. *Twill weave.*

Courtesy Huddersfield Polytechnic

Fig. 36. *Twill weave.*

twill weave (*see* Figs. 35 and 36) is used extensively for overalls and suitings. It is less likely to tear or pull out of shape than a plain woven fabric and may be so closely woven that water and stains take longer to penetrate than other types of woven fabric.

A *satin* weave (*see* Figs. 37 and 38) creates a smooth looking fabric which repels dust. However, these fabrics have a predominance of warp threads and are likely to snag. Their main use is for curtaining.

It is possible to improve the insulating properties of a fibre by weaving it more loosely or in such a way that it has holes (cells) which trap air. A good application of this is hospital blankets,

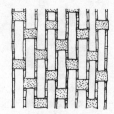

Fig. 37. *Satin weave.*

Courtesy Huddersfield Polytechnic

Fig. 38. Satin weave.

which are made from cotton yarn so that they can be boiled. Because cotton is not particularly warm, the yarns are put together in a cellular weave which will trap air.

A high quality woven fabric has a large number of warp and weft threads per square centimetre ("high count"). It is important for plain weaves to have a high count as these tend to pull out of shape easily. Fabrics with a low count may appear to be of good quality when new but after only a few washes they become limp and may shrink. This usually occurs with cotton fabrics which are coated with a fine powder during manufacture. It is not the method of laundering which causes the change.

CONTROL OF LINEN AND SOFT FURNISHINGS

Textiles may be cleaned either on or off the premises, by washing or dry cleaning. Those which are dry cleaned are maintained *in situ* for as long as possible by vacuuming, brushing and spot cleaning, but will eventually require more thorough cleaning off the premises. Most commercial laundries undertake dry cleaning. Articles which can be washed such as bed and table linen require much more regular attention. Whether washed or dry cleaned maintenance of textile fabrics involves movement of many items. This can result in a high proportion of lost items unless adequate supervision is carried out.

Methods used to control the movement of linen and soft furnishings will vary between establishments. The larger hotels and hostels have a linen room which acts as a central collection, distribution and storage point for both soiled linen and soft furnishings. Establishments using contractors for the supply and maintenance of linen and bedding may not feel the necessity for a linen room. If this is the case, even more attention should be paid to control procedures to avoid damage or loss.

Labelling
When the establishment owns the linen itself, the linen room staff will have to label each item with the name of the establishment and the date it was put into service. This may be done with a marker pen, by ironing or sewing on labels or by machine embroidery. Large organisations may have their name woven into each item during manufacture.

Storage of linen
The main bulk of linen awaiting reuse should be stored in a linen room. Less frequently used items should be protected from dust and pests by polythene, brown paper or dust sheets, and stored either high up or low down, allowing the more frequently used items to be stored where they are easily accessible. All stock should be constantly rotated. Where there is no linen room each department or each floor of bedrooms should have a small linen cupboard or room where supplies can be kept.

All storage areas whether large or small should be:

(*a*) kept locked when not in use;
(*b*) warm in order to air the linen;
(*c*) well ventilated to prevent dampness;
(*d*) well lit to ensure thorough cleaning and so reduce pest infestation (linen, particularly blankets and quilts, can create considerable dust), and to enable staff to see that each item is fit for use.

Storage, collection and despatch of soiled linen
Wherever possible soiled linen should be kept away from clean items to avoid the transfer of germs and smells. Poor handling of soiled linen can often cause damage to the fabric. Soiled linen

should be neatly stored for despatch to the laundry as items such as pillowslips and serviettes are easily mislaid and mistakes can occur when counting the number of items.

Soiled linen should be dealt with as soon as possible. It is usually the responsibility of the assistant housekeeper or linen supervisor to ensure that the following procedures are carried out, whether the linen is washed on or off the premises.

(*a*) Sort all soiled items into type, e.g. serviettes, single sheets, hand towels.

(*b*) Count the number of items in each group before placing them into baskets, skips, bags, etc.

(*c*) Record the number of items in each group in a laundry book (*see* Fig. 39). This should be of a duplicate type so that one copy can be sent with the soiled linen to the laundry and the other kept for reference in the linen room. It is important to record the date of despatch. Some establishments also keep departmental laundry books so that a record can be kept of the laundry costs of each department.

Sorter: 6		Packer: 2	Date 28/6/-7		
Check	Customer's entry	Articles	For Laundry use		
			Sorter's description	£	p
✓	253	SINGLE WHITE SHEETS	B. Sheet (W)	128	—

Fig. 39. *Sample page from a laundry book.*

(*d*) Spot checks should be carried out of all areas likely to harbour soiled linen, e.g. outside service lifts, behind bars, kitchen areas, maids' service rooms and staff changing rooms. These checks will also highlight any damaged linen which has been discarded by staff and which in many cases is automatically sent with soiled linen to be washed again causing unnecessary expense.

(*e*) Items which are badly stained or require special treatment by the laundry should be sent separately and a record made of the number of items and the type of treatment requested, e.g. special stain removal, repair or replacement (hired linen).

Return of clean linen
Clean linen is usually returned at the same time as despatch of the soiled linen. It should be unpacked as soon as possible and checked to ensure that:

(*a*) the correct amount of linen has been returned (refer to despatch date in laundry book);
(*b*) laundering is of a satisfactory standard;
(*c*) the items belong to the establishment (if the linen is owned by the establishment).

Having noted any discrepancies, the linen should then be stored methodically:

(*a*) folds facing the edge of the shelf to ease counting;
(*b*) in piles of equal number to speed up issuing;
(*c*) according to type, e.g. small, medium, large table-cloths.

Some establishments, usually those which own the linen themselves, undertake to carry out their own repair work. Tears, darns, stains, re-ironing, re-making, etc. are dealt with at this stage, either in the linen room or in a separate sewing room.

Distribution of clean linen
The distribution of clean linen may occur at the same time as the collection of soiled linen, i.e. one clean item for one soiled item. This is a very satisfactory method of control in a hostel where the number of residents is fairly constant. However, there is a fluctuating demand for linen in a hotel and unless adequate records are kept of the number and type of articles distributed, linen will be mislaid and pilfering becomes easy. To overcome this problem, food service areas and bedroom areas may have a small stock of linen which can be topped-up at regular intervals and a record made of the amount and type of linen despatched to each store.

Stock checks
These should take place whether linen is owned or hired, and the results noted in a linen room stock book (*see* Fig. 40). The frequency of stock checks varies from place to place but it is advisable to check launderable stock every month if possible, and certainly not less frequently than every six months. Where computers are used it is possible to obtain an accurate record of stock within minutes. Bedding and soft furnishings may be checked less

Date : 26/7/- 4							
Article	Stock in hand	New stock	Total	Less condemned	Total	Actual stock	Discrepancies
SHEETS (SINGLE)	1,120	25	1,145	15	1,130	1,125	5
SHEETS (DOUBLE)							
SHEETS (COT)							

Fig. 40. *Sample page from a linen room stock book.*

frequently, but when they are checked, time should be spent on inspecting them for wear and tear and soiling so that arrangements can be made for repair, replacement, dry cleaning or laundering. This should be carried out at the same time as periodic cleaning of the area (*see* Chapter 7 and Fig. 69).

Hospital linen

Hospital linen is sent direct to the hospital laundry to avoid the risks of cross-infection. Hospital laundries are organised in a similar way to commercial laundries and are a separate department from housekeeping.

Hospital housekeeping staff have little to do with the maintenance of textiles except to ensure that curtaining is kept free of dust and to assist with the taking down and rehanging of screen and window curtains. Bed linen is usually the responsibility of nursing staff and the laundry department, although domestic assistants and ward orderlies may help to bag it and store it safely before despatch/collection. Infected linen is placed in special laundry bags which can be placed into a washing machine without being unpacked. The bag is made from a fabric which will dissolve during the washing process.

Maintenance of personal linen

When people stay away from home it is necessary to offer them facilities for cleaning their clothing. Arrangements will vary according to the type of establishment.

Hostels, local authority homes and holiday camps

These will usually provide laundering equipment for residents to use. In fact, residents may be expected to provide and launder their own bed linen. It is important to keep this equipment in working order and to ensure it is not mistreated—regular, i.e. daily, inspection of these areas is recommended.

Hospitals

In special circumstances hospitals will undertake to launder personal clothing; for example, if a patient has no relatives to do their washing, or in the case of geriatric and long-stay psychiatric patients where the hospital is their home.

Hotels

These may offer a twenty-four hour personal laundry, dry cleaning and valeting service. If this is the case, laundry bags and lists are provided in each bedroom, and if the guest wishes, he may place his soiled clothes in the bag, write the contents on the list and leave it for the room maid to take to the linen room or to the supervisor responsible for linen despatch. She will record the contents in the hotel laundry book by referring to the list attached to the packet and noting the guest's name and room number. The packet will then be despatched and returned with the hotel linen. The cost should be attached to the packet so that reception can be informed of the extra charge to put on the guest's bill.

LAUNDERING PROCEDURES

Residential establishments may undertake to launder their textile fabrics in their own laundry (On Premises Laundry or OPL) or they may decide to use a contractor and send them to a commercial laundry. Whichever system is adopted it is useful for a supervisor to know how they are cleaned—it helps her to communicate knowledgeably with laundry staff and it may be necessary for her to help out in an OPL if staff are absent or on strike.

Sorting

The soiled linen is unpacked and checked against the list in the laundry book. Non-hired items are marked with a temporary tag which is removed before returning the linen. Items are then sorted into groups according to wash codes or items and weighed into manageable quantities. Before placing each load into the washing machines, pockets should be emptied, zips done up and apron strings, etc. tied together to prevent them tangling and pulling off.

Washing

Items are washed in automatic machines with starch or conditioner added with the final rinse. The more sophisticated equipment found in commercial laundries is controlled by a computer which can be programmed to maintain the correct water temeprature and to dispense the correct amounts and type of detergent, bleach, starch, etc. at the right stage of the washing programme. Such equipment will remove water from each load and may be connected directly to a tumble dryer so that on emerging from the machine the articles are ready for ironing. Where the tumble dryer is separate, there must be sufficient baskets and trolleys to assist with the transfer of damp articles from the washer to the tumble dryer as it is often at this stage that damage and resoiling occurs.

Ironing
Cotton and linen items should be slightly damp for ironing. Ironing equipment (*see* Chapter 2) should be kept free of dust, dirt and grease. Establishments with their own laundry may have "easy care" linen, i.e. made from synthetic fibres or mixtures of natural and synthetic fibres, as these can be laundered at lower washing temperatures and need very little drying and little if any ironing, thus reducing heating bills and the cost of equipment.

Folding
All linen items need folding for storage. This may be done by hand or by machine. If done by hand it is possible to vary the position of the folds to avoid wear in the same places. Table-cloths and serviettes should be screen folded, and sheets, pillowslips and towels folded lengthwise to assist with bedmaking and to make towels easier to hang over rails, etc.

Packaging and despatch
At a commercial laundry articles with identically numbered tags are collected together, checked against the laundry list, wrapped in brown paper or polythene and placed back into skips, hampers or bags together with the list. They are then returned to the client. Both commercial and on premises laundries may undertake to package linen in sets, i.e. one sheet, one pillowslip, one hand towel, one bath towel, one bathmat. This saves time when issuing clean bed linen from the linen room.

Points to remember when laundering textile fibres
(*a*) Carry out the correct order of laundering:
- (*i*) check;
- (*ii*) sort;
- (*iii*) wash;
- (*iv*) bleach;
- (*v*) starch/add conditioner;
- (*vi*) spin;
- (*vii*) tumble dry;

Symbol	Washing temperature		Agitation	Rinse
	Machine	Hand		
1 95	Very hot (95°C) to boil	Hand hot 50°C or boil	Maximum	Normal
2 60	Hot 60°C	Hand hot 50°C	Maximum	Normal
3 60	Hot 60°C	Hand hot 50°C	Medium	Cold to minimise creasing
4 50	Hand hot 50°C	Hand hot 50°C	Medium	Cold to minimise creasing
5 40	Warm 40°C	Warm 40°C	Medium	Normal
6 40	Warm 40°C	Warm 40°	Minimum	Cold to minimise creasing
7 40	Warm 40°C	Warm 40°C	Minimum Do not rub	Normal
8 30	Cool 30°C	Cool 30°C	Minimum	Cold to minimise creasing
9 95	Very hot (95°C) to boil	Hand hot 50°C or boil	Maximum	Cold to minimise creasing
	Do not machine wash (the appropriate hand washing instructions are usually given alongside this symbol)			
	Do not wash at all			

Spinning/ wringing	*Fabric*
Normal	Used for white cotton and linen articles without special finishes, this process provides the most vigorous washing conditions. Wash temperature can be boiling (100°C) and agitation and spinning times are maximum. Ensures good whiteness and stain removal.
Normal	For cotton, linen or viscose (rayon) articles without special finishes where colours are fast at 60°C. Provides vigorous wash conditions but at a temperature which maintains fast colours.
Short spin or drip dry	For white nylon or white polyester/cotton mixtures; less vigorous than either 1 or 2. The wash temperature (60°C) is high enough to prolong whiteness, and cold rinsing followed by short spinning minimises creases.
Short spin or drip dry	For coloured nylon; polyester; cotton and viscose (rayon) articles with special finishes; acrylic/cotton mixtures; coloured polyester/ cotton mixtures. Except for washing temperature, identical to process 3. The lower, hand hot temperature (50°C) safeguards the colour and finish.
Normal	For cotton, linen or viscose (rayon) articles where colours are fast at 40°C, but not at 60°C, this process has warm wash (40°C), medium agitation, normal spinning or wringing. The low wash temperature is essential to safeguard colour fastness.
Short spin Do not hand wring	For those articles which require low temperature washing (40°C), minimum agitation, a cold rinse and a short spin, e.g. acrylics; acetate and triacetate, including mixtures with wool; polyester/ wool blends. These conditions preserve colour and shape and minimise creasing.
Normal spin Do not hand wring	For wool, including blankets, and wool mixtures with cotton or viscose (rayon); silk, which needs low temperature washing (40°C) and minimum agitation but requires normal spinning. Washing in this way preserves colour, size and handle. Do not hand wring or rub.
Short spin Do not hand wring	For silk and printed acetate fabrics, with colours which are not fast at 40°C, requiring to be washed at a very low temperature (30°C), with a minimum agitation and spinning. Unlikely to appear on UK produced goods.
Drip dry	For cotton articles with special finishes which benefit from a high temperature (95°C) wash but require drip drying. Again rarely to be found on UK produced goods.

WASHING TEMPERATURES

100°C	Boil	Self-explanatory.	50°C	Hand hot	As hot as the hands can bear.
95°C	Very Hot	Water heated to near boiling temperature.	40°C	Warm	Pleasantly warm to the hand.
60°C	Hot	Hotter than the hand can bear. The temperature of water coming from many domestic hot taps.	30°C	Cool	Feels cool to the touch.

Fig. 41. *International textile care labelling code: washing.*

DRYING

Care labels may also include one or other of the following symbols recommending a particular drying method.

Tumble drying beneficial but not essential.

Line dry.

Drip dry: for best results hang while wet.

Dry flat: do not hang to dry.

BLEACHING

 This symbol indicates that household (chlorine) bleach could be used. Care must be taken to follow the manufacturer's instructions.

 When this symbol appears on a label household bleach must *not* be used.

IRONING

The number of dots in the ironing symbol indicates the correct temperature setting — the fewer the dots the cooler the iron setting.

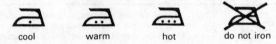

cool   warm   hot   do not iron

Fig. 41. *continued*

(*viii*) remove stains and repair (ideally this should be done prior to washing to prevent stains becoming set and to prevent tears getting worse; however, it can be extremely unpleasant working on soiled linen and in practice linen is washed first);

(*ix*) iron;

(*x*) fold;

(*xi*) store (rotate stock).

(*b*) Adapt the above procedure for the appropriate wash code (*see* Fig. 41). If the incorrect wash code is used irreversible damage can be caused to the fabric, e.g. synthetic fibres which are cooled too quickly or washed at too high a temperature develop creases which cannot be removed with ironing.

(*c*) Remove articles from washers and dryers immediately the cycle is complete to avoid creasing.

(*d*) *Blankets*.

(*i*) These become very heavy when wet and can damage equipment.

(*ii*) Dry clean woollen blankets.

(*iii*) Only wash electric blankets if instructions are given.

(*iv*) Never dry clean electric blankets. It is advisable to return them to the manufacturer for cleaning and servicing.

(*v*) For woollen blankets which have yellowed with age wash in a solution of 15 g eucalyptus oil, 1.5 dcl methylated spirit and 75 g soap flakes.

(*e*) *Pillows*. These should be washed individually if they have synthetic filling. Those with natural fillings should be dry cleaned as they become very heavy when wet.

(*f*) *Bedspreads*.

(*i*) Silk, rayon or wool should be dry cleaned.

(*ii*) Candlewick should not be ironed as this will flatten the tufts.

(*iii*) Crochet should be pulled to shape while drying or ironing.

(*g*) *Quilts*. These should be dry cleaned approximately once a year. Occasionally they will need refilling as they lose efficiency at a rate of 1 per cent per annum.

DRY CLEANING

Some textile fabrics may shrink, crease, distort or lose their colour if washed and therefore have to be dry cleaned. This is usually carried out by a contractor although with the development of non-toxic solvents, it is now possible to dry clean items *in situ*. Uniforms, blankets, quilts, loose covers, pillows, curtains and bedspreads are typical of the items likely to require dry cleaning.

Procedures for dry cleaning

(*a*) Apart from uniforms, articles are usually sent for dry cleaning at the same time as periodic cleaning is carried out (*see* Chapter 7).

(*b*) Loose covers and fitted bedspreads should be marked as to the chair or bed to which they belong unless all chairs and beds are identical.

(*c*) Curtain hooks should be removed and tapes pulled flat.

(*d*) A record is made of the number and type of items sent, in the same way as for laundered items.

(*e*) On arrival at the contractor, each item is temporarily labelled and the dry cleaning symbols checked, if present (*see* Fig. 42).

DRY CLEANING

The letter in the circle refers to the solvent which may be used in the dry cleaning process, and those using "coin op" dry cleaning should check that the cleaning symbol shown on the label is the same as that in the instructions given on the front of the machine.

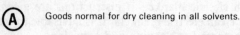 Goods normal for dry cleaning in all solvents.

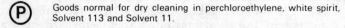 Goods normal for dry cleaning in perchloroethylene, white spirit, Solvent 113 and Solvent 11.

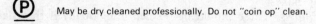 May be dry cleaned professionally. Do not "coin op" clean.

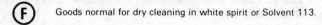 Goods normal for dry cleaning in white spirit or Solvent 113.

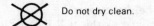 Do not dry clean.

Fig. 42. *International textile care labelling code: dry cleaning. The letter in the circle refers to the solvent which may be used in the dry cleaning process, and those using "coin op" cleaning should check that the cleaning symbol shown on the label is the same as that in the instructions given on the front of the machine.*

(*f*) Loose dust is brushed off and any pockets emptied.

(*g*) Very bad stains are removed prior to cleaning in groups according to colour (light, medium, dark). Heavily soiled items are usually kept separate.

(*h*) Dry cleaning is carried out in machines similar to washing machines, except that a solvent such as trichlorethylene or per-chlorethylene is used in place of water. The solvent is removed by spinning then distilled for reuse.

(*i*) Each item is checked again for stains, as some are water soluble, and if necessary "spotting" is carried out.

(*j*) If requested, special finishes such as retexturing are applied. This involves treating the fabric with a solvent containing resins to improve body and bulk.

(*k*) Each item is pressed, although this might not be necessary, then hung up to allow the toxic solvent fumes to evaporate.

(*l*) Packaging and despatch is carried out in the same way as for laundered items.

REMOVING STAINS FROM TEXTILE FABRICS

The most common stains are those found on table linen and which will be removed in the laundering process. A rather different problem is stains which cannot be laundered. The following procedures should be adopted.

(*a*) Treat all stains as soon as possible after they occur.

(*b*) Treat a ring round the stain then gradually work towards its centre.

(*c*) Dab at the stain as rubbing it may spread it and damage the surface.

(*d*) Use a white, absorbent cloth such as a cotton rag or cotton wool when using a solvent stain remover.

(*e*) Do not over-wet the fabric especially those with a pile which may have a cotton base and be likely to shrink.

(*f*) It is very important to test the action of any stain removal agent on an inconspicuous part of the upholstery.

For more detailed information on stain removal *see* Appendix I.

FURTHER INFORMATION

Inevitably, laundering problems will arise which neither a housekeeper nor her supervisors can solve. Advice can be sought from two well-established associations, the Association of British Launderers and Cleaners Ltd and the British Textile Rental Association Ltd.

Supervisors would be well advised to visit a commercial laundry in order to obtain an insight into the work involved in maintaining the textiles they use in their establishments.

SELF-ASSESSMENT QUESTIONS

1. What are the advantages and disadvantages of:

(*a*) natural fibres;
(*b*) rayon fibres;
(*c*) synthetic fibres?

2. Why is it important for a housekeeping supervisor to know about the characteristics of fibres?

3. What effects can the construction of a soft fabric have on its strength and durability?

4. Suggest two typical finishes which are applied to cotton, viscose rayon and polyamide fabrics and state what precautions are necessary in order to retain them during cleaning.

5. Describe in detail the composition, construction and maintenance of the following fabrics: gingham, repp, dralon, bri-nylon, candlewick, moquette, baize, chiffon, vincel.

6. List six items likely to be stored in a linen room and describe how each should be maintained and stored.

7. Summarise the procedures for the cleaning and general maintenance of:

（*a*）a pair of red cotton velvet curtains;
（*b*）white linen table cloths;
（*c*）navy polyester and cotton overalls;
（*d*）woollen blankets.

Hard Surfaces

CHAPTER OBJECTIVES

After studying this chapter you should be able to:
* identify the types of hard surface which need maintaining by the housekeeping department;
* appreciate why specific types of hard surface are used in certain areas;
* describe the methods used to protect and maintain hard surfaces.

INTRODUCTION

The types of hard surface most likely to be encountered in residential establishments are as follows:

(*a*) metals—aluminium, brass, copper, pewter, gold, silver, stainless steel, steel, tin and iron;

(*b*) wood—solid, plywood, chipboard, hardboard, blockboard, laminated, cork, cane, wicker and bamboo;

(*c*) plastics—thermosetting and thermoplastics;

(*d*) ceramics—earthenware, stoneware, vitreous china, porcelain, bone china, brick and marble;

(*e*) glass—lead crystal, soda lime, borosilicate and glass fibre;

(*f*) rubber—vulcanised.

The wide range found creates many problems for the housekeeping department as they each require different cleaning procedures. Unless measures are taken to standardise them in some way by applying protective coatings or finishes, maintenance can become very costly and time consuming.

Hard surfaces are usually chosen for quite specific reasons; e.g.:

(*a*) hygiene;
(*b*) aesthetic aspects (colour, texture, etc.);
(*c*) insulation;
(*d*) ease of maintenance.

Housekeeping staff should do all they can to ensure that the individual qualities of each surface are retained for as long as possible. Textile fabrics tend to shrink, crease, burn readily, pull out of shape, etc. Hard surfaces, on the other hand, will scratch, crack, chip, perish, splinter, blister and may become dangerously slippery. Such damage is caused by regular subjection to pedestrian traffic and activities such as cooking, washing, scrubbing, etc. Many hard surfaces also undergo rigorous treatment from recreational activities such as weight-lifting, roller-skating and squash.

A cleaning supervisor should ensure that prescribed maintenance programmes are adhered to and that any protective coverings or coatings are kept intact. She should learn to recognise signs of serious damage before repair becomes impossible and be able to identify the causes in order to ensure renovation is carried out correctly and a recurrence is prevented. In order to do this some knowledge of the characteristics of the most frequently found hard surfaces is necessary. This is the subject of the following sections.

METALS

These are used for the construction of beds; chairs; tables; door/window/light fittings; cutlery; and cooking and restaurant equipment. Metal surfaces will tarnish, scratch or rust unless protected in some way. The method of protection will depend on the use to which the metal is put.

Methods of protecting metals

Painting
Paint is usually applied to steel or wrought iron which is to look decorative. Paint prevents the metal from coming into contact with oxygen and moisture, which cause it to rust. The metal must be cleaned thoroughly and all traces of rust removed prior to painting. The paint must be applied very thoroughly and kept in good repair.

Enamelling
This method gives a colourful, gloss or matt finish to steel or cast-iron pans, signboards, blackboards, etc. Molten glass is applied to the surface and sets to form a tough, easily cleaned surface. It may eventually scratch and crack ("craze"), and if this happens to cooking equipment, the item should not be used.

Plastic coating
PVC, acrylic and polyester plastics can be used to cover handrails, table and chair legs, broom handles, etc. This widely used finish has a tendency to scratch which looks unsightly and is difficult to conceal.

Electroplating

Electrolysis is used to deposit metals such as chromium, copper, zinc, tin, silver and gold on to such surfaces as nickel, brass, steel and copper. The finish is widely used for cutlery, restaurant equipment, cooking equipment, and furniture and fittings. It is very durable but will eventually be destroyed by chemical metal cleaning (Silver Dip), constant friction and repeated exposure to high temperatures.

Galvanising

This does not create a particularly attractive finish but is cheap and very durable, and is used extensively for mop buckets, dustbins, pot sinks, etc. The base metal is coated with a layer of zinc to reduce corrosion.

Anodising

This is an electro-chemical process which enhances the appearance of aluminium and increases its resistance to soiling and corrosion. It is used for door and window fittings, etc.

Lacquering

This is usually applied to copper and brass. It is easily applied by painting or spraying and effectively reduces tarnishing to a minimum.

Tin plate

Items such as cheese graters, sieves, wire whisks and copper pans, etc. may be coated with or dipped into molten tin, as this material has good corrosion resistance—an important fact when an item may be exposed to acid or sulphurous foods and frequent washing.

Metals used to provide protection

Metals are very strong and may themselves be used to provide protection, such as on the corner of a wall that is vulnerable to banging from trolleys, wheelchairs and cleaning machines. Sheets of stainless steel may also be placed around light switches and door handles, or on to swing doors which may suffer considerable damage by being opened by people kicking them (waiters carrying trays) or by mobile beds being pushed against them in a hospital. Many bars contain glossy copper or brass tops to the tables with a foot rail beneath the bar itself.

TABLE XIII. MAINTENANCE OF METAL SURFACES.

Metal	Protective coatings	Uses	Maintenance	Special points
Aluminium	Anodising	Saucepans Light fittings Trays Insulating foil Venetian blinds Window frames Furniture Door/window fittings	Use a hot synthetic detergent solution. Do not use soda or bleach. Use abrasives with care. Remove discoloration in saucepans by boiling a solution of water and lemon, rinse and dry, *or* add 15 ml laundry borax to 500 ml washing up solution. Apply a little liquid wax polish to maintain gleam on show pieces.	Damaged by alkalis. Scratches easily. Stained by acids. Lightweight. Varied qualities; very poor qualities bend easily.
Brass Copper	Lacquering Long-term polish	*Brass* Furniture Door/window fittings Foot rails Ornaments *Copper* Table tops Wall panels Saucepans Bowls Kettles	Clean with a paste made of equal quantities of vinegar, salt and flour. Polish with a proprietary polish. Lacquer can be removed with acetone if necessary. Corroded brass should be treated with spirits of salt then rinsed throughly. In very bad cases soak for twelve hours in washing soda solution (approx. 30 g) then rinse and polish.	Will tarnish and scratch easily. Copper is an excellent heat conductor. Copper may also be "beaten" to provide texture. Copper cookware should be lined with tin or nickel as the copper may react adversely with some foods. Pans should be relined as soon as signs of wear can be seen.
Pewter	Lacquering	Tankards Plates Goblets	Wash in warm synthetic detergent solution and rub well when drying. Remove grease with methylated spirit before washing. Polish with a proprietary metal polish.	Should be cleaned regularly and frequently as tarnish is difficult to remove.

Material	Treatments	Applications	Cleaning and care	Notes
Silver } Gold }	Electroplating Long-term polish	Cutlery Restaurant ware Ornaments Vases Bowls	Wash in hot synthetic detergent solution. Occasionally polish with a "dip" or proprietary cleaner. Store silver wrapped in acid-proof tissue paper or tarnish-proof bags and place in airtight containers in a dry atmosphere.	Both are soft metals and will scratch easily. Sulphurous foods such as egg yolk, fish and green vegetables, and salt will create tarnish. Both are valuable metals and items should be stored securely.
Stainless steel	—	Cutlery Restaurant ware Protective panelling Sanitary ware Furniture Trays Cookware	Wash in hot synthetic detergent solution, rinse and dry thoroughly and immediately. Polish occasionally with a proprietary metal polish to remove scratches or spray polish working the way of the grain.	Avoid the use of harsh abrasives. Damage will eventually occur if not kept dry. Will scratch with constant use. Damaged by prolonged contact with acids including silver dips, excessive heat, hot fat, alkalis such as bleach, salt and neat detergent.
Mild steel	Painting Electroplating Galvanising Tin plating	Furniture Cooking utensils Sanitary fitments	Wash or wipe with synthetic detergent solution, rinse and buff up. Remove bad marks from unfinished steel with steel wool. Use bicarbonate of soda on stained chromium followed by a proprietary spray polish.	Avoid abrasives on chromium and tin finishes particularly. Discard tin-plated items as soon as rust marks appear, or have them re-treated.
Iron	Galvanising Enamelling	Cookware Furniture Ornaments Buckets Dustbins Pot sinks	Wash only if necessary unless galvanised when regular washing is necessary followed by thorough drying. Remove rust from galvanised items with fine steel wool dampened with solvent. Wipe unfinished items with a dry cloth while still warm (cookware). Coat lightly with oil or wax occasionally.	Do not use items with cracked enamel. Avoid damp storage areas. Before long-term storage coat with oil, unsalted fat, vaseline or black lead. Prove new iron cookware before putting into use, i.e. warm pan, rub with salt, repeat with fresh salt, heat pan with a little oil until hot then wipe.

Maintenance of metals

Table XIII summarises the uses and characteristics of different metals, and gives guidelines on their maintenance by the housekeeping department.

WOOD

Materials in this group of hard surfaces are porous. They are found in all types of establishment and are used for a variety of reasons:

(*a*) appearance (timber occurs in many colours with an infinite variety of grain patterns);

(*b*) resilience (cork and wood strips);

(*c*) cost (chipboard is a very strong but cheap material to produce);

(*d*) insulation (all these materials will absorb a certain amount of sound and psychologically can create a feeling of warmth and luxury).

Porous materials will absorb not only liquids but also dust. They are also likely to succumb to fungal attack and pest infestation. They therefore require protection against these problems and regular inspection and maintenance if they are to withstand constant use and retain their appearance.

Wood is frequently used in the construction of upholstered furniture (chairs, beds, etc.) when it is covered by upholstery fabrics. Cleaning staff should be aware of this fact in order to appreciate the need for careful handling of such items.

Solid wood (hard or soft)

Hardwood is a very strong, heavy material used for the construction of:

(*a*) floors (strip, board, block, parquet, mosaic);

(*b*) furniture (tables, chairs, chests);

(*c*) walls (panelling);

(*d*) incidental furnishings (lampshades, picture frames);

(*e*) kitchen and restaurant ware.

It has a more refined grain than softwood and the short fibres make it less likely to splinter, swell or dent. Hardwoods are usually darker than softwoods and include teak, mahogany, oak, walnut and beech. Hardwood is expensive and is very often used as a veneer on wood products such as chipboard.

Softwoods such as pine, deal and fir are used for the construction of furniture, subfloors, joists, ceilings, broom handles, etc., where the wood is either covered up or out of public view. Pine has also come into fashion for furniture such as kitchen tables, stools, chairs and dressers (i.e. items which at one time were for use by servants only). Softwood is cheap and lightweight. It is easily damaged by liquids and heavy impact.

Wood products
These have developed to meet the specific demands of furniture manufacture and to reduce the cost of wooden items. The most widely used include:

(a) plywood;
(b) chipboard;
(c) hardboard;
(d) blockboard;

Plywood is made by bonding together a number of thin sheets (plies) of wood—usually hardwood—in such a way that the grain of one sheet lies at right angles to those either side of it (*see* Fig. 43). Plywood is very strong. It can be bent to any shape during manufacture and may have as many as nine plies edged with beading or lipping. It is used for tables, chairs, desks, etc. which need to withstand hard use and is therefore found in schools, colleges and halls of residence. Plywood may be covered with plastic laminate or a hardwood veneer.

Chipboard is used extensively for work-tops, wardrobes, chests of drawers, etc., and nearly always has a wood veneer or plastic laminate. It is heavy, very strong but inflexible. It is made by mixing wood chips with a synthetic resin adhesive (*see* Fig. 44).

Hardboard is more flexible than chipboard and much thinner. It is made from compressed brown fibreboard, smooth on one side with a mesh texture on the other. Hardboard is used for the backing of wardrobes, the base of drawers, door panels, picture backings, and as a base for floor tiles.

Blockboard consists of strips of wood between veneers. The inner strips of wood are fairly thick (up to 30 mm) making it a

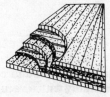

Fig. 43. *Cross-section of 5-ply plywood.*

Fig. 44. *Cross-section of chipboard.*

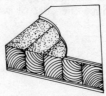

Fig. 45. *Cross-section of blockboard.*

strong material used mainly for shelving and table tops (*see* Fig. 45).

Wood products are nearly always faced with a plastic laminate or wood veneer and so should be cleaned according to the outer surface. Wood products are not generally used for floor or wall surfaces, although hardboard may be used as a backing material for wall tiles and panels as it helps to overcome any unevenness. All of them will deteriorate if excessive amounts of water are allowed to penetrate them.

Cork

Cork is used in the form of tiles or strips in varying widths. It is extremely porous and will easily crumble, dent, burn and stain. Its porosity, however, means that it also has good insulating properties, which make it suitable for use on walls and floors and in areas where more dense surfaces would appear very cold, noisy and inhospitable. It is also an ideal material for such items as noticeboards and bathmats.

Housekeeping staff are likely to encounter cork in varying forms:

(*a*) natural;
(*b*) resin sealed;
(*c*) waxed;
(*d*) vinyl coated.

Natural cork is most likely to be found on walls and should be regularly dusted only, preferably with a vacuum cleaner as dust will be easily trapped by the matt surface. Bathmats, however, should be wiped using the minimum of water to remove talcum powder, etc., then stood on end to allow them to dry naturally as quickly as possible. They are not considered very hygienic. Resin sealed, waxed and vinyl coated cork is usually used as a floor covering and is discussed in greater detail in Chapter 6.

Cane, wicker and bamboo

These are the names given to items of furniture made from thick grasses (bamboo), palms (cane) and willow shoots (wicker). They have similar characteristics to timber products but are usually woven or plaited into chairs, tables, baskets, bedheads, etc. They are easily damaged if not used or stored carefully and regular cleaning is necessary to avoid a build up of inaccessible dust, dirt and grease. Cleaning involves brushing or vacuuming each day and wiping approximately once a week with a solution of warm water and washing soda or a solution made up of 5 ml borax and 50 ml water. Both methods should be followed by rinsing in a cold saline solution (15 g salt in 1 l water) to help stiffen the strands. It should be allowed to dry naturally and overwetting should therefore be avoided. Oil or wax polish may be applied if desired to polished surfaces and spray polish to those which are varnished or painted gloss. Polish should not be used on items used with food.

Protecting wood surfaces

Unprotected wood will absorb moisture which causes the grains to swell and so create gaps into which dirt and germs can fall and become trapped when it dries. Liquids, such as coffee and wine, leave a stain on the surface which is difficult to remove and scratching is difficult to avoid particularly on floors. The following are the most frequently found methods of protection and may be referred to as wood finishes.

Cellulose lacquer

This is a fairly durable matt or gloss finish, applied mainly to solid timber furniture during manufacture. It should be dusted and wiped with a damp cloth then dried with a soft one. Cream or spray polish may be applied to the gloss finish. Heat, water and solvents will cause damage.

French polish

This is used on small decorative items of furniture only as it is easily damaged by heat, water and solvents. Deterioration is caused by light and the atmosphere in general. French polishing is produced by rubbing the solid wooden surface with a solution of shellac (a dark red resin) and methylated spirits. It should be polished up well, working the way of the grain, while dusting on a daily basis. If desired a cream, liquid or paste polish may be applied occasionally to remove light soiling and improve the gloss.

Oil

Solid wooden furniture can be given a matt protective finish by rubbing the surface with a mixture of oil (usually linseed oil) and resin. This process gives very little protection although it will help to reduce the absorption of water. Daily dusting is essential as the matt finish does little to repel dust. Marks can be removed by lightly rubbing with very fine steel wool and about twice a year the surface should be rubbed with a mixture of equal quantities of turpentine and raw linseed oil. Proprietary polishes should be avoided.

Paint

This is very widely used on furniture, window frames, door surrounds, skirtings, staircases, etc. Unlike most other finishes it can be very colourful. Gloss paint is tougher than matt or silk and will withstand more frequent washing. All painted wood should be dusted daily and wiped with a synthetic detergent solution or solvent each week. Spray or cream polish can be used to retain the shine on gloss surfaces. Although paint is easily damaged by heat, alkalis and abrasives, it is easy and inexpensive to renew.

Resin (varnish)

Natural and synthetic resins such as polyesters, melamines and polyurethanes are used extensively on wooden furniture, window frames, door surrounds, skirtings, floors and staircases. The finish may be very glossy or matt, and is frequently applied to furniture made from chipboard. Resin is extremely tough. It will resist heat, water, solvents and abrasives but once damaged by scratching or chipping it is very difficult to repair. Dust should be removed daily and cream or spray polish used on the gloss surfaces after damp wiping. Matt surfaces should be rubbed up occasionally using a mixture of 500 ml turpentine, 100 ml boiled linseed oil and 500 ml vinegar.

Wax (beeswax)

This is applied to solid wood furniture or floors. The degree of protection depends on the number of coats of wax which are applied and the efficiency with which it is rubbed in. This will also affect the degree of gloss. It provides a very attractive finish, exposing the pattern of the wood, but is easily damaged by heat, water and solvents. Waxed surfaces should be dusted daily, cleaned each week with cream or liquid polish, and when considered necessary, rubbed with a thin coat of wax which should be allowed to dry before rubbing up well.

Summary
It can be very difficult to identify a wood finish and most housekeepers should keep a record of the manufacturer's recommended cleaning methods when new furniture is purchased or new finishes are applied. As a guide, dull surfaces should be maintained with oils, matt and satin surfaces with pastes and creams, and gloss surfaces with creams or spray polish. Heavily carved furniture is usually made of hardwood and should be maintained with silicone-free pastes and creams, ensuring none becomes lodged in the carving, which would cause a dull white appearance. (Detailed information on wooden floor surfaces can be found in Chapter 6.)

Removing stains from wooden surfaces
(*See also* Appendix I.)

Alcohol
Polish well. If the stain persists rub along the grain with a metal polish or a mixture of linseed oil and cigarette ash.

Burns (black marks)
Rub with metal polish working in the direction of the grain. For wax or oil finishes, rub the mark hard with turpentine. In the case of severe damage, seek expert advice to avoid further harm.

Heat marks (white rings)
Rub with turpentine in the direction of the grain.

Ink
Dab with a little vinegar, leave for 2–3 hours then wipe. If unsuccessful, use a matchstick or cotton wool and carefully dab with hypochlorite bleach, immediately wiping with a clean cloth or absorbent paper.

Scratches
Mask with a similar colour wax crayon, shoe polish or liquid polish dye.

Water marks
Rub with turpentine the way of the grain. If the stain persists, rub with metal polish followed by a suitable furniture polish.

PLASTICS

Plastic is a man-made material with an infinite number of uses:

    (a) tableware;
    (b) kitchenware;
    (c) protective coatings;
    (d) wall coverings;
    (e) floor coverings;
    (f) furniture
    (g) cleaning equipment, etc.

Plastic can be rigid or pliable and can be moulded into a shape during manufacture. It can also occur in many colours, both pastel and bright. It is, of course, difficult to generalise about a material which is so adaptable that it is possible to eliminate any unwanted characteristics during the manufacture of a specific item. Nevertheless it is possible to identify the following advantages over natural materials:

    (a) lightweight;
    (b) quiet in use;
    (c) a non conductor of electricity;
    (d) resistant to most chemicals;
    (e) reasonably priced.

However, most types of plastic material have a tendency to scratch, discolour and in some cases melt or crack. Plastics do not burn when they get hot but will smoulder giving off potent fumes which may be toxic. The fumes can be extremely dangerous and the heat given off from smouldering plastic is so great that it should be regarded as a flammable material. Its chemical resistance also makes many plastics non-biodegradeable.

Plastics found in a residential establishment fall into two categories, thermosetting and thermoplastic.

Thermosetting plastics

These are very strong and are not softened by heat. There are two qualities likely to be encountered by housekeeping staff, as follows.

Melamines
(Formica, Wareite, Laminex) These are used for tableware, trays and laminated work tops, wall panels and shelves.

Phenolics
These are used for buckets, trays, telephones, door handles, toilet

seats, electrical fittings and also laminates. Phenolic plastics can be boiled and so are suitable for use in kitchen areas and hospitals.

Thermoplastic plastics

The majority of plastic materials found in hotels and institutions fall into this group, some being very sensitive to heat and others withstanding sterilisation temperatures.

Acetal resins (Delrin)

These resist boiling, chipping, scratching and corroding, and are used for knife handles in particular.

Acrylics (Perspex, Lucite)

Although extremely lightweight and strong they will scratch easily and are damaged by contact with very hot liquids. They are used for sanitary ware, trays, telephones, furniture and protective panels.

Cellulose Acetate and Nitrate (Celluloid, Xylonite)

This is a pliable plastic used for brush handles, door handles, light fittings, lampshades, etc.

Polyamide (Nylon)

This is used for kitchenware, knife handles, brushes (bristles), curtain fittings, abrasive pads, etc. It will withstand sterilisation.

Polyester

This may be used on its own for trays, lampshades, etc. or it may be reinforced with glass fibres and moulded into laundry skips, sinks, furniture, etc. It is also used in the construction of resin seamless floorings.

Polyethylene/Polythene (Crinothene, Alkathene)

This may be flexible in which case it will not withstand boiling liquids and is used for plastic bags, squeeze bottles, etc. In a more rigid form it is used for sanitary ware, kitchenware, trays, lampshades, etc. and can be boiled.

Polypropylene (Propathene, Ulstron)

This may be rigid and used for laundry skips, dustbins, buckets and sanitary ware, or it may be extremely pliable and used for matting. Both types will withstand sterilisation.

Polystyrene (Styron)

This may be found in three formats. The crystal type is clear, glossy and brittle and used for domestic kitchen utensils and equipment. Toughened varieties are less brittle and are used for refrigerator linings, fan blades, etc. Expanded polystyrene has a cellular structure and is therefore light and warm with excellent insulating properties which make it an ideal material for ceiling tiles. These are very difficult to clean, however, as the slightest pressure may cause damage. A flame retardant emulsion paint will give a certain amount of protection but will not reduce its absorbent nature. Tiles should be kept clear of dust by vacuuming or light dusting and if necessary washed with a mild, warm synthetic detergent solution followed by rinsing and thorough drying. Replacement is often easier than washing and is not particularly expensive.

Polyurethane foam

This may be a rigid fabric used for insulation but it is more frequently found as a flexible material used in the manufacture of furniture (mattresses, cushions), carpet underlays, sponges and mops. It can be boiled without harm and will withstand dry-cleaning fluids.

Polytetrafluoroethylene (PTFE)

This is used in kitchenware and on the base of irons. It is bonded to iron or aluminium to give a smooth, non-stick surface which is quite tough but sensitive to extremes of heat such as those used when grilling.

Polyvinyl chloride (PVC)/fluoride

This is often referred to as "vinyl" and is used a great deal in institutional establishments. It may be rigid, when it is used for curtain tracks, plumbing fitments and suspended ceilings, or flexible, when it is used as an upholstery fabric, wall covering, curtain fabric, etc. It is used to coat wallpaper and wood products to render them washable and as a rust inhibitor on kitchen wireware. Housekeeping staff are most likely to come into contact with vinyl as a floor covering in either tile or sheet form.

Acrylonitrile

This plastic is used for tableware and for the outer casings of vacuum cleaners, etc.

Maintaining plastics

Very little effort is required to clean plastics. They tend to attract dust and so occasional use of a spray polish while dusting should be considered. Light soiling can be removed by wiping with a warm synthetic detergent solution followed by rinsing, drying and buffing. Textured surfaces may need scrubbing with a soft brush. Stains can be removed by rubbing with a clean cloth soaked in methylated spirit or by rubbing with a metal polish. Small items may be soaked occasionally in a mild solution of hypochlorite bleach. Where plastics come into contact with food, for instance refrigerators, a solution of 18 ml sodium bicarbonate to 600 ml water should be used for cleaning as the odour from a detergent may contaminate the food. The surface should be rinsed thoroughly afterwards. Proprietary plastic cleaners may be used but they are expensive. (The care of plastic floor coverings is discussed in Chapter 6.)

Points to remember when maintaining plastics

(a) Keep away from direct heat or flames, e.g. cigarette ends, hot ashes, hotplates, hot pipes.

(b) Do not use harsh abrasives.

(c) Do not drag heavy objects over plastic surfaces or chop or cut on them.

(d) Keep away from strong acids and alkalis.

(e) Some plastics are damaged if heavy objects are dropped on to them or if they are dropped from a height.

CERAMICS AND STONEWARE

These materials are made from a base of sand and clay and are extremely porous unless a glaze or seal is applied to the outer surface during or after manufacture. They are used internally and externally in all areas of a residential establishment as construction materials and for decorative finishes. They are also used for sanitary fittings, tableware and kitchenware. The most frequently found ceramic materials are:

(a) earthenware;
(b) stoneware;
(c) vitreous china;
(d) porcelain;
(e) bone china;
(f) brick;
(g) marble;
(h) concrete/cement;
(i) terrazzo;
(j) granolithic.

Items (h)–(j) are used mainly as floor surfaces and are discussed in detail in Chapter 6.

Earthenware

Earthenware is a thick, heavy and very porous material which is usually glazed. It chips easily and must be cleaned, stored and handled with care. It is cheap to produce, however, and is used in the majority of residential establishments for mugs, jugs, bowls, vases, goblets, ashtrays, etc.

Stoneware

This is similar to earthenware but has a higher stone content. It is fired at a higher temperature giving a stronger material which is impervious and so needs no glazing. Some stoneware is oven and flameproof.

Vitreous china

This is also fired at a higher temperature than earthenware. It contains more flint which makes it very strong but very heavy. Some types of vitreous china have a high chip resistance (Steelite, Micratex) and are used throughout hotels and institutions for crockery and sanitary ware.

Porcelain

This is a translucent earthenware containing china clay, stone and feldspar. It is very strong but very expensive and therefore rarely found in institutions. Its main use is for cups, saucers, etc.

Bone china

This is similar to porcelain but contains bone ash and less feldspar. It is fired at very high temperatures making it very thin but also strong and impervious. Designs are applied to the outer surface and so care should be taken when washing. Bone china is used for cups, saucers, etc.

Cleaning and storing

Great care should be taken in the cleaning and storage of these five ceramic materials to avoid chipping, cracking, scratching and pattern erosion. Extremes of temperature should be avoided and they should be cleaned or soaked as soon as possible after use so that harsh abrasives are not necessary. A hot neutral synthetic detergent solution should be used followed by rinsing and drying, preferably in a washing machine where rinse aids can be used and drying occurs naturally. Stains, particularly those made by tea and coffee, can be removed by rubbing with a damp cloth and bicarbonate of soda.

Staff should be shown how to stack crockery correctly both

before and after washing to avoid damage and breakages. It should be remembered that ceramics are heavy and only a few should be carried at one time. Shelves must also be strong and secure.

Brick

Bricks are also made from clay and are frequently left uncovered to create a natural, textured finish to a wall or floor. They are very porous and may be sealed or painted to make cleaning easier although the areas of mortar will trap dust. Unpainted or unsealed brick surfaces require only vacuuming with the correct attachment approximately once a week and occasional scrubbing with hot water where necessary. Painted brickwork tends to show soiling more easily and will require daily dusting if possible. Washing can create a streaky effect unless the entire surface is cleaned each time. A tough paint containing polyurethane and silicone should be used along corridors and in areas of heavy use.

Marble

Mable is highly polished limestone and may be used for floors, walls and staircases and in the construction of statues and ornaments often found in the entrances of hospitals and hotels. It is a very hard, dense material but is slightly porous and may be damaged by abrasives, acids and alkalis. Daily dust removal and damp wiping is all that is required to maintain its appearance, with an occasional application of spray polish, well rubbed in. Marble flooring is also discussed in Chapter 6.

GLASS

Glass is a brittle material made from a base of sand. It is found in all types of building where it is used not only for windows but for table and kitchenware, furniture, light fittings, mirrors and partitions. It may also be used as a protective cover for tables. To satisfy the demands of these areas of use, glass is made in varying strengths; as follows.

Lead crystal glass

This contains lead oxide which produces a lustrous glass, soft enough to enable the outer surface to be cut away into attractive designs. It is very expensive and used mainly for bowls, drinking glasses, vases, etc. which are not in constant use. Lead crystal glass should always be washed by hand.

Soda lime glass

This contains soda ash and limestone and is much cheaper to produce than lead crystal. It is used for general purpose glassware—tumblers, plates, cups, saucers, ashtrays, bottles, shelving, windows, pictures and mirrors.

Plate glass or sheet glass, such as that used for windows, shelves and table tops, is made from a soda lime base. It may be textured so that light passes through but it is not transparent (e.g. bathroom windows) or it may have wire incorporated into it. The latter is a type of safety glass as, if broken, the glass will be held in place by the wire until knocked out for repair. It is used for door panels and fire screens. Glass doors and panels are usually made from specially toughened sheet glass. This may be done in two ways; as follows.

(*a*) *Laminated:* here the glass contains two thin sheets with plastic between. If the glass becomes broken the pieces will stick to the plastic.

(*b*) *Toughened:* In this type, the glass sheet is heated then thoroughly cooled so that a skin is formed which will cause the glass to shatter into tiny fragments and be less likely to fall out of its frame.

A combination of both these methods creates a very strong, tough glass.

Silvered glass (for mirrors) is made by coating one side of a glass panel with silver, and in some cases copper, followed by a coat of paint and a layer of stove enamel. Silvered glass may be used as tiles or mosaics or as reflective sheets. Care should be taken not to damage the backing when cleaning. Do not soak in water but wipe with a damp cloth or one soaked in a solvent such as methylated spirit which will evaporate before it can attack the backing. Mirror glass looks very unsightly with only the slightest marks on it and so frequent attention is essential.

Borosilicate glass

This contains borax which enables the glass to withstand heat. It is therefore used mainly for cookware and is frequently referred to as toughened glass or flameproof glass (e.g. Pyrex).

Glass fibres

These have already been discussed in Chapter 4 (Textiles). However, they may also be manufactured as rigid sheets which can be moulded in the same way as plastic materials and used for sanitary ware, furniture, wall panels, etc. as well as for thermal, sound and electrical insulation. They are non-combustible, impermeable and immune to attack by pests.

Maintaining glass surfaces

Glass surfaces are easily marked and easily damaged. They therefore require frequent attention and should be treated with respect. Apart from the aesthetic reasons for keeping glass clean, there are some areas in hospitals where observation of patients in intensive care and baby units is carried out through glass partitions—these should be kept scrupulously clean to avoid cross-infection.

Daily care involves damp or dry dusting, preferably with a lint-free cloth such as paper or scrim. Light soiling and greasy finger-marks can be removed by wiping with a solution of equal quantities of vinegar and water or a mixture comprising approx. 18 ml ammonia to half a bucket of warm water. More stubborn marks such as make-up and toothpaste deposits found on mirrors can be removed by wiping with a solvent such as methylated spirit. Newspaper print contains solvents and can be used to remove soiling from windows, particularly the external surface. Textured or engraved glass should be cleaned occasionally using a very soft brush. Glass polish or spray furniture polish is an expensive method of maintenance but is very effective. Care should be taken to ensure all traces of polish are removed while buffing up. A lime deposit often occurs on water jugs, vases and tumblers. This can be reduced by soaking the items in distilled water followed by scrubbing with a soft brush and washing in a neutral synthetic detergent solution. Discoloured or stained decanters and vases can be cleaned by filling them with a mixture of vinegar, water and potato pieces, and gently shaking until the marks disappear. Where glass is used for table tops, mats should be provided to protect the surface from scratching. The use of abrasives should be avoided.

RUBBER

Rubber is a natural material although synthetic rubber can also be produced and is usually combined with the natural product to improve its resistance to oils and solvents. Chemically it is similar to thermosetting plastic. Rubber is an ingredient in many adhesives and is also used for chopping boards, spatulas and floor coverings, as a protective surface around cleaning equipment and food trolleys, and for drive belts, etc. in vacuum cleaners. Internal hospital doors may be made from rubber as they will withstand the constant impact from mobile beds, food trolleys, wheelchairs, etc.

Rubber is very soft and very quiet and is therefore used as a floor covering in areas where noise is to be kept to a minimum e.g. (hospitals and lecture areas).

It is a warm material with good thermal insulation but is softened by excessive heat. Care should therefore be taken to avoid placing buckets of hot water on to a rubber floor.

Rubber is a very hygienic material as it resists attack by all pests and is unharmed by water, mild acids or mild alkalis. It will eventually scratch, however, with constant use and very little can be done to repair the damage. (More information on rubber floors can be found in Chapter 6).

NOTE:

For methods of cleaning individual items and specific areas containing these materials, *see* Chapter 7.

SELF-ASSESSMENT QUESTIONS

1. What are the signs of damaged or worn hard surfaces?

2. Why is it important for a cleaning supervisor to have a knowledge of hard surface materials?

3. What causes tarnishing of metals? How can it be prevented?

4. What is the common ingredient in mixtures used for cleaning metals?

5. Suggest the types of wooden surface suitable for use as:

(*a*) upholstered furniture;
(*b*) dining tables;
(*c*) wall panelling;
(*d*) wardrobes.

6. Why is polish used for the maintenance of wooden surfaces?

7. What advantages do plastic surfaces have over wooden surfaces?

8. What is the difference between thermoplastic and thermosetting plastics?

9. Why should plastics be treated as flammable materials?

10. What are the signs that incorrect cleaning has been carried out on a plastic surface?

11. Briefly describe the general maintenance of ceramic materials.

12. What is meant by safety glass?

13. How might the replacement of vitreous china sanitary ware with plastic affect cleaning?

CHAPTER SIX

Floor Surfaces

CHAPTER OBJECTIVES

After studying this chapter you should be able to:
* appreciate the importance of correct floor maintenance,
* appreciate the importance of providing a good subfloor;
* describe the characteristics of the main types of floor surface found in hotels and institutions;
* show how to protect and maintain different types of floor surfaces;
* diagnose and rectify damage caused to floor surfaces.

INTRODUCTION

Importance of good floorcare

Floor surfaces are subjected to more wear than practically any other area in a building. They are also expensive to buy and therefore replaced less frequently than other furnishings. If they are neglected or are incorrectly maintained they can become hazardous and irreparably damaged so that considerable and unnecessary expenditure is incurred. Floorcare plays a large part in the cleaning programme of a building, and housekeeping managers and supervisors should have some knowledge of the composition of floor surfaces and their subfloors if they are to make decisions about their maintenance. The condition of a floor is often an indication of the general standards of cleanliness in a building.

Hard and soft floors

Floor surfaces may be either hard or soft and usually form the basis for a décor. The desire for individuality, in hotels particularly, means that the housekeeping department may have to deal with more unusual floorings as well as the very familiar ones. Hard floor surfaces are usually of a more permanent nature than soft floor coverings and tend to be more resistant to wear. Soft floor surfaces, however, provide a safer, quieter, more luxurious surface and offer a very wide choice of colours and patterns.

Subfloors

Both hard and soft floor surfaces are laid on to a subfloor or screed. This may be made of concrete (solid floors), softwood boards (suspended floors) or hardboard sheets (suspended or solid floors). A subfloor must be completely free of dust, dirt, dampness and unevenness. If it is not, the upper floor covering will quickly become dirty, may rot with dampness and wear thin, split or crack in areas of unevenness. Soft floor surfaces are particularly vulnerable to these problems; an underlay should always be placed between the subfloor and the carpet.

HARD FLOOR SURFACES

The majority of hard floorings are made up from fillers and binders. The filler forms the main bulk of the floor covering and is held together by the binder. The filler may be porous and so liable to damage by liquids. The binder may be more susceptible to damage from solvents, alkalis and acids although these may also react with the filler. Continual cleaning causes hard floor surfaces gradually to deteriorate but this can be kept to a minimum on the less resistant types of surfaces by the application of a suitable seal or polish (*see* Figs. 46 and 47).

Not all hard floors require sealing or polishing, e.g. ceramic tiles, but even with this type of hard floor surface, the grouting between the tiles may become damaged and a seal may have to be applied.

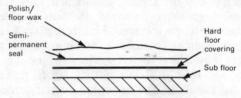

Fig. 46. *Cross-section of a sealed and polished hard floor covering.*

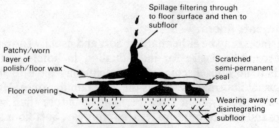

Fig. 47. *Cross-section of a hard floor covering with worn polish and damaged semi-permanent seal.*

Hard floor coverings can be divided into three groups according to their composition:

(*a*) stone-based;
(*b*) wood-based or timber;
(*c*) resilient.

Stone-based
These floor surfaces are extremely durable and hygienic. They are frequently found in hospitals and in such areas as kitchens, bathrooms, corridors and storerooms. They have a tendency to crack, however, and can become dangerously slippery.

Concrete
This is made from cement and sand and is naturally grey in colour although pigments may be added (red or brown). It is very porous and can create a large amount of dust unless sealed, but it is extremely strong and will withstand tremendous weights. Concrete is damaged by acids, alkalis, grease and oil.
Seal. Pigmented. Water/polyurethane.
Polish. Water-based.

Granolithic
This is made by mixing ground granite into fine cement. It is naturally grey but may also have pigments added. It is used in similar areas to concrete. It is less porous, however, and has more resistance to acids.
Seal. Pigmented. Water/polyurethane.
Polish. Water-based.

Marble
Marble is metamorphosed limestone. It may be white, black, red or green and when used for decorative purposes is cut into blocks, carved if desired, then highly polished. Although unharmed by water, it is sensitive to acids, strong alkalis, oil and therefore oil-based products. Marble is slippery when wet, although this can be reduced by applying a water-based polish. It is an expensive flooring, usually found in entrance areas, etc.
Seal. Water-based (optional).
Polish. Water-based if sealed first.

Terrazzo
This looks similar to marble but is cheaper. It is used in many hotels and institutions for entrances, corridors, cloakrooms, restaurants, operating theatres, etc. It is often curved at the edges

to form a skirting so that more hygienic cleaning is possible. Terrazzo is made by mixing crushed marble with cement. The marble chips and cement may be coloured to give a white, green, grey or black effect. Terrazzo may be laid *in situ* in a similar way to concrete, or be pre-cast and laid in the form of tiles. That which is laid *in situ* is usually divided into panels by plastic or brass strips and is more inclined to crack. Terrazzo floors are porous and, although unharmed by water, are damaged by acids, alkalis, grease and oil. They have good slip resistance when polished.

Seal. Acrylic (optional).

Polish. Water-based if sealed first.

Ceramic tiles

Ceramic floor tiles are usually unglazed as the glazing creates a slippery surface. They are made from fired clay and are usually red, black or cream. They are impermeable and so very hygienic and therefore used in kitchens, bathrooms, canteens, bars, etc. with either a smooth or slip-resistant surface (e.g. ridged). A mosaic floor is made from very small squares of glazed ceramic tile. Quarry tiles are resistant to acids, oil, grease and water but may be damaged by strong alkalis. When wet or polished incorrectly, however, they can become dangerously slippery. Cracked or chipped tiles are dangerous and unhygienic and should be repaired as soon as they occur.

Seal. None.

Polish. Water-based (optional).

Others

Natural stone, slate and brick are also used for floor surfaces. Stone is frequently found in older types of building, in entrances and corridors. They are all porous and likely to be damaged by chemicals and so sealing is recommended. Water-based polishes only should be used.

Wood-based

These floor surfaces are used in all types of establishment for corridors, games rooms, dance floors, dining rooms, bathrooms, etc. They are usually considered more attractive than stone and composition floorings but are very porous and are easily damaged. They are also susceptible to attack from fungi and insects.

Timber

Well-maintained timber floor surfaces can remain in an attractive, hygienic and serviceable condition almost indefinitely, while neglected and misused timber floors deteriorate rapidly and look extremely unattractive. They are found in all types of building both new and very old and are particularly suited to hallways, gymnasia, ballrooms, dining rooms, libraries, linen rooms, corridors and entrances. The characteristics of a timber floor surface vary with the type and shape of wood used. There are three main designs:

(a) strips and boards;
(b) blocks;
(c) parquet and mosaic.

Wood strip floor surfaces are constructed from hardwood such as maple. The strips of wood are quite narrow (under 10 cm) and when joined together and attached to the subfloor, create a resilient floor, suitable for dancing on or for sporting activities. A wood strip floor may have springs placed under the floor joists to improve its resilience. It is then described as "sprung".

Floor boards are usually made from softwood and so are less resistant to wear. They are also thicker and wider than wood strips and may be sanded, sealed and polished or left in their natural state and used as a subfloor.

Wood block floor surfaces are constructed from hardwood blocks, e.g. oak and teak. These vary in size and are laid on to a cement type base. They are used to create a number of attractive designs, the most popular being a herringbone or basket pattern. Wood block floors are frequently used in entrance halls, corridors, carpet surrounds, linen rooms, offices and generally areas where appearance is important. They are not particularly resilient.

Parquet flooring looks similar to wood block but is more expensive and decorative. The wood pieces are laid in similar designs but different hardwoods are used to give added interest and a greater sense of pattern. The pieces of wood, however, are much thinner and will not withstand constant sanding. If such treatment is considered necessary abrasive nylon discs should be used with a rotary floor machine.

Mosaic wood floor surfaces are made in the same way as parquet but with smaller pieces of wood. These may be attached to bitumen sheeting for easy laying. Both parquet and mosaic wood floor surfaces are used in similar areas to wood blocks.

Seal. Solvent-based (optional).

Polish. Solvent-based (if unsealed). Water-based (if well sealed).

Cork
Cork comes from the bark of the cork oak tree. As a floor surface it is found in varying shades of brown and is used in the form of

tiles. Cork is the least resistant of the hard floor surfaces. Care should be taken therefore to prevent indentation occurring from heavy furniture and equipment. Cork also contains a high proportion of air. This trapped air is a poor conductor of heat and so the cork feels warm and acts as an insulating material. For this reason it is often used in bathroom suites. It is quiet to walk on and ideally suited for use in hospitals, libraries, music rooms, etc. Cork is unaffected by moisture and has a high degree of slip resistance. However, an excess of water may cause the tiles to lift, and contact with grease, oil and alkalis may cause damage.

Seal. Solvent-based (optional).

Polish. Solvent-based (sealed or unsealed). Water-based (if well sealed).

Wood composition

(Chipboard, Granwood) This type of floor surface is made by mixing wood chippings or sawdust with resins or cement, followed by subjection to heat and pressure. The material is then cut into strips, blocks or tiles. A wood composition floor surface is usually fairly light in colour and will usually be sealed by the manufacturer. Unlike timber floor surfaces it will not warp or split. It is warm and resilient but porous and easily damaged by grease, oil, alkalis and water. It is used for corridors, dining areas, lecture rooms, sports halls, storerooms, etc.

Seal. Solvent-based.

Polish. Solvent-based (if unsealed). Water-based (if well sealed).

Magnesite

(Magnesium Oxychloride, Oxychloride composition, Magnesite jointless composition, Magnesite composition, jointless flooring, Oxychloride, Composition) Magnesite flooring is formed by combining powdered calcined magnesite, which consists mainly of magnesium oxide, with magnesium chloride. These two substances react chemically and when added to a sawdust filler give a cement-like mixture which is applied *in situ* to provide a jointless floor surface. Squares can be created, however, by using wooden dividing strips. This also enables a pattern to be created by using different coloured magnesite in the squares (red and black usually). Magnesite floors look like smooth cement but are not as hard or cold underfoot. They are fairly resistant to abrasion and impact and are unharmed by oil and grease. Damage may be caused, however, by contact with acids, alkalis and water. They will become dangerously slippery with poor maintenance.

Seal. Solvent-based.

Polish. Solvent-based (if unsealed). Water-based (if well sealed).

NOTE:
   All wood-based floors are porous and liable to damage by grease,
   oil, alkalis, water and pests (*see* Chapter 8 for pest control).

Resilient

This group of floor surfaces includes mainly plastic materials which
are semi-porous and is used extensively in hospitals and institutional buildings, particularly those built since the Second World
War. Linoleum, rubber, asphalt and bitumen are also included,
however, as they have similar characteristics and are used in similar
areas, i.e. corridors, lecture rooms, dining areas, lifts, offices,
cloakrooms, patient areas, etc. If well maintained, these floor
surfaces have an attractive gloss and will last for many years. They
are unaffected by pests or fungi.

Linoleum

This is one of the oldest types of resilient floorings. Its name derives
from the two main ingredients—*linum* (flax) and *oleum* (oil). The
oil, usually linseed oil, is combined with ground cork, resins and
sometimes mineral fillers. Pigments are added to form colour and
pattern. This mixture is compressed on to a flax or jute backing and
cut into tiles or sheets. Linoleum is fairly quiet underfoot and
insulates well. It will, however, crack if laid on a poor subfloor and
fail to recover from severe indentations caused by heavy furniture
or equipment. It is fairly easily damaged by acids, alkalis, oil,
grease and cigarette burns although it is non-flammable. Industrial
quality linoleum is used in hospitals, hostels and hotels, in areas
such as corridors, study bedrooms, offices and utility rooms.
   Seal. Water-based.
   Polish. Water-based.

Bitumastic/asphalt

These floor surfaces are usually dark in colour—black, red, brown
or green, Bitumen is a solid or viscous liquid derived from
petroleum, as well as occurring as a natural deposit. Asphalt
consists of bitumen and minerals. When used as floor surfaces these
two materials are mixed with grit or limestone and laid *in situ*. They
are both strong and resilient. They are sensitive to changes in
temperature, however, and tend to be cold and noisy. They are
used mostly in heavy traffic areas such as corridors, workshops,
changing rooms in sports complexes, etc. Care should be taken,
however, to prevent them coming into contact with oil, grease and
solvents.
   Seal. Acrylic (optional).
   Polish. Pigmented water-based.

Rubber

The main characteristics of a rubber floor surface are quietness, resilience and thermal insulation. It is produced in bright, attractive colours and in smooth or textured designs which improve its inherent non-slip properties. Rubber floor surfaces are usually made from a combination of natural and synthetic rubber and laid in sheet or tile form. They are used extensively in hospitals but are also found in hotels, hostels, sports centres, transport termini, etc. in areas such as entrances and corridors. Grease-resistant rubber flooring may be found in kitchens and canteens. Rubber is likely to be damaged by excessive heat and should not be used where there is underfloor heating. It is also sensitive to oil, grease and strong alkalis and will react by stretching and swelling if it comes into contact with solvent-based products. It has very good resistance to water, however, withstanding repeated mopping with neutral detergent solution. Rubber floors are immune to mould growth, bacterial decay and pest infestation.

Seal. Acrylic.

Polish. Water-based.

Thermoplastic

This type of flooring occurs in tile form only and is sometimes referred to as asphalt tiling. It is a cheap form of resilient flooring, constructed from asphalt, asbestos fibres, pigments, mineral fillers and sometimes PVC (polyvinyl chloride). The tiles are usually a dark colour which has a tendency to fade. They are the least resilient of this group of floor surfaces and so need protecting from sharp, heavy furniture and heavy impact. They are durable, however, and although they have a cold appearance and are rather noisy to walk on they have good thermal insulation. Like most resilient floor surfaces, thermoplastic tiles are semi-porous. They have excellent resistance to water, withstanding repeated scrubbing, but may be harmed by heat (including very hot detergent solutions), solvent-based products, strong acids and alkalis. They are used in all types of building, generally in corridors.

Seal. Acrylic.

Polish. Water-based.

Vinyl

This type of floor surface is constructed from polyvinyl chloride (PVC), fillers and pigments and may be in the form of flexible tiles and sheets or rigid tiles. Vinyl tiles contain asbestos fillers and are very similar in appearance to thermosplastic tiles. Flexible PVC tends to be smoother and shinier and is frequently backed with plastic foam or cork to improve its resilience, sound insulation and appearance. PVC sheets may also be welded together to create a jointless floor covering which is very hygienic and ideal for use in hospitals. Both types of vinyl floor are used in all types of establishment for corridors, dining areas, lifts, wards, offices, common rooms, study bedrooms, etc. Vinyl floor coverings have similar properties to thermoplastic tiling, the higher grades having improved resistance to chemicals. Both types, however, are damaged by direct contact with heat, particularly cigarette burns, and so adequate provision of ashtrays is essential. They may also be damaged by gel cleaners as these contain pine oil which softens the plastic and eventually dissolves it. The floor will also shrink even if use of the gel cleaner ceases.

Seal. Acrylic.

Polish. Water-based.

SPECIAL FLOOR SURFACES

Certain floor areas in a building may be treated to make them slip resistant or anti-static. These treatments are expensive and so are only found where it is imperative for the floor to have such characteristics. Maintenance of these floors must therefore be thorough in order to prevent damage and consequent deterioration of performance.

Slip-resistant floors

These are used mainly in kitchens, shower areas and where there are ramps or sloping corridors. They are usually constructed from flexible PVC which has had chips of carborundum added during manufacture to render the surface less slippery. Ridged quarry tiles or textured rubber floorings are also reasonably slip resistant. Whichever type is used it must be kept free of grease, oil and an excess of water.

Conductive floor surfaces

Pedestrian traffic, movement of equipment or human activity of any kind, particularly if it involves contact with synthetic materials, can cause a build up of static electricity, particularly on the floor surface. If the atmosphere is charged with a flammable substance such as ether or solvent cleaner, the slightest spark could cause a fire or even an explosion. It is most important therefore in, for example, operating theatres, treatment rooms and computer areas that anti-static floors are laid. They are made from terrazzo, magnesite, linoleum, rubber or flexible PVC. These will have had carbon black or copper salts (magnesite) added during manufacture. Consequently they will have a much darker appearance than the non-conductive varieties. Terrazzo and magnesite may have a galvanised wire mesh laid over the subfloor (screed) prior to being laid *in situ* to improve their conductivity. Linoleum and PVC may also contain wire mesh. In addition, an electrically conductive adhesive may be used to stick down the linoleum, PVC and rubber flooring.

Maintenance of conductive floors
Correct maintenance is essential if these floors are to retain their conductivity and therefore safety. Care should be taken to prevent the slightest film from forming on the surface and so soaps, polishes and seals should be avoided. Soft water only should be used with a neutral or bactericidal detergent for mopping or scrubbing with spotlessly clean equipment. This should be followed by thorough rinsing. It is also important that adjacent floor areas are kept very clean and it is advisable in high risk areas for footwear to be changed before entering. Conductive floors have to undergo regular testing to ensure that their level of conductivity is within the specified safety limits.

MAINTAINING HARD FLOOR SURFACES

Maintenance of hard floors involves the following procedures:

(*a*) removal of dust;
(*b*) removal of dirt;
(*c*) spray buffing;
(*d*) application and removal of polish;
(*e*) application and removal of semi-permanent seal.

Some floor surfaces require only two or three of these processes, while others require all five. Most floors require daily attention of some kind, usually dry suction cleaning, buffing or mopping.

Removal of dust
This can be achieved by sweeping or suction cleaning or with the aid of dust control equipment, depending on the circumstances and the type of building. Hospitals, for instance, rarely use sweeping as brooms tend to redistribute the dust. Suction cleaners are very quick and efficient, but can be noisy and cumbersome. Dusting mops, however, can be expensive and require adequate supervision if they are to be effective.

Sweeping
This method should be limited to the removal of dust which is inter-
mingled with litter, e.g. paper, cigarette ends, etc. Such conditions
are likely to be found in common rooms, canteens, vending areas,
etc.

Equipment. (*See also* Chapter 2.)

(*a*) Long-handled broom.
(*b*) Dustpan with a ridged edge.
(*c*) Short-handled, soft-bristled brush.
(*d*) Waste sack or bin.

Method.

(*a*) Work in a forward direction.
(*b*) Use long, even, smooth strokes.
(*c*) Follow straight, overlapping lines.
(*d*) Remove dust trapped in corners by using the broom
sideways.
(*e*) Gather up the dust frequently and place carefully into the
waste bin or sack.
(*f*) After sweeping, remove any fluff and cotton threads from
the bristles and when necessary or when instructed, wash in a
germicidal solution and leave to dry. Wipe the handle of the broom
and the dustpan with a damp cloth.
(*g*) Store correctly (*see* Chapter 2).

Suction cleaning
This is a very efficient method of dust removal, although the
availability and positioning of electric sockets can be a problem.
The noise from the machine can also be uncomfortably loud when
it is resting on a hard floor surface. Dry suction cleaners, however,
are excellent for removing dust trapped in corners, along skirtings
and behind furniture.

Equipment. (*See also* Chapter 2.)

(*a*) Suction cleaner.
(*b*) Attachments for hard floor surface (large head with bristles,
crevice nozzle).

Method

(*a*) Clear as much of the floor area as possible.
(*b*) Check flex, hose and plug for damage. Record and report
any damage to supervisor or housekeeper.
(*c*) Ensure that sockets with switches are turned off before
fitting in the plug. Use the nearest socket and ensure the flex or hose

is not stretched tight or lying in a position which will cause an accident or allow it to become trapped by the machine.

(*d*) Using slow strokes work systematically across the floor, overlapping each line slightly.

(*e*) Use the crevice attachment for awkward corners and skirtings and around immovable furniture.

(*f*) Use the upholstery attachment for staircases.

(*g*) Disconnect and remove hose and attachments. Clean them and store correctly (*see* Chapter 2).

(*h*) Check dust bag and change if necessary. Seal full dust bags and place in rubbish sack. (This should be done in a service room or cleaners' closet.)

(*i*) Check cloth bag for tears.

Dust control cleaning

This method involves the use of mops which attract and retain dust. It is a very quiet, quick and efficient method of removing dust but staff must be given clear instructions on how to use the equipment if the dust is to be collected properly. The mops have removable heads which may be made from cotton impregnated with a mineral oil solution, synthetic fibres (nylon/acrylic), or disposable, synthetic fibrous strips.

Impregnated cotton mop heads need to be vacuumed after use and when very badly soiled or at the end of an agreed period, they should be laundered and re-impregnated. This is a service which may be carried out by a contractor who will collect the soiled mop heads and replace them with clean, impregnated ones.

Mop heads made from synthetic fibres create static electricity and therefore attract the dust when passed over the floor. These are maintained in the same way as the impregnated type, without the necessity for re-impregnation.

Disposable synthetic fibrous strips attract the dust in the same way as the synthetic fibre mop heads but cannot be laundered and so are expensive. They do, however, provide an extremely hygienic system for dust removal.

Unless adequate training is given in the use of these mops, and unless sufficient supervision is carried out to check they are being used, stored and cleaned correctly, the system can be expensive and unhygienic.

Equipment. (*See also* Chapter 2.)

(*a*) Dry dust control mop.

(*b*) Spare fringe or disposable strips.

(*c*) Waste bin.

Method

(*a*) Remove any waste bins, mats, etc.

(*b*) Place mop on floor at the far end of the area to be cleaned and push forward working in parallel lines until the whole area has been covered. Do not lift the mop from the floor until the entire floor has been mopped.

(*c*) When turning, turn mop on half circle and continue pushing forward.

(*d*) Any accumulation of dust should be placed out of the way and removed by dry suction or dustpan and brush as soon as possible.

(*e*) When the work is complete, replace the furniture and take the mop to a service area or cleaners' room to remove the dust from the head. This can be done with a vacuum cleaner or by placing the mop over a rubbish sack and brushing. Remove and dispose of disposable mop heads.

(*f*) Remove badly soiled heads, place in special box or bag ready for collection by contractor or laundry, and replace with a clean head.

(*g*) Store mop with head uppermost and covered, to keep it clean until next required.

Dust should be removed by this method at least once a day using dry, clean equipment, on floors which are dry and free from stickiness.

Removal of dirt

(*See also* Chapter 3.) This can be carried out by either wet or dry methods, and involves the use of a cleaning agent. It is important to use the correct type of cleaning agent and machine attachments if the floor is to be cleaned efficiently and economically. The wrong choice can in some cases cause irreparable damage to a floor or its protective coatings. A neutral detergent is sufficient for the majority of hard floor surfaces.

Wet methods

There are three main methods of removing dirt from floors which involve the use of water:

(*a*) damp mopping;
(*b*) deck scrubbing;
(*c*) machine scrubbing.

Damp mopping

This will only remove surface soiling and is fairly time-consuming, although it is a quiet method and convenient for removing spillages, etc. However, unless the equipment is maintained correctly (*see* Chapter 2) contamination can easily occur. Mopping equipment should be kept for use in specific areas to reduce the dangers of cross-infection especially in hospitals.

Equipment. (*See also* Chapter 2.)

(*a*) Warning signs.
(*b*) Suitable mop with appropriate bucket.
(*c*) A supply of hot or warm water.
(*d*) Appropriate detergent.
(*e*) Protective cloth (if bucket has no castors).

Method.

(*a*) Place warning signs in position.
(*b*) Ensure dust is removed.
(*c*) Place mop in detergent solution and wring out thoroughly. Shake mop head slightly to open it out.
(*d*) Work backwards moving the mop from side to side in a figure of eight action. Do not touch the skirting until the centre of the floor area has been mopped, then mop parallel to it. This avoids splashing the wall.
(*e*) Rinse the mop frequently and change the cleaning solution and rinsing water before they become too dirty.
(*f*) When work is complete wash, rinse and dry the mop head. If possible remove it and send it for heat treatment (hospitals). Wipe the handle and store with the head uppermost (*See* Chapter 2).
(*g*) Empty, wash, rinse and dry buckets. Store upside-down.
(*h*) Replace cleaning agent.
(*i*) Remove signs when the floor is dry.

Deck scrubbing

A deck scrubber should only be used in areas too small for machine scrubbing, such as toilets and storerooms.

Equipment.

(*a*) Warning signs.
(*b*) Deck scrubber.
(*c*) Bucket large enough to allow total immersion of the bristles.
(*d*) Mopping unit or wet suction machine.
(*e*) Neutral detergent solution.

Method.

(*a*) Place warning signs in position.

(*b*) Ensure dust is removed.

(*c*) Place bristles into a warm neutral detergent solution (avoid wetting the wooden base as this can become unhygienic when wet) and commence scrubbing with short strokes, parallel to the skirtings to avoid splashing the walls.

(*d*) Change the cleaning solution and rinsing water frequently and before they become dirty.

(*e*) Remove the excess water with a clean mop and bucket (*see* mopping above) or wet suction machine.

(*f*) When work is complete, wash, rinse and dry the brush, mopping unit or wet suction machine tank. Wipe the handle. Store it horizontally to allow any water to drain away from the head. (If possible the brush should be heat treated.)

(*g*) Remove warning signs when the floor is dry.

(*h*) Replace cleaning agent.

Machine scrubbing

This is a very quick and efficient method of removing dirt. Basic machines will scrub only, and detergent solution must be applied to the floor first. Wet suction or mopping is used to remove the soiled water afterwards. Machines fitted with a tank (*see* Fig. 9 in Chapter 2) allow detergent solution to be applied during scrubbing. This makes the process safer and quicker but still requires the use of a mopping unit or wet suction machine and consequently more than one operative. The most sophisticated scrubbing machines will dispense detergent solution, scrub and vacuum up the soiled solution all in one operation. This obviously speeds up the operation but the machine is rather bulky and tends to be noisy and so is not ideal for floor scrubbing in all establishments. All machine scrubbing should be carried out with a slow speed machine to avoid splashing.

Equipment. (*See also* Chapter 2.)

(*a*) Warning signs.

(*b*) Suitable machine with appropriate attachments, i.e. either:

(*i*) one large medium/coarse synthetic fibre pad, usually green, with drive disc; or

(*ii*) one large or two or three small nylon or polypropylene bristle brushes.

(*c*) Mopping unit or wet suction cleaner.

(*d*) Clean dry cloth and abrasive pad.

Method.

(*a*) Position warning signs.

(*b*) Clear area of obstructions, waste and dust.

(*c*) Check condition of plug, flex and machine, then connect correct attachments.

(*d*) Make up detergent solution according to manufacturer's instructions and place in tank or bucket.

(*e*) Plug into most convenient socket, then with the flex over one shoulder commence scrubbing at a point farthest from the entrance to the area being cleaned.

(*f*) Gradually walk backwards working with a side-to-side motion (single-brush machines) or a back and forwards motion (multi-brush machines). Overlap each line to ensure total coverage.

(*g*) Dispense a minimum of detergent solution at regular intervals.

(*h*) Mop or scrub the edges where the machine has not been able to reach, and wipe any splash marks from the walls.

(*i*) Move the plug to another socket if the flex begins to pull tight. Make sure the flex is kept clear of the brushes or pad.

(*j*) Remove soiled solution from the floor with a wet suction machine or mopping unit.

(*k*) Rinse the floor with clean water either dispensed from the cleaned tank or using a clean mopping unit.

(*l*) Ensure the floor is as dry as possible after rinsing.

(*m*) When thoroughly dry replace furniture, etc. and remove warning signs.

(*n*) Clean and dry all equipment thoroughly.

(*i*) Remove tank, rinse and leave open to dry.

(*ii*) Remove brushes or pad. Rinse and hang to dry in such a way that they are not damaged, preferably in a vertical position.

(*o*) Wipe drive disc and machine casing. Wind up flex neatly and store correctly.

Spray buffing

This is a method of floor cleaning used in areas which cannot be easily evacuated for regular scrubbing and polishing, e.g. hospital wards, entrances and corridors. It involves spraying the floor surface lightly with a one-in-eight solution of emulsion polish in water, or a proprietary spray buff solution, and then machine buffing with a pad while still damp. The pad will absorb the soil and so will need changing frequently.

Equipment

(*a*) Polishing machine, preferably fast speed, with drive disc and a supply of synthetic pads (red, maroon, blue).

(*b*) Spray bottle with a fine nozzle.

(*c*) Spray buff solution.

(*d*) Bucket of hot water.

(*e*) Dust control mop.

Method.

(*a*) Check condition of flex, plug and machine and connect to nearest socket.

(*b*) Attach drive disc and clean pad. Place flex over shoulder.

(*c*) Spray up to two metres ahead of the machine but not right to the wall, and buff immediately. (Too much polish can damage the surface, dull the floor and cause strain on the machine.)

(*d*) Keep the machine moving until it has covered the sprayed area.

(*e*) Change the pads regularly and place soiled ones in a bucket of hot water, to prevent them from drying out, until it is possible to wash, rinse and dry them thoroughly.

(*f*) On completion, the floor should be dust mopped.

(*g*) Wipe down the machine, check and store flex neatly.

(*h*) The spray bottle should be emptied and rinsed out thoroughly, particularly the nozzle. Containers of proprietary spray cleaner should be replaced.

Application and removal of polish

A polish or floor wax is applied to a thoroughly clean and sound floor surface to protect it and provide an attractive sheen or gloss. The floor may or may not be sealed. There are two types of polish or floor wax, water-based emulsion wax polish and solvent-based wax polish, and it is important that the right one is applied. Further information on the nature of floor polishes and waxes can be found in Chapter 3.

Water-based emulsion polish can be used on:

(*a*) concrete;

(*b*) granolithic;

(*c*) asphalt;

(*d*) linoleum;

(*e*) rubber;

(*f*) thermoplastic;

(*g*) vinyl;

(*h*) marble;

(*i*) terrazzo;

(*j*) cork;

(*k*) wood composition;

(*l*) magnesite;

(*m*) timber;

although (*h*)–(*m*) must first be protected with a semi-permanent seal.

Solvent-based polish can be used on:

(*a*) cork;
(*b*) wood composition;
(*c*) magnesite;
(*d*) timber.

Floor waxes should be applied thinly, evenly and methodically. Several thin coats should be applied, each one being allowed to dry thoroughly before applying the next. The application of fewer thick coats should be avoided as these will take longer to dry and create a softer, less durable finish. Where an establishment needs to use both types of floor wax two sets of equipment should be kept. These must be labelled or be of different colours or materials for easy identification so that the two types of polish do not become mixed. This situation could result in a newly polished floor looking patchy and feeling sticky, and may cause damage to the floor surface. When only parts of the floor finish become worn, a thin coat of undiluted polish can be applied to the worn areas to restore the general appearance of the floor. This can usually be done four or five times before a build up of polish occurs and the floor begins to look dark and dust begins to stick to the surface. At this stage the polish should be stripped off and a fresh coat applied.

Applying floor wax/polish
  Equipment

(*a*) Warning signs.
(*b*) Applicator mop or spray containing polish.
(*c*) Polish tray or container.
(*d*) Suitable polish.
(*e*) Buffing machine with soft brush or drive disc and soft pad (tan or white).

Method

(*a*) Position warning signs.
(*b*) Remove obstacles, dust and dirt.
(*c*) When floor is dry, apply approximately three thin coats of polish allowing each to dry thoroughly (30–40 minutes). Commence at the farthest point and work towards the exit.
(*d*) Use long, even strokes working in small sections.

(*e*) Apply each coat at right angles to the previous one to ensure complete coverage.

(*f*) Buff each dried coat with machine. This hardens the film.

(*g*) Wash, rinse and dry all equipment and store correctly (*see* Chapter 2).

(*h*) Replace furniture, etc. and remove warning signs when completely dry (up to twenty-four hours).

Removing floor wax/polish
Equipment

(*a*) Warning signs.

(*b*) Polishing machine with drive disc and coarse nylon/polyester pad (brown, black).

(*c*) Hand abrasive pads.

(*d*) Stripping agent:

    (*i*) alkaline (pH 10–11) for water-based waxes;

    (*ii*) solvent cleaner for solvent-based waxes.

(*e*) Wet suction machine or mopping unit.

Method

(*a*) Ventilate area.

(*b*) Position warning signs and remove obstacles.

(*c*) Place stripping solution in tank or bucket and apply to floor with a mop using long, even strokes, or by dispensing from a machine. (Do not overwet the floor as this may loosen tile adhesives and grouting, etc.)

(*d*) Commence at the farthest point and work towards exit.

(*e*) Scrub the floor thoroughly working in sections.

(*f*) Scrub edges and corners with a deck scrubber or by hand with an abrasive pad.

(*g*) Leave the stripping agent on the floor for 5–10 minutes to allow penetration of the wax. If solvent cleaner is left on too long, the solvent content will evaporate and dirt will be deposited on to the floor again.

(*h*) Remove solution with wet suction or a clean mopping unit.

(*i*) Rinse floor thoroughly.

(*j*) Where an alkaline cleaner has been used, neutralise the floor surface by adding 35 ml of vinegar to the final rinse water. (Unless the alkali is completely removed it will attack any newly applied floor wax; therefore test with litmus paper after rinsing.)

(*k*) Clean all equipment thoroughly, dry and store it correctly. (Use turpentine substitute for equipment used to remove solvent-based waxes, and neutral detergent for that used to remove water-based waxes, followed by a final rinse in a mild acid solution.)

Application and removal of a semi-permanent seal

Before applying a seal, all traces of dirt, grease, wax and detergent must be removed. This can be done by sanding (wood, wood composition, magnesite and cork) or by using an alkaline detergent containing a solvent (resilient and stone group of floors). Sanding is usually carried out by a contractor using a special machine or an abrasive nylon disc, grit 120 or finer, under a scrubbing machine. Sanding creates considerable amounts of dust and so should be done during less busy periods and a day or two before the new seal is to be applied. This allows time for the dust to settle so that it can be removed more easily. A solvent-based seal which is applied to these types of floor surface should last for three to five years.

If a water-based seal is to be removed (approximately every three years) the stripping agent should be applied and left to soften the seal for about five minutes. The floor is then scrubbed using a black synthetic fibre pad or metal fibre pad under a scrubbing machine. The floor should then be rinsed thoroughly and dried. (*See also* Chapter 3.)

Applying a floor seal

It is important to make sure the correct seal is applied and that the correct set of equipment is used.

Equipment

(*a*) Warning signs.
(*b*) Cotton mop or lambswool applicator.
(*c*) Tray or bucket for seal.

Method

(*a*) Position warning signs.
(*b*) Ventilate area to be sealed.
(*c*) Tape over sockets less than 60 cm from the floor.
(*d*) Facing natural light if possible, apply two or three coats of seal, working in small sections and using long, smooth strokes.
(*e*) Use straight lines taking care not to overlap and in the case of wood, work the way of the grain.
(*f*) Join up sections using light, feather-type strokes.
(*g*) Allow each coat to dry and sand any roughness or unevenness before applying the next.
(*h*) Allow the seal to harden for 12–16 hours.
(*i*) Wash equipment with appropriate cleaner (*see* Chapter 3).
(*j*) Do not smoke when applying solvent-based seals.

Table XIV lists some common problems and possible causes. The use of dust control mats at the junction of a waxed floor with a

TABLE XIV. REASONS FOR SOME COMMON FLOOR TREATMENT PROBLEMS.

Fault	Possible causes
(1) Overall poor quality finish	Insufficient rinsing of alkaline cleaner. Too little polish applied. Coats of polish not allowed to dry before application of subsequent ones. Too much polish applied.
(2) Slippery floor	Too much polish applied. Transfer of polish from another floor. Insufficient cleaning of floor before application.
(3) Powdery finish	Contaminated floor. Humidity too low or too high while applying seal. Underfloor heating. Incorrect pad used for regular maintenance.
(4) Poor durability	Traffic too heavy for type of floor protection. Wrong type of cleaner used. Wrong type of pad used for regular maintenance. Too little polish applied. Polish applied to a soiled floor. Insufficient rinsing of alkaline cleaner.

carpeted floor or where a solvent-waxed floor is adjacent to a water-based wax emulsioned floor greatly reduces "treading off" problems.

SOFT FLOOR COVERINGS

(Carpet, carpeting, rugs, mats and tiles.) Soft floor coverings have many advantages over hard floor coverings. In addition to offering an infinite variety of colours, textures and designs, they are quiet, warm, slip-resistant and fairly simple and economical to maintain. Durability, however, depends very much on the type of carpet and the amount and type of wear it receives. Buyers of carpets in hotels and institutional establishments should have made reference to information produced by the Federation of British Carpet Manufacturers to ensure that the correct quality of carpet is used in the various areas of the building, e.g.:

(*a*) light contract for hotel bedrooms, etc.;

(*b*) medium contract for public areas with medium traffic, e.g. lounges, TV rooms;

(*c*) general contract for such areas as entrances, restaurants, bedrooms, offices, etc.;

(*d*) heavy contract for areas with heavy traffic such as bars, stores, corridors, etc.

A good quality carpet should be able to withstand wear from constant pedestrian traffic, spillages, cigarette ash and grit, and have the ability to recover from the effects of heavy or sharp furniture. Its shape and colour should be stable when deep cleaned or when constantly exposed to sunlight. The pile should be dense and made from strong fibres held firmly in position.

The housekeeping department should keep a record of construction details for reference when new shampooing techniques or materials are to be used. These can also be referred to before attempting to remove stubborn stains. Soft floor coverings should be vacuumed daily and deep cleaned at least twice a year depending on the amount of traffic they receive.

Construction of soft floor coverings

The majority of soft floor coverings consist of a pile, a backing and an underlay (*see* Fig. 48). The pile is held into the backing with knots (woven carpets) or with adhesives. An underlay is essential if a woven carpet is to be laid but many manufacturing techniques provide carpets with backings of sufficient resilience to make an underlay unnecessary.

Underlay/underfelt

There are four reasons for using an underlay, as follows.

(*a*) It acts as a shock absorber between the carpet backing and any unevenness in the subfloor which could cause the carpet pile to wear unevenly.

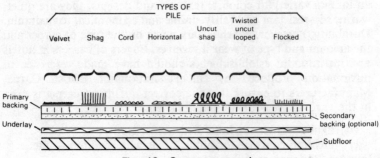

Fig. 48. *Carpet construction.*

(*b*) It tends to make the carpet feel softer and more luxurious and helps it to absorb pressure from furniture.

(*c*) It provides increased sound and heat insulation.

(*d*) It helps protect the carpet from rising dust and dirt.

An underlay may be attached to the carpet backing, when it may be referred to as the secondary backing, or it may be a separate item. Attached underlays make for quicker and easier laying of the soft floor covering, and so reduce installation costs, but they are easily damaged by dampness, and may be adversely affected by underfloor heating. Separate underlays may add to the cost of providing a soft floor covering but they last for many years and can easily be replaced. Types of underlay include:

(*a*) plain needlefelt;

(*b*) impregnated felt;

(*c*) waffled rubber foam;

(*d*) rubber foam or crumb with a jute or polypropylene backing;

(*e*) rubber foam and needlefelt.

Backing

The type of fabric used for backing a carpet has a considerable effect on its lifespan. Natural materials used include jute, hemp, cotton, rubber, bitumen, glue and starch. Synthetic materials may be used alone or in conjuction with natural ones and include polypropylene, nylon, resins and synthetic rubber. Aluminium thread may also be used.

A primary backing is the one into or on to which the pile is anchored. A secondary backing may be added to help the carpet keep its shape and to improve its resilience. It can also protect the primary backing from moisture or dirt and act as an underlay. Secondary backings are not considered necessary on woven carpets.

Pile fibres

The pile of a carpet takes most of the wear and so the fibres from which it is made must be strong and resilient. They should if possible be shrinkproof, mothproof and flameproof. Table XV examines the characterictics of various carpet pile fibres.

A carpet pile is frequently made from a blend of fibres, e.g.:

(*a*) wool and polyamide (usually 80 per cent/20 per cent);

(*b*) wool and viscose;

(*c*) acrylic and viscose;

(*d*) polyamide and viscose;

(*e*) polyamide, viscose and wool.

TABLE XV. COMPARISON OF THE MAJOR PILE FIBRES.
(*See also* Chapter 4)

Fibre	Resilience (resistance to flattening)	Resistance to soiling	Ease of cleaning	Remarks
Acrylic Modacrylic "Acrilan" "Courtelle" "Dralon" "Teklan"	Very good	Shows dirt easily Resists stains well	Easy to clean Requires frequent attention	Looks like wool Teklan is flame resistant
Cotton	Poor	Shows dirt easily Fair resistance to stains	Easy to clean Requires frequent attention Colours may run Liable to shrink	Carpets often thin and so edges may curl Burns readily
Polyamide "Anso" "Artron" "Bri-Nylon" "Nylon" "Enkalon" "Timbrelle"	Good	As acrylic	As acrylic	Melts when exposed to flame Generates static so should be treated
Polyester "Dacron" "Terylene" "Trevira"	Fairly good	Shows dirt easily Stain resistant except to oil	As acrylic	As polyamide Has soft texture
Polypropylene "Merkalon"	Fair	Good	Very easy	Melts when exposed to flame Harsh texture
Viscose "Rayon"	Poor	As cotton	Easy Avoid excessive shampooing	Soft, warm texture Burns easily
Modified viscose "Darelle" "Evlan"	Fair	As cotton	As viscose	As viscose Darelle is flame resistant
Wool	Very good	Good	Easy	Soft, warm texture Does not burn easily Must be moth-proofed

Each blend is intended to fulfil specific requirements, for example low cost with good durability.

Classification of soft floor coverings

Soft floor coverings are made from textiles and may be manufactured in a variety of shapes, sizes and qualities, as follows.

(*a*) *Contract carpet:* a term frequently used to describe tufted carpets because of their suitability for industrial use.

(*b*) *Broadloom carpet:* carpet woven on a very wide loom. Maybe up to 10 m wide.

(*c*) *Body or strip carpet:* usually used for fitted carpeting. Measures up to 90cm in width.

(*d*) *Carpet square:* all edges are neatened. This is not necessarily a square. Usually larger than 210 cm × 120 cm.

(*e*) *Mat/rug:* all edges are neatened and may be edged with rubber. Much smaller than a carpet square. May be round, square, hexagonal, etc. May have a fringe.

(*f*) *Stair carpet:* similar to body or strip carpet but with a border.

(*g*) *Tiles:* smaller than a square, mat or rug. Edges are not neatened but do not fray. Vary in size from 50 cm^2 to 77 cm^2.

Carpets are usually classified according to their method of construction, as this is an important factor when considering maintenance procedures. New kinds of soft floor coverings are constantly being developed, but those most frequently used are:

(*a*) woven;
(*b*) tufted;
(*c*) needle-punched felt;
(*d*) pile bonded;
(*e*) electrostatically flocked.

Woven

Woven carpets are those where the pile and backing are produced simultaneously. In this way the pile is secured with a knot and is therefore very strong. The pile may be either cut or uncut (looped), the uncut variety giving 5–10 per cent more wear. The type of weave may be varied to give different effects, e.g. sculptured or velvet. There are two methods of manufacturing woven carpets, each taking its name from the town where it was first developed— Axminister and Wilton. Both methods produce extremely durable carpets.

Fig. 49. *Patterned Wilton carpeting.*

Wilton carpeting is produced in four varieties—patterned, plain, brussels and cord.

Patterned. This is woven on a special type of loom known as a Jacquard Loom, which draws one thread up at a time to form the pile while the remainder stay hidden in the backing, giving added strength, warmth and resilience (*see* Fig. 49). The use of too many colours would create a very bulky carpet and so no more than five colours are used in the construction of a patterned Wilton. They are often characterised therefore by a regular two or three tone design suitable for use in corridors or in small areas where a carpet with a large, multi-coloured pattern could be overpowering.

Plain. This type of Wilton has extra jute threads ("stuffers") added to the backing to compensate for the lack of spare coloured yarns (*see* Fig. 50).

Brussels. This type of Wilton has an uncut pile and is always patterned.

Cord. This type of Wilton also has an uncut pile but is always plain.

Axminster carpet manufacture allows for much greater use of coloured yarns because each pile tuft is individually inserted into the backing, leaving no "dead" threads to reinforce it. The backing is, however, very durable and has a distinct ribbed effect (*see* Fig. 51).

Although woven carpets are expensive they are very durable and are frequently used in hotels for reception areas, corridors, dining

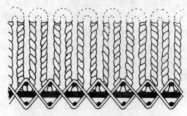

Fig. 50. *Plain Wilton carpeting.*

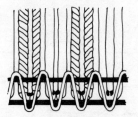

Fig. 51. *Axminster carpeting.*

rooms and bedrooms. They may also be found in entrance areas, lounges and common rooms of institutional establishments.

Tufted

(*See* Fig. 52) This type of carpeting is cheaper to produce than woven. It accounts for over 50 per cent of carpet production and may be referred to as contract carpeting. Its low cost is attributed to its speedy method of manufacture: the backing is woven first then the pile tufts are punched through at a very rapid rate. The pile may be cut or uncut and is held in place with an adhesive made from latex or PVC compounds. Tufted carpeting is used throughout hotels and institutional establishments as it is strong and very easy to install. Care is necessary, however, when deep cleaning as overwetting or the application of an over-strong shampoo solution can cause damage to the synthetic backing.

Needle-punched felt (needleloom)

This is a felt-like carpet in which the backing is punched between two layers of compacted carpet yarn with the aid of needles (*see* Fig. 53). The finished material is then impregnated with resin.

Pile bonded

In this type of carpet the pile is compacted into an adhesive backing

Fig. 52. *Tufted carpeting.*

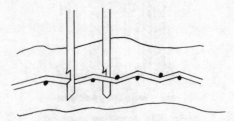

Fig. 53. *Needle-punched felt carpet construction.*

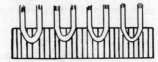

Fig. 54. *Construction of pile bonded carpet.*

and then heated and dried. Alternatively the fibres may be bonded by melting, causing them to fuse together on to the backing. The pile may be cut or uncut (*see* Fig. 54).

Cleaning of felted and bonded carpets

Felted and bonded carpets tend to have a less luxurious appearance than the woven or tufted varieties. The closeness of the pile fibres makes them fairly resistant to superficial soiling but unless they are cleaned regularly the dirt becomes trapped and is very difficult to remove; stains particularly are difficult to remove. They will, however, withstand fairly rigorous methods of cleaning. The use of a suction cleaner with a powered brush attachment is recommended for these carpets. They are frequently found in the form of tiles.

Electrostatically flocked

These carpets are made with synthetic fibres which are molecularly-bonded into a glass fibre reinforced vinyl base to create a very smooth, dense pile which dirt and liquids have difficulty in penetrating (*see* Fig. 55). They will withstand very rigorous methods of cleaning and are used throughout hotel and institutional establishments for entrances, corridors, dining areas, cloakrooms and kitchens. They are, however, vulnerable to cigarette burns.

Fig. 55. *Construction of electrostatically flocked carpet.*

Matting

Mats and rugs are used for one or more of the following reasons:

(*a*) To remove dirt, mud or water at the entrance to a building so that the internal floor areas will not become heavily soiled or damaged. Mats used in such areas may be referred to as "walk-off mats" and may take the form of either a metal grating interspersed with rubber or material, or an open rubber grating with a built-in scraper action. Both types are usually sunk into a well so that the surface is flush with the floor. Coir, sisal, jute and rush mats are used in many establishments but they are not very efficient, and if large, are so heavy to lift for cleaning that this task has a tendency to be neglected.

(*b*) To provide comfort while walking or standing in specific areas, e.g. behind a service counter, or beside a bath.

(*c*) To eliminate the dangers of slipping in areas such as shower rooms and around swimming pools.

(*d*) To control noise.

(*e*) To reduce the transfer of germs.

Mats may be constructed from textile fibres or hard materials such as vinyl, cork, wood and rubber. One type of mat used internally or externally to simulate grass ("Astro-turf") is made from polyethylene with a skid-resistant sponge backing. Such mats may be used for displays or in leisure complexes.

Hospitals are very sensitive to floor hygiene and where possible try to install barrier zones at entrances. These are of sufficient length (1.8 m minimum) to remove the majority of soil from shoes and wheels before the start of the internal floor covering (*see* Fig. 56).

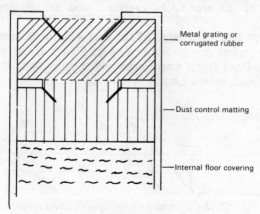

Fig. 56. *Barrier zone.*

There are two types of dust control matting:

(*a*) impregnated cotton mats which are usually supplied and maintained by a contractor in a similar way to impregnated mops;

(*b*) static mats constructed from synthetic fibres which, as a result of the friction created by footwear, build up static electricity and thus attract and retain dust and dirt.

Good supervision of dust control mats is essential if any benefit is to be gained by their use. Like all mats, they should not be allowed to curl at the edges (many are edged with rubber to prevent this) and must be changed before they become saturated with dirt. The frequency of change should increase during the winter months or during redecoration periods. This type of matting has largely replaced the use of druggets.

Fitted carpeting

The majority of soft floor coverings used in hotels and institutional establishments are fitted from wall to wall and although a housekeeping department is not expected to be responsible for the initial fixing of the carpet, it may be involved in the removal of areas of carpet for cleaning, repair, redecoration or when preparing a room for a function. A housekeeping supervisor should therefore be familiar with both the semi-permanent methods of fixing carpet and those which allow for fairly frequent lifting.

Semi-permanent methods

Tackless gripper. The carpet is stretched on to narrow strips of wood with protruding tacks (*see* Fig. 57(*a*)). The strips line the perimeter of the area to be carpeted, and are dangerous when exposed.

Turn and tack. The edge of the carpet is turned under like a hem, then tacked into position (*see* Fig. 57(*b*)). Unless well fitted, this method can create unevenness which traps dust. It is usually only used with woven carpets.

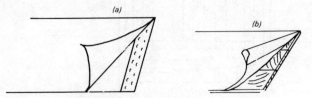

Fig. 57. *Semi-permanent methods of fixing carpets.*
(a) *Tackless gripper;* (b) *turn and tack.*

Sunken. This method may be used where there is a change in floor level. The carpet is placed into a "well" and edged with metal or wood strips.

Glued. This is more permanent than the other methods. It is usually used with rubber or foam-backed carpets and can cause early wear unless the subfloor is very even.

Temporary methods

These usually involve the addition of tape sewn round the edge of the carpet. This tape may contain pegs, hooks, press-studs or "touch and close" loops ("Velcro") which will attach themselves to corresponding sockets, loops, or hooks attached to the floor surface immediately beneath the carpet. Sometimes the carpet is edged with rubber so that it will lay firmly in place without any additional anchorage.

Stair carpeting

This should be firmly fixed to prevent accidents occurring. (*see* Fig. 58). Tackless grippers, rods or clips are usually used as they allow the carpet to be taken up for "jogging"—a process which involves moving the carpet up or down a few centimetres to even the wear on the tread.

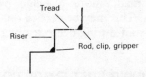

Fig. 58. *Fixing stair carpet.*

Special treatments applied to soft floor coverings

Table XV above illustrates that very few carpet pile fibres are able to fulfil all the requirements of a soft floor covering. Wool appears to be the most suitable but it is very expensive and still requires protection from moths. Many carpets therefore undergo special treatment either during manufacture or *in situ*, in which case housekeeping staff are responsible for carrying out the treatment. The following finishes are frequently applied:

Flameproofing

This is an essential treatment for carpets containing rayon and cotton. It should be carried out by specialists to ensure thorough treatment.

Mothproofing
This should be applied to carpets with a high proportion of wool. It involves spraying the carpet with a moth deterrent such as naphthalene.

Water/stain resistance
A silicone solution can be sprayed on to a carpet and left for about two hours. The spray coats each pile fibre with an invisible film, so that it effectively seals the carpet. This seal, however, is vulnerable to hot liquids and is usually only applied to carpets with a dense pile.

Anti-static treatment
Carpets made from synthetic fibres are prone to a build up of static electricity which is increased when the volume of traffic on the carpet increases, or when the relative humidity in the area of the carpet is low. Anti-static agents may be sprayed on to the carpet to attract moisture from the atmosphere so that the relative humidity immediately above the carpet pile is high and the electricity is able to leak away. The addition of metal fibres in the carpet construction can also aid conductivity.

Disinfection
A carpet may be made more hygienic by treatment with a disinfectant solution. This may be carried out during manufacture or by housekeeping staff during deep cleaning or while vacuuming each day.

MAINTAINING SOFT FLOOR COVERINGS

Soft floor coverings are easily soiled and damaged. Frequent, regular care is therefore essential if early replacement is to be avoided. There are four stages in the care of soft floor coverings:

(*a*) protection from soil and damage (*see* Table XVI);
(*b*) daily attention;
(*c*) periodic attention;
(*d*) removal of stains as soon as they occur.

Daily attention
This involves the removal of dust using dry suction equipment or a carpet sweeper. Some establishments, e.g. hostels and some hotels, feel that daily attention is unnecessary. If this is house policy the carpets should have a short pile or be of a cord construction as these trap dust less easily.

TABLE XVI. PROTECTION OF SOFT FLOOR COVERINGS FROM SOIL AND DAMAGE.

Causes of soil or damage	Methods of protection
Dust	Regular use of dry suction equipment.
Dirt	Removal of dust before it is allowed to turn into dirt by contact with grease or moisture. Treatment with a soil-resistant finish.
Grit	Provision of matting at entrances. Regular use of dry suction equipment. Provision of paved areas outside the entrance areas.
Stains	Treatment with a stain-resistant finish. Regular inspection of carpeted areas for stains. Provision of a suitable stain removal kit for staff.
Spillages	Mop up as soon as possible with absorbent cloth followed by immediate treatment of any resulting stain. (Rubber-backed carpets may be damaged if spills are left.)
Cigarette burns	Provision of sufficient metal ashtrays and waste bins of adequate size, which must be frequently emptied. Treatment with a flameproof finish.
Indentation from furniture	Move furniture frequently. Fit castors to chair and table legs or place "cups" beneath them.
Inefficient removal of shampoo	Provision of adequate training and supervision of staff in shampooing techniques.
Pest infestation	Regular use of dry suction equipment. Treatment with mothproof finish.

Equipment. (*See also* Chapter 2.)

(*a*) Dry suction equipment or carpet sweeper.
(*b*) Appropriate attachments.
(*c*) Spot cleaning kit.

Method

(*a*) Remove scraps of paper, pins, etc.
(*b*) Remove stains with spot remover.
(*c*) Check plug and flex then connect to nearest socket, keeping flex over shoulder.
(*d*) Vacuum or sweep area methodically using crevice attachment around the edges of fitted carpeting and around the base of furniture.

(*e*) Remove threads, fluff, etc. from equipment.

(*f*) Unplug electrical equipment and check bag. Change if necessary.

(*g*) Empty carpet sweeper pans into paper and place in rubbish sack.

(*h*) Replace spot cleaner and deal with soiled cloths.

(*i*) Store equipment correctly (*see* Chapter 2).

Periodic attention

This involves deep cleaning. The frequency with which it occurs depends on the amount and type of traffic the carpet receives, the type of soft floor covering and the area in which it is situated. The housekeeping manager should have prepared a deep cleaning programme for soft floor coverings which should take into account these factors as well as bearing in mind room availability at various times of the year. Consultation with other departments is essential as it may be necessary to close off certain areas completely.

The majority of establishments take it upon themselves to deep clean the soft floor coverings. However, contractors may be employed to carry out the work either on or off the premises. In both cases any department involved in using the carpeted area should be consulted well before any definite arrangements are made, and housekeeping staff should be made aware of such arrangements as work schedules may need to be adapted.

A soft floor covering is in need of deep cleaning when it shows signs of:

(*a*) colour loss;

(*b*) staining;

(*c*) flattening;

(*d*) strong odour or mustiness.

Before attempting to deep clean a new carpet an inconspicuous area should be tested for colour loss. If this occurs, advice should be sought from the manufacturer or a professional carpet cleaning company.

There are three methods of deep cleaning soft floor surfaces:

(*a*) shampooing;

(*b*) hot water injection and extraction;

(*c*) dry powder.

Shampooing

This can be done by hand or with electrically operated equipment. Shampooing by hand is very tiring and time-consuming and is only

used in areas where machines cannot reach, such as the edges of
fitted carpets, corners and stairs. It is also used when spot cleaning.
Care must be taken when hand shampooing to avoid excessive
amounts of shampoo solution soaking into the carpet as this may
damage the backing and extend the drying time.

There are two types of carpet shampoo, liquid and dry foam.
Both belong to the anionic group of synthetic detergents (*see*
Chapter 3) and must be diluted accurately if they are to be effective
and safe. Liquid shampoo acts in a similar way to washing up
detergent but with less foam. This type of shampoo, however,
tends to leave a residue which traps dirt making it necessary to
shampoo the carpet fairly frequently. Dry shampoo contains some
solvent in addition to detergent to assist in the removal of solvent
soluble dirt. It is in fact a liquid which leaves a dry foam on the
surface of the carpet after application. The foam loosens and lifts
the dirt holding it on the surface of the carpet pile until it can be
removed by dry suction. Dry shampoos deposit about 90 per cent
less liquid on to the carpet than liquid shampoos and so require
considerably less drying time. They are to be recommended for use
on carpets with rubber backings.

Both liquid and dry shampoo solutions can be dispensed from an
ordinary scrubbing machine fitted with a tank, but special brushes
should be fitted to prevent damage to the carpet pile. In addition,
special shampooing machines may be used in conjunction with dry
foam shampoo. These feed the diluted solution through a foam
generator on to a revolving cylindrical brush which works foam
into the carpet. This has the advantage of preventing any water
being deposited on to the carpet.

Hot water injection and extraction
This method of deep cleaning requires a special machine. The noise
level for this type of machine is high and so extra piping and hosing
may be necessary in hospitals and nursing homes, to enable the
machine to be left outside the patient area. Special shampooing
solution which does not foam is necessary for this type of machine;
in fact a de-foamer should be used to reduce any foam created by
reactivation of deposits of old shampoo lying dormant in the
carpet. The machine injects the solution under high pressure
through the pile to the back of the carpet where it loosens and
emulsifies dirt and grease deposits. At almost the same time the
machine sucks up the solution together with the dirt and grease and
deposits it into a separate tank (*see* Fig. 59). This simultaneous
action leaves the carpet only slightly damp so that drying time is
very short. All methods of deep cleaning should be followed by dry

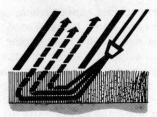

Fig. 59. *Hot water injection/extraction.*

suctioning to restore the carpet pile and to allow air to reach through to the backing.

It is very important that sufficient time is allowed for a carpet to dry thoroughly after either of the above methods has been used. If the carpet is put back into use too soon, soiling will occur much more rapidly and the damp backing and underlay may become damaged. The use of a wet suction machine after shampooing will greatly accelerate drying time.

Dry powder

This method of cleaning a carpet does not strictly deep clean, but helps to prolong the periods between deep cleaning. A powder containing absorbent materials such as sawdust, solvents and drying agents is sprinkled on to the carpet, left for several minutes then removed together with the absorbed dirt and grease, with a dry suction machine or special looped cotton pad beneath a floor machine "soil-sorb"). Water-absorbent dirt is not removed by this method, and it should not be considered as an alternative to the other methods of deep cleaning.

How to deep clean a soft floor covering

Staff involved in the periodic maintenance of soft floor coverings should be thoroughly trained in the procedure to be followed and be conversant with the equipment to be used.

Equipment

(*a*) Dry suction equipment with appropriate attachments.

(*b*) Wet suction machine (not necessary for hot water injection and extraction).

(*c*) Shampooing machine.

(*d*) Deep clean solution correctly diluted.

(*e*) De-foamer (optional).

(*f*) Stain removal kit.

(*g*) Plastic material.

(*h*) Warning signs.

Method

(*a*) Seal off the area to be cleaned and position warning signs.

(*b*) Ventilate the area (many shampoos contain a high proportion of ammonia which creates strong fumes).

(*c*) Remove furniture or push neatly to one side.

(*d*) Protect the bottom and legs of furniture with plastic material to prevent rust marks appearing on the carpet.

(*e*) Remove dust thoroughly with dry suction equipment, attending to both sides of rugs and loose laid carpets.

(*f*) Remove stains or sticky marks (*see* Appendix I).

(*g*) Test an inconspicuous area for colour fastness (especially new carpets).

(*h*) Attend to carpet edges by hand shampooing.

(*i*) Check flex and plug, then connect electrical equipment to nearest socket making sure the flex is in no danger of being caught up with the brushes, etc.

(*j*) Shampoo methodically according to the manufacturer's instructions, overlapping each line of work.

(*k*) Remove excess moisture immediately using wet suction equipment.

(*l*) Empty equipment including tanks and hoses. Rinse and dry them. Store safely and correctly.

(*m*) Replace furniture when thoroughly dry (allow twenty-four hours if possible depending on the method used).

(*n*) Remove warning signs when completely dry.

Removing stains from soft floor coverings

Stains can be kept to a minimum if spillages are wiped up as soon as they occur and if housekeeping staff are trained to look out for and remove stains when carrying out daily cleaning. The longer a stain remains the more permanent it becomes and the more difficult and expensive it is to remove.

The general principles of stain removal are dealt with in Appendix I but the following points are specific to the removal of carpet stains:

(*a*) Work in a well-ventilated room as a fitted carpet will retain solvent fumes longer than textiles which can be laundered.

(*b*) If possible identify the stain and the pile fibres then test that the stain removal agent will not damage the carpet.

(*c*) Remember that a stain removal agent could damage a special finish.

(*d*) Remove liquids with absorbent paper.

(*e*) Scrape up semi-solids with a blunt knife or brush lightly to loosen the stain.

(*f*) Freshly spilled liquids can be flushed out by squirting with a soda syphon.

(*g*) Dirty marks and water soluble stains can usually be removed with carpet shampoo, correctly diluted or slightly under-diluted. This should ideally be followed by deep cleaning the whole carpet to prevent patches showing.

(*h*) Rub stains gently with a lint free cloth dipped into a suitable solution. If rubbed too hard the stain will be forced further into the carpet pile.

(*i*) Work from the outer edge of the stain towards the centre.

(*j*) Rinse thoroughly after using a water-based remover. Allow a solvent-based one to evaporate completely.

(*k*) Avoid overwetting the carpet and if possible cover the damp area with a chair or table until it has dried.

(*l*) If possible raise woven carpets and treat the back as well as the front.

(*m*) Take care with solvent cleaners as these may damage rubber or foam-backed carpets.

(*n*) After treatment suction clean or smooth the carpet pile in the correct direction and allow it to dry naturally.

SELF-ASSESSMENT QUESTIONS

1. Suggest five reasons why a supervisor should have a knowledge of floor construction.

2. What advantages and disadvantages do soft floor coverings have over hard floor coverings?

3. What are the five procedures involved in the maintenance of hard floor coverings?

4. Suggest suitable floor coverings for the following areas, giving reasons:

      (*a*) an operating theatre;
      (*b*) a study bedroom;
      (*c*) a hotel lounge bar;
      (*d*) a sauna suite;
      (*e*) a geriatric hospital ward.

5. Suggest five substances likely to cause damage to hard floor coverings.

6. What is the difference between a resilient floor covering and one which has good resistance?

7. What is a barrier zone?

8. What procedure should be followed by staff about to use electrical floor cleaning equipment?

9. Why is an underlay used beneath soft floor coverings?

10. What preparation work is necessary before deep cleaning a soft floor covering?

CHAPTER SEVEN

Housekeeping Control

CHAPTER OBJECTIVES

After studying this chapter you should be able to:
* understand how the duties of a housekeeping department are organised and performed;
* appreciate the important role played by the supervisor in the efficient running of a housekeeping department;
* define the levels of responsibility attached to the various grades of housekeeping staff;
* calculate staffing requirements;
* describe the methods used to control standards within the housekeeping department;
* understand what is meant by a cleaning programme and how to implement it.

DUTIES AND RESPONSIBILITIES OF STAFF

The part played by the housekeeping department in the various sectors of the accommodation industry is outlined in Chapter 1, where Table I indicates that it is the frequency of cleaning rather than the type or amount of cleaning which differs from establishment to establishment—the basic housekeeping techniques remain very similar. The different grades of housekeeping staff therefore have to perform similar duties whichever establishment they work in.

Housekeeping staff can be divided into the following categories:

(a) managerial;
(b) supervisory;
(c) unskilled.

Their duties are outlined below.

Managerial duties
The housekeeping manager is responsible for the efficient and economic running of the department and must have the administrative ability to:

(a) utilise manpower effectively; this involves delegating tasks to housekeeping staff in such a way that the work of the department is carried out correctly and on time;

(b) develop and instigate control procedures for cleaning materials, equipment, linen, staff and standards of performance;

(c) plan and forecast the department's needs, to do this it is necessary to:

(i) keep records of the amount, type and cost of all work carried out annually:

(ii) frequently reassess the cleaning routines;

(iii) search contantly for and test new techniques and products;

(d) develop a good working relationship with all other departments so that time and effort are not wasted when co-operation from them is required;

(e) implement the legal obligations of the department (health and safety, lost property, fire precautions, etc.; *see also* below);

(f) create and organise training programmes for all grades of housekeeping staff.

A housekeeping manager therefore requires a background of training and experience in all types of housekeeping work. This should provide him/her with confidence and the ability to command respect and loyalty from the staff.

Supervisory duties

Staff on a supervisory grade should have had sufficient experience in the practical aspects of housekeeping to be able to implement the housekeeper's instructions with confidence and clarity. A housekeeping manager needs to rely on the supervisory staff to control and maintain satisfactory standards of work.

The duties of a housekeeping supervisor are illustrated in the selection of job descriptions in Appendix II. Such posts are filled either by people with several years of experience at the unskilled level and who are prepared to accept the degree of responsibility offered by a supervisor grade, or by people who have received formal supervisory training and who have perhaps undergone a short period of practical experience. Anybody who is in a supervisory position, however, must have certain personality traits if they are to be successful. They must be:

(a) competent at practical housekeeping skills;

(b) punctual;

(c) trustworthy;

(d) reliable;

(e) observant;

(f) adaptable;

(g) tactful;

(h) firm but approachable.

They must also be able to pass on information in a clear concise way to the operative staff as well as to management.

Duties for unskilled staff

The unskilled staff of a housekeeping department are, in some sectors of the industry, quite a transient body of workers—hotels, for instance, often employ staff for six to eight months in the year only and re-recruit at the start of the next season. Many areas of the industry rely on large numbers of part-time unskilled staff to assist during peak periods such as changeover days, or in the mornings when the majority of cleaning duties are carried out (hostels).

Although their work may be classed as unskilled they may be expected to operate large electrical equipment and need to be given training in how to carry out even the most basic cleaning tasks, if they are to contribute to the efficient running of the department. This type of work is physically strenuous and usually involves working unsocial hours, e.g. week-ends and very early or late shifts.

They are frequently in a position where they meet guests/customers/patients at their most vulnerable—in a state of undress or while suffering in hospital—and so the attitude they adopt in such situations can play an important part in the marketing policy of the establishment. Employees on this grade should have a neat appearance, a healthy constitution and hygienic habits. They should be punctual, polite, tactful, cheerful and able to adapt to new situations when they arise.

Relations between the three grades

Table XVII illustrates the links between the three grades by showing how the responsibilities of the manager are reflected in the duties of his subordinates.

Job titles

The titles given to staff employed in these three grades of work vary from establishment to establishment. The following is a guide to the most frequently used titles.

(a) Managerial: executive housekeeper, head housekeeper, housekeeper, domestic bursar, domestic services manager and their deputies.

(b) Supervisory: Assistant head housekeeper, assistant housekeeper, assistant domestic bursar, assistant domestic services manager, floor housekeeper, linen keeper, storekeeper, domestic supervisor, ward housekeeper, ward orderly.

TABLE XVII. DELEGATION OF HOUSEKEEPING DUTIES.

Managerial duties	Subsequent supervisory duties	Subsequent unskilled duties
Engagement and dismissal of housekeeping staff.	Report on standards of individual staff performance.	Welcome and assist new staff as much as possible. Report any knowledge of misconduct by colleagues.
Liaise with other departments.	Respect the skills of all grades of staff from other departments when they are working in the housekeeping department.	Co-operate as much as possible with staff from other departments.
Organise the provision of staff welfare facilities meals on duty, uniform changing facilities, recreation areas, parties, etc.	Inform staff of such facilities and where necessary supervise the cleaning of them, e.g. cloakrooms, uniforms.	Co-operate when requested to maintain or use such facilities, e.g. arrive on time for meals, look after uniform, clean cloakrooms.
Plan induction and training sessions. Organise short courses, lectures, etc.	Arrange work schedules and work rotas to allow all staff to undergo a period of induction and to attend training sessions, etc. Instruct staff in cleaning routines, etc. Participate in or attend training courses.	Undergo a period of induction and be willing to attend training sessions when requested.
Compile duty rotas.	Make sure staff are aware of their hours of work and that the rota is adhered to. Solve any problems or queries if possible.	Be punctual and attend work when requested. Inform management promptly if attendance is not possible.

Table Continued

TABLE XVII. (*Continued*).

Managerial duties	Subsequent supervisory duties	Subsequent unskilled duties
Control standards of cleaning.	Regular completion of cleaning and maintenance checklists and inventories.	Perform allocated cleaning duties as instructed.
Maintenance of room status records.	Inspect and record room status regularly. Liaise with reception.	Be aware of the state of room occupation and report when requested on customer/patient comfort.
Organise and control linen provision.	Check and record the amount and state of linen during collection, despatch, storage, repair and use.	Ensure beds are well made with clean linen in good repair. Provide regular supply of clean towels, etc.
Custody of room keys and lost property found within department.	Issue and receipt of keys. Receipt of lost property handed in by housekeeping staff.	Receive and look after required keys while on duty. Hand in lost property immediately
Provision and responsibility for safety and security within the housekeeping department.	Instruct staff in the rules of safety and security while at work. Supervise fire practices.	Be aware of safety and security procedures. Co-operate during fire practices. Attend security talks, films, etc.
Organise stock control system and provision of supplies.	Check stock regularly. Issue supplies to staff. Check deliveries.	Use supplies and equipment correctly and economically.
Advise on the choice of décor schemes and furniture provision.	Report on the durability and suitability of fabrics used for furniture and decoration from the point of view of cleaning.	Adhere to pre-planned cleaning procedures to help prolong the life of internal decorations and furniture.

Table Continued

TABLE XVII. (*Continued*).

Managerial duties	Subsequent supervisory duties	Subsequent unskilled duties
Organise the provision of rooms/areas for meetings, functions, periodic cleaning and the necessary equipment.	Supervise staff involved in the cleaning and setting up of function and meeting rooms, etc.	Carry out non-routine duties as instructed by supervisor.

(*c*) Unskilled: chambermaid, room maid, room attendant, cleaner, cloakroom attendant, domestic assistant, linen maid/ assistant, house porter.

ORGANISING THE WORK

A well-managed housekeeping department relies on the ability of its manager to organise work efficiently. It is also important that the supervisors have a working knowledge of how this is done as they are responsible for controlling and carrying out the allocated work.

When a building is first put into commission the housekeeping manager must compile a list of which duties top management expect the department to perform. This will vary from establishment to establishment and in hospitals will alter with the type of ward or area. Alongside these duties there should be an indication of the frequency with which each duty is to be performed, e.g. in a new hotel:

Areas to be covered	Frequency of cleaning
Reception	Twice daily and when considered necessary in between
Bedrooms	Daily or whenever room occupancy changes (this could be as many as three times a day if it is used for business during the day)
Staircases	Once a day
Lifts	Once a day
Staff changing rooms	Twice a week

Subsequent organisation involves the preparation of:

(*a*) work specifications;
(*b*) work schedules;
(*c*) job procedures;
(*d*) duty rotas.

Work specifications

These are detailed descriptions of the work to be carried out in specific areas, e.g. bedrooms, common rooms, waiting areas, general wards, intensive care wards. There should be a work specification for every type of area covered by the housekeeping department. The information contained in such a document should include the following.

(*a*) The work to be covered.

(*b*) The equipment and materials required to carry out this work.

(*c*) The area of responsibility of the worker. (For example, hotel dining rooms are maintained by restaurant staff on a daily basis but deep cleaning may be carried out by housekeeping staff. Nursing staff may make up patients' beds but the housekeeping staff clean the surrounding areas.)

(*d*) The time allowed for completion of the job.

A work specification is a useful reference document for newly appointed managers and supervisors. It also provides the necessary information for calculating staff and equipment requirements. Some example specifications are given below.

WORK SPECIFICATION: CLEANING CORRIDORS

1. Store equipment neatly in corridor to be cleaned.
2. Empty waste bins and ashtrays, etc., dust them and wash if necessary.
3. Remove dust from walls including window surrounds, curtains, doors and any pictures or notice-boards, etc.
4. Spot clean, using a damp cloth and synthetic detergent solution, areas such as light switch panels, door handles and hinges, windowsills, skirtings, etc.
5. Remove dust and dirt from floor using appropriate methods, but if the floor is to become damp, attend to one-half of the corridor at a time and position warning signs at the appropriate points.

The frequency of corridor cleaning will depend on its situation. Guidance should be given by the appropriate supervisor.

WORK SPECIFICATION: SERVICING A BEDROOM WITH PRIVATE BATHROOM
1. Check that room and bathroom are free for cleaning.
2. Leave door open while cleaning to warn guest that cleaning is taking place.
3. Ventilate room.
4. Strip bed and remove soiled linen including towels, etc.
5. Empty ashtrays and remove litter.
6. Remove or wash dirty crockery, etc.
7. Clean bathroom area and replenish toilet paper, tissues, soap, shampoo, shower cap, etc.
8. Remake bed with clean linen.
9. Close window then dust all horizontal surfaces which can be reached and remove sticky marks.
10. Replenish beverage facility, information folder, and update magazines.
11. Vacuum floor, removing stains as soon as they are noticed.
12. Check room for general appearance and to ensure no equipment has been left inside.
13. Close and lock door and proceed to next room.

WORK SPECIFICATION: STUDY BEDROOM (TERM TIME)
1. Ventilate room.
2. Empty ashtrays and remove litter. (Do not wash dirty crockery, etc.)
3. Tidy bed.
4. Clean wash-basin and surround, including mirror.
5. Adjust window.
6. Dust and remove any sticky marks from all horizontal surfaces within reach. (Do not disturb desk top.)
7. Attend to floor, removing stains as they occur.
8. Check that no equipment is left in room.
9. Close and lock door. Proceed to next room.
Thursday: place one clean sheet and one clean pillowcase outside each bedroom.
Friday: collect one soiled sheet and one soiled pillowcase from outside each bedroom. Count them and take to linen room. Inform surpervisor of any absence of soiled linen or failure to remove clean linen.
Periodic cleaning: to be carried out at the end of each term or at least once a year.
This specification is to be followed twice a week. Students should be informed of which days their room is to be cleaned so that they can vacate it.

The above specification is likely to become more like that for a hotel if the room is to be let during vacation periods.

Work schedules

These list the actual work to be carried out by one member of staff during a particular period of the day. They should include meal breaks and allow time for clearing away and tidying equipment, etc. The amount of work to be done by the housekeeping department in one area may take longer than the length of one shift, and so several schedules may have to be compiled for use in one day. The number of schedules necessary is therefore an indication of the number of staff required to clean any one area on one day. A work schedule should allow for flexibility, especially in a hospital where cleaning has to be carried out between visiting times, meal periods, etc. It should be clear, concise and readily available for reference by staff after it has been explained to them. An example is given below.

WORK SCHEDULE: DOMESTIC ASSISTANT, WARD 3

7.00 *Waiting Room:* static mop floor. Damp dust tables.
Clinical Room: static mop then damp mop floor. Spray clean twice weekly.
Sister's Office: as above. Vacuum mat.
Kitchen: wash pots as they become available using pot washing machine. Wipe down work surfaces. Check and spot mop floor.
Playroom: remove large items of debris and food spillage. Static mop and wet mop floor. Spray clean twice weekly.
Ward Areas (cubicles and 6-bed wards): as available, static mop and wet mop floors. Spray clean twice weekly.

9.45 Break

10.00 *Ward Areas:* continue as above.
Corridor and Nurses' Station: static mop and wet mop floor. Spray clean twice weekly.
Clinical Room: check clean floor area.
Patients' bathroom: thoroughly clean sinks and toilets. Replenish supplies of toilet rolls. Wet mop floors.
Staff Toilets: as above.
Sluice: wet mop floor.
Waiting room and Landing: static mop and wet mop floor. Spray clean twice weekly.

12.00 *Kitchen:* wash all pots using pot washing machine. Wipe down all working surfaces. Mop floor. Empty swill bucket and wash.

Clear away equipment. Wash hands.

13.00 Off duty.

Weekly: high dusting, radiators, paintwork, defrost fridge (Friday), clean cooker, scrub grocery basket, wash tiles, floor maintenance, internal glass, cleaning cupboard. All these tasks to be completed at some stage during each week.

Job procedures

These specify the way in which a job is to be done, and relate to one task only such as bedmaking or toilet cleaning. They should be used during induction and training sessions and be kept for reference. Updating is necessary as and when changes in equipment, cleaning materials, furniture, furnishings, etc. occur. One example of a job procedure is given below, and more can be found later in this chapter. A housekeeping supervisor should be fully conversant with the job procedures used throughout the department.

JOB PROCEDURE: CLEANING A TELEPHONE

Equipment: damp cloth;
duster;
sanitiser/detergent or special "wipe";
disinfectant (optional).

Method

1. Dust then wipe with synthetic detergent solution, or sanitiser.
2. Pay particular attention to the dial numbers, mouthpiece, earpiece and flex.
3. Depress receiver buttons if possible while cleaning.
4. Wash, rinse and dry cloths. Replace cleaning agents.

Duty rotas

A duty rota or roster can only be drawn up after the work schedules have been prepared. They are necessary for ensuring that there are sufficient staff to cover each schedule and therefore enough staff to carry out the work indicated by the work specification. A duty rota is usually prepared by the housekeeping manager but it is often the supervisors who have to sort out any difficulties or alterations. They must therefore know how it works. A well-planned duty rota should be easy to understand and read. It should be displayed in the area to which it applies, and in the housekeeper's office, at least seven days before it is to come into operation and should indicate:

(*a*) where each member of staff is to work;

(*b*) their hours of duty;

(*c*) days off and holiday periods;

(*d*) overtime to be worked and by whom.

In some establishments such as hostels, a fixed rota can be used. This type is simple to compile, as staff are kept on the same duties and days off each week, although slight alterations may be necessary when conferences are catered for and during holiday periods. In establishments which need to provide a seven-day-week coverage, a rotating rota is usually operated as this enables week-end work and overtime to be shared by the staff. This type of rota has to cover more than a seven-day period, and is usually planned on a fourteen or twenty-eight day basis.

How to compile a duty rota
Basic information.

(*a*) Full-time staff usually work forty hours a week, i.e. eight hours per day for five days.

(*b*) Each eight-hour shift should include drinks breaks and paid meal breaks.

(*c*) Some establishments include time for changing and signing in and out in each eight-hour shift.

Special considerations

(*a*) Split duties should be avoided as far as possible as they are considered "unsociable" and may be liable to extra pay.

(*b*) The bulk of the staff should be on duty during peak periods. These may be at certain times of the day, week or season.

(*c*) The personal commitments of individual staff should be catered for as far as possible.

(*d*) Overtime and week-end work which deserve extra pay should be kept to a minimum.

(*e*) Days off should be consecutive if possible.

(*f*) Only two people should be off on any one day in each area, if maximum efficiency is to be maintained.

(*g*) Each area should have one person on duty who is familiar with the regular routine.

(*h*) Allow two full-time relief staff for every five full-time staff in any one area, when a seven-day operation is required.

Fixed duty rotas

These will usually be used in establishments or areas requiring staff Monday to Friday only. Saturday and Sunday therefore

Name	Shift	Mon. hours	Tues. hours	Wed. hours	Thurs. hours	Fri. hours	Sat. hours	Sun. hours	Total hours
M. Black	8-4	8	8	8	8	8	DO	DO	40
R. Green	9-5	8	8	8	8	8	DO	DO	40
S. White	9-5	8	8	8	8	8	DO	DO	40
F. Brown	9-5	8	8	8	8	8	DO	DO	40
L. Grey	8-12	4	4	4	4	4	DO	DO	20
TOTAL		36	36	36	36	36	0	0	180

Fig. 60. *Fixed duty rota.*

automatically become their two days off (*see* Fig. 60). Part-time staff are frequently employed to cover holiday periods—unlike the rotating rota where shifts can be altered more readily. It is advisable to begin by listing the number of staff necessary for the area in which the rota is to be used, and then to add the desired number of relief staff.

Rotating duty rotas

To even out the workload when a seven-day-week coverage is required, days off should be moved forward by one day each week, assuming all staff are able to work any day and any shift (*see* Fig. 61). In some establishments, however, the level of service required

Week commencing 28.3.-4								Area Annex	
Name	Duty No.	Mon. hours	Tues. hours	Wed. hours	Thurs. hours	Fri. hours	Sat. hours	Sun. hours	Total hours
A. Shaw	1	8	8	8	DO	DO	8	8	40
B. Kent	2	8	8	8	8	8	DO	DO	40
C. Riley	3	8	DO	DO	8	8	8	8	40
D. Boffin	4	DO	8	8	8	8	8	DO	40
L. Moon	5	8	8	8	8	DO	DO	8	40
Relief 1		DO	DO	8	8	8	8	8	40
Relief 2		8	8	DO	DO	8	8	8	40
TOTAL		40	40	40	40	40	40	40	280

Fig. 61. *Rotating duty rota.*
The duty number will refer to the work schedule number.

can be reduced at week-ends and so this should also be taken into account.

Having worked out a rota it is advisable to check:

(*a*) the number of people off on one day;

(*b*) the experience of the staff remaining on duty;

(*c*) that the staff have no more and no less than four days off over a period of fourteen days.

(*d*) that all work schedules are covered.

New staff should if possible be prepared to accept the hours made available by the vacant post otherwise the rota will need altering and this can cause upset and annoyance to the existing staff. Staff should also be prepared to accept the days off they are allocated—any alterations they desire should if possible be through direct exchange with a colleague.

CONTROL OF HOUSEKEEPING DUTIES: FLOW OF INFORMATION

Physical control of cleaning standards is the responsibility of the supervisory staff. They pass on information from the housekeeper to the housekeeping staff and vice versa, and from housekeeping to other departments such as reception, maintenance, personnel, etc. This information can take several forms, as outlined below.

Management to workforce

The majority of information is passed on during a period of induction and subsequently during regular training sessions.

Induction

Every new employee should be "introduced" to the establishment whatever department he is to work in. This introduction should include:

(*a*) a summary of the aims of the establishment;

(*b*) the staffing structure of the establishment and the new employee's immediate superiors;

(*c*) the policy of the establishment towards treatment of guests/residents/patients—be respectful, polite, helpful, etc.;

(*d*) fire procedure;

(*e*) accident procedure;

(*f*) security procedures;

(*g*) grievance procedures and location of union office;

(*h*) a brief tour of the establishment.

This type of induction may be carried out by personnel staff or general management, although such information may be passed on during a more specific induction session which relates to the work of the housekeeping department. The latter will include information regarding the following.

(*a*) Uniform: what is correct, where and when to change it, the importance of personal hygiene. How to clean it. Cloakroom facilities.

(*b*) Pay and hours: checking in and out procedure, explanation of rota system, when and where pay is received.

(*c*) Meals and breaks: where, when, duration, payment if any.

(*d*) Absence: procedure required by establishment and by law.

(*e*) Holidays: entitlement, when and how to book periods required.

(*f*) Termination of employment: notice required, return of uniform.

(*g*) Grievances: introduction to departmental union representatives.

(*h*) Complaints: what to do in the event of a complaint by a customer.

(*i*) Lost property: prompt action. Procedure to follow.

Training
Shortly after the induction period, which may last for a morning or possibly two or three days, new employees should atend a training session or a series of training sessions so that they can be instructed in:

(*a*) how to use and care for equipment;
(*b*) how to use and store cleaning materials;
(*c*) how to obtain supplies of cleaning materials;
(*d*) linen/laundry procedure;
(*e*) how to perform the tasks required of them to the desired standard.

The last of these items should be prefaced by an explanation of the general principles of cleaning, i.e.:

(*a*) close windows before dusting;
(*b*) perform any process likely to create dust at an early stage, e.g. bedmaking, removal of debris and cigarette ash;
(*c*) complete all processes involving the use of water prior to dusting and polishing (except floor areas);
(*d*) work safely, e.g. stack equipment neatly, replace lids on

cleaning agents immediately after use, do not stretch flexes, use warning signs where surfaces may be slippery;

 (*e*) remove stains as soon as they occur;

 (*f*) remove dust from high surfaces first then work downwards;

 (*g*) start cleaning at the furthest point to the main exit of the area and work towards it.

Terminology should also be explained at this stage to assist with communication. There are some terms used by housekeeping staff to describe the standards of cleaning required which may be ambiguous unless defined adequately at the commencement of employment. The following are some examples.

Dust Remove all dust, stickiness, marks and streaks.

Wipe Remove all dust, dirt, grease, and marks with a well wrung out cloth.

Sweep Remove all dust and debris from a floor surface.

Dry mop Bring a light shine to a floor surface without the aid of a polish.

Damp mop Remove all dirt, marks, streaks, liquid and detergent solution from a floor surface.

Scrub Remove all ingrained dirt, grease, marks.

Rinse Remove all traces of dirt or cleaning agent.

Training sessions may be carried out by the housekeeping manager or the supervisory staff and should take the form of a concise talk with practical demonstrations. Existing staff should be expected to attend regularly to renew and update their knowledge. Such sessions also enable staff to air their views on aspects of their work which they find unsatisfactory. In this way staff are encouraged to take an interest in their work and to consider attending college to become more qualified. Other advantages of induction and training sessions are:

 (*a*) they help to maintain the desired standards of cleaning;

 (*b*) they require managers and supervisors to keep up to date and encourage the adoption of new, more efficient methods;

 (*c*) employees are made to feel needed.

Legal obligations of the housekeeping department
There are some rules laid down by the housekeeping manager for staff to follow which stem from the requirements of law. They should be stressed during induction periods and training sessions.

 Guests' property. The housekeeping department must undertake to safeguard guests'/residents' belongings while performing their duties. (Hotel Proprietors Act 1956.)

An innkeeper is only responsible for guests' property if at the time of loss the guest had reserved sleeping accommodation and the loss took place between midnight before the reservation and midnight after the final reservation date. Loss or damage must therefore be reported immediately and a liability notice must be displayed in a prominent place (usually in the reception area).

Guests' behaviour. Housekeeping staff should report to management any cases where guests' behaviour leaves something to be desired. If damage to property has been caused staff must be precise over what they report. The damage will have to be the result of negligence on the part of the guest, e.g. standing on furniture. This is very difficult to prove, however. (Law of negligence.)

Illness and death. If a guest becomes ill, he will be confined to his bedroom, and housekeeping staff must carry out the doctor's instructions. This may involve instructions by the medical authorities to fumigate the room, but this is usually only the case if an infectious disease has been contracted. Reception should be informed if a room is to be fumigated so that it can be taken off the letting list. Deaths should be treated discreetly: double lock the bedroom door and do not touch anything in case there are any suspicious circumstances surrounding the death. (Hygiene Regulations.)

Lost property. This must be handed in immediately to the housekeeping manager who may pass it on to reception, as this reduces any accusations of theft. If the item is valuable it should be handed in to the police within forty-eight hours. (Hotel Proprietors Act 1956.)

Health and safety. The housekeeping manager must ensure that guests/residents/patients do not come to harm as a result of:

(*a*) badly lit corridors or stairs;
(*b*) slippery floors;
(*c*) defective equipment;
(*d*) infectious diseases;
(*e*) negligence by staff.

Housekeeping staff must also be safeguarded from injury while at work, equipment must be maintained and a uniform should be provided. (Health and Safety at Work etc. Act 1974.) Staff are entitled to claim state benefit under the National Insurance (Industrial Injuries) Act 1965.

Common law. There are also certain common law obligations which employees and employers should be aware of as follows.

(*a*) Employers must:
(*i*) provide work as arranged;

(*ii*) pay wages when due;

(*iii*) take all reasonable precautions for the safety of employees during the course of their employment.

(*b*) Employees must:

(*i*) devote the agreed amount of time to the performance of their duties;

(*ii*) obey all reasonable and authorised orders;

(*iii*) use reasonable care and skill in the performance of their duties;

(*iv*) act honestly and in good faith to their employer;

(*v*) account for all money and property received on behalf of their employer;

(*vi*) refrain from disclosing confidential information obtained in the course of their duties;

(*vii*) disclose any fellow-worker's misconduct likely to affect the employer's business.

Workforce to management

This type of information is usually passed on by completion of a list or pre-typed document, such as the following.

Room status report

A room status report is completed by either room cleaning staff or supervisors. It usually takes the form of a preprinted sheet (*see* Fig. 62) listing the bedroom numbers against which a note is made indicating:

(*a*) if the room is let (i.e. occupied by a guest);

Date: 28/3/-4		Signed: B. Jones	
Room no.	State of occupancy	Room no.	State of occupancy
50	1	116	0/0/0
51	2	117	2
52	2	118	L
53	3	119	1
	✓	120	L

Key: 1 = 1 person; 2 = 2 persons; L = Luggage still in room;
V = Vacant; 0/0/0 = Out of order

Fig. 62. *Housekeeping report: occupancy list.*

(*b*) if it is vacant but has not been serviced;
(*c*) if it is vacant and ready for reletting;
(*d*) if it is unavailable owing to redecoration or repairwork.

In large establishments this information can be passed on automatically by the use of electronic equipment (the chambermaid presses the appropriate button in the housekeeper's office or the service room or enters the information into a computer). Accurate up-to-date knowledge of the state of room occupancy is vital to a hotel reception department and the hotel housekeeper. It is also necessary in hostels, nurses homes, etc. as it affects laundry costs, cleaning schedules and staff rotas. In small establishments this information is usually passed on verbally.

Maintenance report
(*See* Fig. 63.) This is completed during regular inspection of each area maintained by the housekeeping department, and records the state of all furniture, furnishings, room decoration and services (heating, plumbing, electric fittings, drainage, etc.). Inspections may take place daily, weekly or monthly depending on the type of establishment and the standard of accommodation offered, although any serious faults should be reported as soon as they occur. The more frequently such items are checked the less chance there is of a guest becoming irritated by the lack of a light bulb or failure of a television to work. It also means that a

Date: 15/5/-5											Signature: V. White
Rooms	Lights	Radio	TV	Heating	Ventilation	Plumbing	Drainage	Furniture	Fittings	Décor	Remarks
23	✓	✓	✓	✓	✓	✓	✓	✓	✓	✓	
24	✓	✓	✓	✓	✓	✓	✓	✓	✓	✓	
25		✓	✓	✓	✓	✓	✓	✓	✓	✓	LOBBY LIGHT NOT WORKING
26	✓	✓		✓	✓	✓	✓	✓	✓	✓	BBC 2 RECEPTION V. POOR
27	✓	✓	✓	✓		✓	✓	✓	✓	✓	ONE WINDOW WILL NOT CLOSE COMPLETELY
28	✓	✓	✓	✓	✓	✓	✓	✓	✓	✓	CRACKED TILES IN BATHROOM

Fig. 63. *Maintenance report.*

hostel housekeeper can recoup the cost of any damage caused by residents before they leave. As soon as the lists are completed (by chambermaids or supervisors) any problems should be attended to immediately and if necessary the maintenance or portering departments notified that their services are required.

The importance of regular maintenance inspections should not be minimised, as early attention to such faults as leaking radiators, blocked toilets, loose chair legs, etc. will prevent the occurrence of major repairwork and premature replacement of costly furniture and furnishings. It will also help to maintain a safer environment for guests and staff who might otherwise become injured.

Room inspection reports

These reports record the standard of cleanliness in each area for which the housekeeping department is responsible. They are completed by supervisors during a daily or weekly inspection. Inspection may be carried out informally as staff are visited each day, or formally when a checklist is completed (*see* Fig. 64). From these checklists it is possible to compile an overall inspection report. Spot checks help to keep staff alert and enable the supervisor to pinpoint staff who require further instruction in certain procedures or who constantly neglect certain duties. A tour of inspection should always include a cleaner's store cupboard or service room as the state of these areas is often an indication of a member of staff's attitude to work. It will also reveal any existence of stockpiling.

Condition and efficiency of equipment and cleaning materials

This type of information can be acquired by speaking to the people who use the equipment and supplies and by informal inspection. It should be possible, however, to assess the performance of cleaning

Rooms	Bed	Bathroom	Floor	Dusting	Replacements	Remarks
23	✓	✓	✓	✓		No menu card or sugar portions
24	✓	✓	✓	✓	✓	
25	✓		✓	✓	✓	Splashes on mirror
26		✓	✓	✓	✓	Untidy pillows & bedspread

Date: 15/5/-5　　　　Signature: A. Smith

Fig. 64. *Room inspection checklist.*

materials by referring to a monthly consumption sheet compiled from recorded issues of stock. These issues relate to staff requisitions for supplies (*see* Chapter 3).

Grievances
All staff should be encouraged to take any complaints they may have to their departmental head as problems are often easily settled without the involvement of the union. However, a supervisor should be conversant with the grievance procedures adopted by the establishment, as these may need to be explained to staff. Any complaints which operative staff receive from residents or guests, however, should be passed on to the supervisor and eventually the housekeeper even if they have been rectified, as measures can then be taken to ensure that the problem does not occur again.

Inter-departmental information
No department in any accommodation establishment can work in isolation. A willingness to co-operate together with the assistance of efficient methods of communication are essential if the establishment is to run smoothly. Methods of communication differ from place to place but the most frequently used methods involve memoranda, telephones, bleeps, preprinted forms, lights, two-way radios and computers.

Figure 65 indicates some of the issues on which housekeeping will need to liaise with other departments. In most cases the supervisor

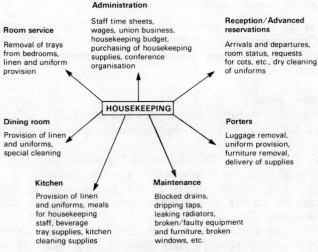

Administration
Staff time sheets, wages, union business, housekeeping budget, purchasing of housekeeping supplies, conference organisation

Room service
Removal of trays from bedrooms, linen and uniform provision

Reception/Advanced reservations
Arrivals and departures, room status, requests for cots, etc., dry cleaning of uniforms

HOUSEKEEPING

Dining room
Provision of linen and uniforms, special cleaning

Porters
Luggage removal, uniform provision, furniture removal, delivery of supplies

Kitchen
Provision of linen and uniforms, meals for housekeeping staff, beverage tray supplies, kitchen cleaning supplies

Maintenance
Blocked drains, dripping taps, leaking radiators, broken/faulty equipment and furniture, broken windows, etc.

Fig. 65. *Inter-departmental communication.*

provides the link between departments and so such a person must have an appreciation of the workload of each department and have the ability to communicate clearly either verbally or in writing or be able to operate the appropriate communication equipment such as a computer display unit.

CLEANING PROGRAMME

The majority of staff employed in a housekeeping department are involved in practical cleaning and room servicing. Their work is part of a planned cleaning programme (consisting of work specifications, work schedules and job procedures) which ensures that all areas of a building, both internal and external, are kept clean and in good condition all the time. A cleaning programme is tailored to the specific needs of an individual establishment but there are some factors which affect the content and design of any programme as follows:

(a) the required standards of cleanliness;
(b) the type and amount of work to be covered;
(c) the time allowed to cover the work;
(d) the most convenient times when work can be performed;
(e) the skills of the staff;
(f) the amount and type of equipment and cleaning materials;
(g) the type and condition of the building;
(h) the amount and type of furniture/fittings/decorations;
(i) the general outside environment.

It is impossible in most establishments to clean every part of a building thoroughly every day. The amount of cleaning and the methods used will vary according to the type of activity being pursued in each area.

Sanitary areas
(Toilets, sluices, bathrooms, urinals and showers.)
(a) Toilets, urinals and sluices should be cleaned thoroughly every day.
(b) Dripping taps should be reported immediately to prevent staining of the fitments to which they are attached.
(c) Avoid constant use of bleach or ammonia as they can damage the surface of a fitment. (Ammonia especially damages stainless steel.)
(d) Avoid the use of coarse abrasive detergents or pads except for extreme cases as they scratch smooth surfaces making them less hygienic.

(*e*) Toilet brushes and their containers should be inspected weekly for damage, and washed, disinfected and dried after use.

(*f*) Iron and copper stains caused by metal salts, precipitated from the inside of water pipes through taps or toilet cisterns, are removed with an acid cleaner.

(*g*) Limescale, commonly found around the base of taps and around the water level in toilets and urinals, is also removed with an acid cleaner.

(*h*) Remember that strong acids burn, therefore rubber gloves must be used when applying acid cleaners and instructions must be followed carefully. It they are used too frequently, the fittings can become damaged and so it is advisable to keep a record of the occasions when they are used.

(*i*) Never mix acid cleaners with other cleaning agents as dangerous gases can be produced.

(*j*) Use disposable cloths or ones which can be boiled after use.

(*k*) Clean equipment thoroughly before using in another sanitary area. Never use sanitary cleaning equipment in another type of area—labelling or colour coding is advisable.

JOB PROCEDURE: CLEANING A TOILET/URINAL
Equipment: toilet brush and container;
damp cloth;
detergent/abrasive detergent/disinfectant/toilet cleaner;
small hand mop;
mopping unit/floor cloth;
bowl or bucket;
supply of toilet paper.

Method
1. Ventilate room.
2. Flush cistern to obtain fresh water for cleaning.
3. Brush down the U-bend with strong movements to reduce water level and expose any water mark which may need removing (toilets).
4. Turn off automatic flushing system (urinals).
5. Apply a solution of neutral detergent with a cloth or brush. If considered necessary use abrasive detergent.
6. Using detergent solution and a cloth, wipe the cistern, flushing handle, pipework, both sides of lid and seat, inside and outside of bowl, sides and base of pedestal.
7. Flush to rinse and if necessary apply disinfectant or toilet cleaner using a brush or small mop. Allow time for scale to soften then remove it with a non-metal scraper. Flush again.

8. Leave lid and seat up until the pedestal rim is dry to avoid staining.

9. Check supply of toilet paper and wipe round the roll holder and door lock, and surrounding tiles or paintwork.

10. Wipe or mop floor.

11. Empty bucket, rinse and dry.

12. Dispose of cloth or boil and dry it.

13. Rinse then wash brush and holder thoroughly and leave to dry.

JOB PROCEDURE: CLEANING A BASIN/BATH/SHOWER
Equipment: damp cloth;
　　　　　　dry cloth;
　　　　　　abrasive detergent;
　　　　　　mopping unit/floor cloth;
　　　　　　supply of soap, etc.

Method

1. Clear fitment of soap, glasses, etc. and pull shower curtain to one side.

2. Dampen cloth and surface of fitment.

3. Place a small amount of detergent on to cloth and wipe entire surface of fitment including underside of basin and pedestal if exposed, the side of the bath and any surrounding tiles. Do not apply abrasive detergent to taps unless considered necessary as this will scratch the surface.

4. Wipe shower curtain and leave loose to dry.

5. Rinse cloth.

6. Rinse fitment thoroughly and wipe taps and mirror if there is one.

7. Dry surfaces and polish up taps and mirror.

8. Replace soap, nailbrush, tooth glasses, etc. Tidy shower curtain.

9. Wipe or mop floor.

Ceilings and walls
(*See also* Chapters 4 and 5.)

(*a*) Clean walls in kitchens and bathrooms frequently as dust will turn to dirt in a damp, greasy environment.

(*b*) Use dust control or dry suction equipment to remove dust.

(*c*) Clean a ceiling before the walls. (Maintenance or portering staff frequently clean ceilings.)

(*d*) When removing dust start at the top of the wall and work down.

(*e*) When washing walls, begin at the top unless it is very dirty when cleaning should begin from the bottom as streaking will occur if dirty water is allowed to run down a badly soiled wall.

(*f*) Cover electric sockets with tape to prevent the entry of water.

(*g*) Remove or cover all furniture and fitments before washing.

(*h*) Remove curtains, pictures, notice-boards, etc.

(*i*) Cover floor area with dust sheets.

(*j*) In a hospital, consult nurses if patients are to remain in the ward area.

(*k*) Use firm step-ladders, tall enough for cleaning to be carried out comfortably when standing one step from the top.

(*l*) Never rest buckets, etc. on windowsills: they are easily knocked down and may leave marks.

(*m*) Protect vulnerable wall areas, e.g.:

(*i*) convex corners, use metal or perspex corner strips;

(*ii*) where chairs may rub, use dado rails or place wooden strips on the floor parallel to the skirting;

(*iii*) around light switches, use metal or plastic plates;

(*iv*) door stops or stays should be fitted.

(*n*) When cleaning, signs of deterioration should be reported, e.g. blistering paint, peeling and damp wallpaper, discoloration on a wall.

(*o*) Care should be taken to ensure ceiling tiles are not loosened or knocked down and that water is not too hot when cleaning near smoke detectors.

(*p*) Light fittings should be cleaned at the same time as a ceiling or wall.

JOB PROCEDURE: WASHING WALLS
Equipment: warning signs;
damp cloth/sponge mop/electric wall washer;
step-ladders;
synthetic detergent;
bucket;
scrubbing brush.

Method
1. Position warning signs.
2. Dilute detergent correctly. Do not overfill bucket. Change solution frequently.
3. Using the minimum of solution on cloth, wipe in small sections using pipes, windows, etc. as landmarks.
4. Use a circular motion, overlapping each stroke slightly to ensure complete coverage.

5. Wash window surrounds by hand, using a small brush for awkward areas.

6. Empty, rinse and dry bucket. Wash, rinse and dry cloth and brush.

7. Remove step-ladder and warning signs.

Tiled surfaces: polish with soft cloth after washing.

Fabric surfaces: test first to ensure adhesive is not water-soluble. Do not overwet at seams. Remove and wash or dry clean curtaining/screens.

Marble surfaces: do not use abrasive detergent, steel wool or acid cleaner. Polish after washing.

Water-based painted surfaces: test first to make sure it will withstand washing.

Unprotected plaster, cement, brick, wood: do not wash but remove dust frequently.

Wallpaper: check if washable by testing a small area. Do not overwet or adhesive may be damaged. Take care with textured papers, e.g. "Anaglypta", imitation grass, suede, etc.

Windows/glass partitions/mirrors

(*a*) If time permits remove curtains, blinds, etc. or tie out of way.

(*b*) Protect floor and base of wall below window with dust sheet.

(*c*) Make sure step-ladders are safe, if used.

(*d*) Observation windows in swing doors or in hospitals require constant cleaning.

(*e*) Do not use abrasive detergents or pads.

(*f*) If possible use lint free cloths to avoid untidy "bits" being left on the surface.

(*g*) Remove stains with vinegar solution or spirit, e.g. methylated spirit.

(*h*) Glass may be polished after cleaning.

(*i*) Avoid wetting the back of mirrors as this may eventually cause damage to the silver. Attend to any framework after washing.

JOB PROCEDURE: CLEANING WINDOWS

Equipment: two buckets;
        one dry cloth (preferably lint free);
        two damp cloths/squeegee/sponge mop (for high windows);
        one polishing cloth, e.g. chamois leather;
        newspaper (optional);
        glass polish (optional);

one of the following solutions:

18 ml ammonia in half a bucket of warm water;
warm synthetic detergent solution;
18 ml vinegar in half a bucket of warm water.

Method

1. Remove dust and superficial dirt with dry cloth or newspaper (the solvent in the print also helps to remove grease).
2. Fill one bucket with cleaning solution and one with warm water for rinsing.
3. Wash and rinse frame, paying attention to corners.
4. Wash glass from top using circular movements or as shown in Fig. 66 if using a squeegee.
5. Dry and polish to a shine using polish if desired. (Do not use polish with a chamois leather.)
6. Wipe dry and polish up windowsill and fittings. Replace curtains, etc.
7. Empty, rinse and dry bucket. Wash, rinse and dry cloths.

Curtains and blinds

The frequency with which these items are cleaned depends on their situation—at windows, around beds, along walls. A daily task is to check that the suspension mechanisms are in order and that the curtains or blinds hang neatly. Once a week dust should be

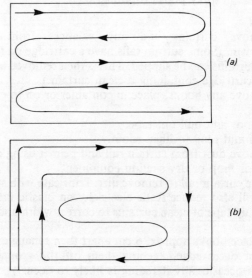

Fig. 66. *Two methods of washing glass using a squeegee.*

removed using dry suction equipment with the high dusting or upholstery attachment or with a soft brush. For venetian blinds a special tool may be used which collects dust from both sides of each strip simultaneously. Periodically, curtains and blinds need washing or dry cleaning. This may be done *in situ* using hot water injection/extraction equipment (curtains) but generally they are removed and laundered or dry cleaned, or scrubbed in the case of blinds. There should be sufficient spare curtains and blinds to allow periodic cleaning to be carried out without disruption to any area, i.e. putting a room out of use while they are cleaned. Net curtains require frequent laundering, e.g. monthly, but as they dry quickly, there should be no problem of room usage. Where there are windows of varying sizes curtains and blinds should be labelled to avoid time being wasted when rehanging. When removing roller blinds, care should be taken not to damage the spring.

JOB PROCEDURE: PERIODIC CLEANING OF CURTAINS
Equipment: step-ladders;
                    container for hooks, rings, etc;
                    clean set of curtains;
                    dust control mitten or mop or dry suction
                        equipment with high dusting or upholstery
                        attachments;
                    soft brush;
                    spray polish (optional).

Method
1. Remove curtains and any valances from suspension mechanism. (Some curtain rails have a cartridge on to which the soiled curtains can be slipped. This is then removed and replaced with a cartridge containing a clean curtain.)
2. Remove any hooks, place in container or on to clean pair of curtains.
3. Unknot and pull out tape.
4. Fold and send to linen room.
5. Remove dust from curtain rail and pelmet using dust control mitten or mop or dry suction equipment.
6. Wipe curtain rail to remove dirt. Lubricate with spray polish. (This will also reduce static electricity on plastic fittings.)
7. Pull up tape of clean curtains to correct width and knot cords neatly.
8. Replace hooks approx. 6 cm apart then rehang curtains with cord on outer edge, keeping them off the ground. (Reverse curtains occasionally if fading is likely to occur.)
9. Test that rehung curtains draw properly.

Curtains with a flame-resistant finish should be checked and retreated if necessary after laundering (*see* Chapter 4 for treatment and care of flame-resistant finishes).

JOB PROCEDURE: PERIODIC CLEANING OF BLINDS (ALUMINIUM, PLASTIC, PAPER, WOOD, CLOTH)

Equipment: step ladders;
dry suction equipment and high dusting
attachment/dust control mitten or mop;
two buckets;
damp cloth/venetian blind tool/scrubbing brush;
dry cloth;
duster;
appropriate polish.

Method
1. Remove blinds unless to be cleaned *in situ*. Do not allow venetian blinds to bend.
2. Extend blinds fully (close slats if venetian or vertical slats).
3. Remove dust from slats, tapes, rollers, etc. using dry suction or dust control equipment.
4. Repeat on reverse side.
5. Wipe with detergent solution (not paper blinds which should not be washed). Scrub fabric blinds gently. Avoid abrasives on plastic and aluminium sufaces.
6. Rinse cloth then, using rinsing water, wipe again.
7. Allow to dry or wipe with dry cloth.
8. Apply furniture polish or rub up with a duster.
9. Empty, rinse and dry buckets. Wash, rinse and dry cloths.
10. When thoroughly dry, rehang carefully.

Furniture (wood, plastic, metal, rubber, textiles, wicker, cane)

(*a*) Dust hard surfaces daily with a duster or damp cloth, checking for sticky marks on all areas including the under-side of chairs and tables.

(*b*) Use dry suction equipment with an upholstery or crevice nozzle to remove dust from upholstered furniture and the inside of wardrobes, drawers, etc.

(*c*) Occasionally wash using a minimum of synthetic detergent solution and a soft brush or cloth.

(*d*) Allow furniture to dry naturally in a well-ventilated area. Do not place near gas or electric fires. (Upholstered chairs should remain out of use until thoroughly dry.)

(*e*) Rub suitable furniture polish well in as any residue will attract and retain dust.

Fig. 67. *Label indicating furniture is fire-resistant.*

(*f*) Test upholstery for colour fastness before washing or refer to records relating to furniture construction.

(*g*) Reline drawers after washing.

(*h*) Check fire resistance cautiously after washing furniture claiming to have a fire-resistant finish (*see* Fig. 67).

(*i*) When furniture has both upholstery and hard surfaces wash the upholstery before attending to the hard surfaces.

(For further information *see* Chapters 4 and 5 and Appendix I.)

JOB PROCEDURE: PERIODIC CLEANING OF UPHOLSTERED FURNITURE

Equipment: dry suction equipment with upholstery and crevice attachments;

soft brush or electric upholstery cleaner;

duster;

solution of dry foam shampoo;

damp cloth;

bucket;

spot remover;

dust sheet or similar;

hot water injection/extraction machine (do not use on foam rubber filled furniture).

Method

1. Protect surroundings from splashes with a dust sheet.

2. Remove dust, crumbs, etc. paying particular attention to corners, sides of seats and under-sides of seats.

3. Deal with seat cushions separately, gently applying shampoo solution with damp cloth, soft brush or shampooer. Do not allow surface to become too wet.

4. Allow to dry.

5. When thoroughly dry remove shampoo residue containing dirt with dry suction equipment.

6. Inspect for stains and treat accordingly (*see* Appendix I).
7. Report any damage, e.g. loose legs, missing castors, etc.

Upholstered chairs may be revitalised with a loose cover. When washing loose covers check first for shrinkage. Furniture should be periodically cleaned on a rotation basis. Records should therefore be kept of when each item has been attended to.

JOB PROCEDURE: CLEANING A WARDROBE/CHEST OF DRAWERS
Equipment: duster;
  dry suction equipment with dusting attachment;
  damp cloth;
  synthetic detergent solution/vinegar solution/
    abrasive detergent;
  lining paper;
  spare hangers.

Method
1. Remove all contents including hangers (if possible).
2. Remove and dispose of lining paper.
3. Dust inside and outside (including top) with appropriate equipment. Pay particular attention to the base of sliding doors.
4. Wipe inside and outside thoroughly using the minimum of detergent or vinegar solution and abrasive detergent if necessary, followed by rinsing.
5. When dry apply appropriate polish externally where considered necessary.
6. Replace lining paper and hangers (check quantity).
7. Clean equipment.
8. Report any damage to furniture, e.g. drawers sticking, handles broken.

Use spray polish for wood and plastic veneers, varnish and gloss paint. Use wax and cream polish for porous surfaces, e.g. wood finishes with wax, oil or french polish. Remember that freestanding wardrobes can be unstable when empty.

Beds
Daily care of a bed may involve either tidying the bedding and sheets, etc. or stripping and remaking. Periodic cleaning involves the removal of bed linen and bedding and then the following procedures (*see* also Fig. 68).

(*a*) Removal of dust from base and mattress using a soft brush or dry suction machine with the upholstery attachment. Particular attention should be paid to the areas around the quilting, buttons or tufts.

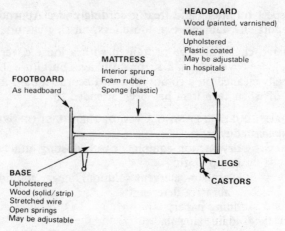

Fig. 68. *Bed components which require cleaning.*

(*b*) Removal of any stains on the base or mattress.

(*c*) Turning of upholstered (interior sprung) mattresses.

(*d*) Removal of dirt and sticky marks from the base surround, legs, footboard if there is one and headboard where grease may also be found.

(*e*) Polishing of any plastic, wood or metal areas (not the springs).

(*f*) Removal of fluff and dust from castors and the application of a little oil if they seem to squeak or are stiff (efficient castors ease bedmaking).

(*g*) Replacement of a clean mattress cover if used.

(*h*) Inspection of mattress and base for tears and spring damage. (Check that there is an underlay on wire mesh bases as this helps to prevent the mattress from becoming snagged.)

JOB PROCEDURE: CHANGING BED LINEN

Equipment: two pillowcases;
two sheets of appropriate size;
one hand towel;
one bath towel/sheet;
face cloth (optional);
one bathmat.

Hotels with private bathrooms will usually change these items of linen at the same time. They are not usually provided in hostels or hospitals.

Method

1. Move bed away from wall if possible.
2. Untuck all sides of bed. Place chair by bed.

3. Remove pillowslips from pillows, fold and place to one side. Place pillows on a chair.

4. Stand at bottom of bed and pull each item of bed linen towards the end and fold over into three. Lift folded sides on to bed and place item on chair.

5. Collect soiled linen and place neatly by door. (Early removal of soiled linen helps to air the room quickly.)

6. Stand at one side of the bed and place underblanket on mattress. Smooth out.

7. Remain at side of bed, open out bottom sheet so that the fold line runs down the centre of the mattress.

8. Walk round the bed and tuck in each corner using a mitred fold.

9. Stand at the side again and open out the second clean sheet so that the fold line is again central and the top edge of the sheet reaches 8–10 cm beyond the headboard end of the mattress. Tuck in the bottom end only.

10. Place each blanket (usually two) on separately in the same way as the sheets but so that they just reach the headboard end of the mattress. Tuck in at the bottom only.

11. Turn the top end of the sheet over the top edge of the blankets (unless the sheet has a decorative edge), then fold the sheets and blankets together down the bed far enough to leave space for the pillows.

12. Tuck in the top sheet, and blankets, mitring the bottom corners.

13. Place pillow slips on pillows making sure the corners are filled and the open end is neatened, i.e. enclosed in a flap, tied, buttoned or folded over.

14. Place on bed with openings away from the door.

15. Replace bedspread so that it covers the pillows, tucks under them slightly and hangs about 1.5 cm off the ground all round. Tuck corners under to prevent accidents.

When continental quilts are used, a top sheet may also be used to help reduce laundry bills. Quilt covers should be put on in the same way as a pillow. Quilts require shaking every day to even out the filling or to make it fall to one end for use in hot weather.

There are many different ways of making a bed. The one described above is recognised as an efficient and quick method, suitable for use in most establishments.

Hotels may expect staff to "turn down" beds. This involves removing or turning back the bedspread then folding back the edge of the sheets and blankets to form either a triangle or an oblong so that the bed looks prepared for sleeping in. This is one of the duties performed by housekeeping staff in establishments were an evening schedule is operated. At the same time, they will also draw the curtains and generally tidy the room. Some hotels compromise and "turn down" before placing the bedspread on after remaking the bed. If a bed board is requested, it should be placed between the mattress and the bed base. It should be removed as soon as the guest leaves.

Cleaning frequencies

Table XVIII gives a summary of cleaning frequencies. Daily cleaning of public areas such as entrances, reception areas, waiting rooms, etc. may be carried out at night, often by contractors, in which case supervision by the housekeeping department should be provided. Unoccupied rooms/areas should always be dusted each day and checked that they are ready for use.

Weekly cleaning can be organised in either of the following ways.

(a) All weekly tasks may be carried out in one room on a certain day each week. This will occur in four or five rooms in rotation. This system may not be possible in a hotel where occupied rooms will need servicing with the minimum of intrusion for the guest.

(b) One or two weekly tasks may be added each day to the daily routine so that by the end of the week all weekly tasks have been completed.

Much of the periodic cleaning may be carried out by contractors or maintenance or portering staff. If this is the case, housekeeping staff should co-operate in any way they can. A well-organised department will keep a record of when and where periodic cleaning has taken place (see Fig. 69) so that no area is neglected. Reference to this record also enables the housekeeping manager to co-ordinate periodic cleaning with maintenance work so that they can be done simultaneously and therefore with as little inconvenience as possible.

Cleaning special areas

There may be certain areas in a building which require special care when cleaning, e.g. rooms containing sensitive equipment or dangerous chemicals such as laboratories and computer rooms, intensive care units and isolation areas.

Staff who clean these areas should be trustworthy and responsible. They must not tamper with equipment or unplug machinery to use cleaning equipment. They should be able to work quietly and quickly and be prepared to obey any special rules regarding hand-

TABLE XVIII. SUMMARY OF CLEANING FREQUENCIES.

Area	Daily	Weekly	Periodically
Sanitary areas	Remove litter. Wash all fitments and related areas. Empty sanibins. Check supply of soap, toilet paper, towels, barrier cream, nail brushes, etc. Mop or scrub floor.	Wipe walls and windows.	Wipe ceiling and light fittings. Clean any window coverings. Check plumbing and drainage. Check condition of décor.
Ceilings, walls and windows	Remove dust and stickiness from radiators, noticeboards, pictures, windowsills, ledges, etc. Spot clean vulnerable areas such as door handles.	Damp wipe internal window areas and glass partitions. Apply polish if policy to do so.	Wash ceilings then walls and window frames and outside of windows. Check condition of décor.
Furniture, fittings and light fittings	Remove dust and stickiness.	Damp wipe or spray polish.	Empty shelves, cupboards, drawers. Remove dust then wash or shampoo. Reline drawers. Remove and clean light fittings. Check bulbs/tubes. Check condition and safety.

Table Continued

TABLE XVIII. (*Continued*).

Area	Daily	Weekly	Periodically
Window coverings	Check for neatness. Shake curtains slightly.	Remove dust from curtain /blind, pelmet and suspension track.	Remove for washing or dry cleaning. Wipe track and check condition and safety.
Beds	Tidy or remake. Dust head and footboards.	Strip and change sheets (hostels). Damp wipe headboard and polish if policy to do so.	Vacuum mattress and base. Check cleanliness of legs and castors. Polish or shampoo headboard. Turn interior sprung mattresses. Check for damage. Dry clean or launder bedding.
Floors	Sweep, vacuum or dust mop. Damp mop (kichens, bathrooms).	Buff, dry buff, damp mop if not done daily.	Deep clean. Renovate. Polish.

washing and the use of protective clothing. Many hospitals, for instance, require cleaning staff working in theatre areas to wash their hands and scrub their nails before entering the area, before leaving the area and after leaving the area. They are also required to wear rubber gloves while cleaning and to wear special gowns, shoes and masks. The nature of hospital work may also require staff to clean up blood, remove contaminated linen and rubbish and perhaps to work among some unpleasant and disturbing sights. Staff who are prepared to work in these areas are given specific training.

Date	Rooms	Bedrooms	Curtains	Windows	Floor	Walls	Redecoration		Remarks
17/7/-	659	✓	✓	✓		✓			
	660	✓	✓	✓		✓			WINDOW STUCK
	661	✓	✓		✓				
	662	✓	✓		✓				
	663	✓	✓		✓				

Fig. 69. *Cleaning and maintenance record.*

Hotel guests and hostel residents may also become ill and so to prevent any spread of infection the following procedures should be adopted.

(*a*) Use only clean equipment;

(*b*) Dilute cleaning agents accurately;

(*c*) Change cleaning solutions frequently and before moving to another area.

(*d*) Use disposable or boilable cloths only. If possible use several cloths, discarding each after use so that the cleaning solution does not become contaminated.

(*e*) Clean the least soiled areas first.

(*f*) Clean equipment thoroughly after use.

(*g*) Restrict the number of staff using or working in the area.

Preparation of rooms for special events or functions

Special events and functions may require the use of both public areas and bedrooms. The preparation of these areas often involves considerable movement and rearrangement of furniture, often at times when housekeeping staff are not on duty or are busy with routine cleaning. Advance planning and organisation is therefore essential if everything is to run smoothly. The housekeeping manager must work closely with the advanced reservations department and the conference secretary in order to obtain as much information as possible on the customer's room requirements.

A special function may involve as few as two or three people requesting a room for an interviewing session or for changing in after a wedding reception, in which case only the minimum of organisation is required, or it may involve provision of sufficient space for a fashion show or an exhibition of office equipment, etc. However large or small, the preparation procedure remains the same. This involves three stages; as follows.

(*a*) Initial preparation: to be carried out on receipt of a booking.

(*b*) Immediate preparation: physical work to be carried out immediately prior to commencement.

(*c*) Clearing away: to be carried out immediately the event is ended so that the area is ready for another booking.

Initial preparation

(*a*) Ascertain date of commencement, duration, arrival and departure times, approximate numbers, age range, sex and mobility of clientèle. (This may affect cloakroom facilities, etc.)

(*b*) Arrange facilities required—lecture rooms, blackout rooms, storage areas for equipment, audio-visual equipment, tables, chairs, television lounges, bar areas, floral displays, blotters, parking.

(*c*) Arrange staffing for services requested—secretarial, linen/laundry, newspapers, room service.

(*d*) Inspect all areas to be used for cleanliness and maintenance and arrange for any subsequent work to be carried out.

(*e*) Prepare a work schedule for each member of the housekeeping staff to be involved in the event.

Immediate preparation

(*a*) Clean requested rooms thoroughly.

(*b*) Set up rooms according to the customer's requirements with the aid of porters if necessary.

(*c*) Position direction signs, etc.

(*d*) Prepare and position floral decorations.

(*e*) Check visual-aid equipment, and provision of chalk, pens, dusters, etc.

(*f*) Provide adequate ventilation in meeting rooms, etc.

(*g*) Provide adequate ashtrays.

(*h*) Check cloakroom facilities.

Clearing away

This is self-explanatory but must be well organised and particularly well supervised to ensure the area is left clean and in good condition for future use. All equipment and furniture should be accounted for and replaced without damage. Any damages or lost property should be dealt with immediately.

SELF-ASSESSMENT QUESTIONS

1. How does the work of a housekeeping supervisor differ from that of a housekeeping manager?

2. Why is it important to have good supervision in a house-keeping department?

3. Distinguish between a work specification, a work schedule and a job procedure.

4. What are the advantages of a well-planned duty rota?

5. Summarise the information which should be passed on to new employees during an induction period.

6. What measures are taken by a housekeeping supervisor to ensure that no area of a building is left uncleaned?

CHAPTER EIGHT

The Internal Environment of an Accommodation Establishment

CHAPTER OBJECTIVES

After studying this chapter you should be able to:
* explain how to provide and maintain adequate light, heat, and sound insulation in a building;
* appreciate the effects of colour and texture on the atmosphere and cleanliness of a building;
* show how to maintain incidental furnishings and decorations;
* describe how to prevent the entry of pests and the methods used to eradicate infestation;
* appreciate the importance of accident and fire prevention and know what to do if they occur;
* describe the responsibilities of the housekeeping department towards security.

LEGISLATION

General requirements

One of the basic aims of any accommodation establishment is to provide and maintain a comfortable and safe environment for guests, patients, residents and staff (*see also* below, p. 225). In fact, employers have a legal obligation to do so under the Health and Safety at Work etc. Act 1974. Their responsibilities include:

(*a*) securing the health, safety and welfare of persons at work (e.g. provision of uniforms and safe equipment);

(*b*) protecting others from risks arising from work premises or activities (e.g. use of warning signs when cleaning);

(*c*) controlling the storage and use of dangerous flammable substances (e.g. solvent cleaning agents);

(*d*) controlling the emission of noxious or offensive substances into the atmosphere (e.g. polishes, burning refuse).

Failure to adhere to the Act can result in the employer going to prison or having to pay heavy fines.

Specific requirements

More specific legislation regarding the welfare of staff is contained in the Factories Act 1961, the Offices, Shops and Railway Premises

Act 1963 and the Sanitary Conveniences Regulations 1964. These stipulate that the following facilities should be provided.

Cloakrooms

(*a*) Separate peg or locker for each employee.

(*b*) Facilities for drying wet outdoor clothes and overalls worn in wet processes, e.g. sweeping outdoor areas such as yards, entrances, etc.

(*c*) Adequate space for changing clothes and footwear.

(*d*) Adequate precautions against theft, e.g. locker provision.

(*e*) High standard of cleanliness.

(*f*) Adequate ventilation and lighting.

(*g*) Best if located between employee's entrance and place of work.

(*h*) Floor space should allow for changing without crowding.

(*i*) Storage space for clothing should be adequate.

Washing facilities

(*a*) These must be adequate (*see* Table XIX) and provide:

(*i*) a supply of clean running hot, cold or warm water;

(*ii*) soap or cleansing agent, whether liquid, powder, jelly or tablet;

(*iii*) clean towels or other means of drying (*see* (*f*)).

(*b*) They should be conveniently accessible.

(*c*) They should be kept in a clean and orderly condition.

(*d*) Basins should be made of smooth, impervious material with a plug provided.

(*e*) Water should be operated with a foot pedal if possible.

(*f*) Drying facilities should be provided, e.g. one of the following:

(*i*) roller towels, preferably from a machine which is renewed under contract;

TABLE XIX. PROVISION OF WASHING FACILITIES.

Number of employees using changing room	Number of basins necessary
1–15	1
16–30	2
31–50	3
51–75	4
76–100	5
Over 100	5 + 1 for every 25 persons or fraction of 25 in excess of 100

(*ii*) paper towels, which are hygienic and require no laundering, *but* adequate bins for soiled towels must be provided;

(*iii*) warm air blower perhaps combined with paper towels.

(*g*) Employers are legally responsible for laundering and changing towels at least once a week.

(*h*) Where nailbrushes are provided (a legal requirement in food industries) they must be kept clean and in an effective condition.

(*i*) Consideration should be given to the provision of barrier creams and conditioning creams.

(*j*) Careful thought should go into *layout and design*, e.g.:

(*i*)   good lighting;

(*ii*) good ventilation and heating;

(*iii*) impervious material, e.g. tiles, for walls and floors;

(*iv*) coved angles between floors and walls;

(*v*)   good plumbing design and wash-basin outlet pipes well above floor level;

(*vi*) mirrors should not be above basins.

NOISE, HEAT AND LIGHT

Noise

Noise can be defined as sound which is undesirable to the recipient, i.e. that which intrudes, disturbs or annoys.

Excessive noise can affect a person physically, psychologically and socially. It can make speech communication difficult so that instructions may be misunderstood; cause distraction and reduce concentration and therefore be the cause of an accident; interfere with sleep and therefore be irritating to guests, patients or residents; and at high levels cause permanent damage to hearing, even if the hearer finds the sound desirable, e.g. discos and radios.

Noise in a housekeeping department may be generated by floor cleaning equipment, e.g. metal mop buckets and wet and dry suction machines, by laundering equipment, e.g. washing machines and dryers, and by the nature of a cleaning process, e.g. flushing toilets, scrubbing tiles, washing up. The sounds are intensified if several machines are operated at the same time, if they are used in a confined space, and if there are large areas of non-absorbent material, e.g. ceramic and vinyl tiles. Poor or infrequent maintenance of equipment and plumbing systems can also result in irritating noises.

Many hotels, holiday camps, leisure centres, etc. transmit background music in the belief that it helps to create a relaxed atmosphere. Housekeeping staff may find that this helps their morale while performing repetitive tasks but supervisors should ensure that bedroom radios are not turned on so loud that it offends other staff or indeed guests, especially if the noise of a vacuum cleaner is added.

Methods of reducing noise in a housekeeping department

(*a*) Fit silencers to electrical equipment (hospitals).

(*b*) Use plastic rather than metal buckets, etc.

(*c*) Use insulating materials on floors (rubber, cork, carpeting) and on metal tables and trolleys to reduce impact sound.

(*d*) Use rubber shoes on the bottom of metal table legs resting on hard floor surfaces, e.g. kitchen tables.

(*e*) Service equipment regularly.

(*f*) Keep wheels, doors, etc. well-oiled.

(*g*) Instruct staff in the need for using quiet working methods, e.g. place containers on to surfaces carefully, do not shout to colleagues, do not bang into fire doors with equipment, etc.

(*h*) Areas with electronic games and amusement machines should be decorated with sound-absorbent materials such as perforated hardboard, cork, wallpaper, carpet, etc.

It is important to remember that staff must be able to hear the sound made by his/her machine in order to detect any unusual sounds which signify danger.

Heat

Extremes of temperature should be considered as an additional integral part of a work-load. For efficient and healthy functioning the body temperature must be maintained at 37 °C. Slight variances can cause considerable discomfort. The efficiency with which the human body regulates its temperature depends on certain physical properties of the area surrounding it, namely:

(*a*) air temperature;

(*b*) relative humidity;

(*c*) radiant heat;

(*d*) air movement;

all of which can be controlled by maintenance staff, housekeeping staff and sometimes guests or residents.

Air temperature

Optimum air temperatures vary with the individual by about 2–3 °C and with the activity likely to be pursued in the room. The following is a guide as to suitable room temperatures:

(*a*) reception areas, lounges, offices—18–21 °C;

(*b*) bedrooms, bathrooms—16–18 °C;
(*c*) establishments accommodating the elderly, sick or very young—22–24 °C.

These temperatures are for the benefit of guests, residents and patients rather than employees who are likely to be more active. Housekeeping staff should therefore be advised not to wear clothing which will be too warm. They should also be provided with a uniform made from a fabric which will absorb perspiration as well as wash easily.

Relative humidity

This describes the amount of moisture in the air. A high level of humidity (100 per cent) prevents the evaporation of perspiration and people become less alert and lethargic—a situation which should be avoided if staff are to work efficiently. A low level of humidity (below 30 per cent) creates a dry atmosphere. This causes the skin tissues to dry out, particularly in the nose, causing people to contract sore throats and colds and so give rise to absenteeism among staff. Relative humidity should be kept at 40–70 per cent.

Radiant heat

This is the heat emitted by the walls, floors and ceilings. Such areas may be much warmer (underfloor heating and radiators) or much colder (window areas and outside walls) than the general room temperature. Ideally, there should be very little difference between these two temperatures but if there is, increased insulation is necessary (double glazing, curtaining, draught excluders, pipe lagging). Housekeeping staff should make sure that furniture is not left in front of radiators or warm air ducts as this will prevent economic use of the heating system and may possibly cause damage to the furniture. Thermostats should be checked if heat seems to be excessive or lacking.

Air movement

Air movement (ventilation) is necessary to lower the relative humidity in an area and to remove unpleasant smells, smoke and vapours. It also prevents creation of a stale and stuffy atmosphere—conditions which encourage lethargy and which are attractive to bacteria and pests. Ventilation can be provided naturally by opening windows and doors. A certain amount of air movement may also be created by leakage through closed windows and doors or through open fireplaces. However, internal rooms and corridors and double-glazed buildings require mechanical ventilation equipment (fans, etc.) or they should be connected to an air-conditioning system. Such a system works best if all natural forms of ventilation are sealed. It controls the amount of filtered air entering a building as well as its temperature and relative humidity. Establishments fitted with an air-conditioning system provide extremely pleasant working conditions for staff, and help to provide an environment suitable for hay fever and asthma sufferers—a fact which can help to reduce absenteeism. Air inlets and extract gratings must be kept clear of dirt and dust if the system is to function correctly.

Light

Lighting may be natural or artificial. Natural light should be used whenever possible and must be retained by regular window cleaning both inside and outside and by ensuring that curtains, blinds, plants and furniture are not allowed to block out too much window area. Natural light can be intensified by the use of mirrors and light coloured wall surfaces which will reflect light rays. Good lighting is important for several reasons.

(*a*) It prevents the accumulation of dirt and dust.
(*b*) It promotes safety.
(*c*) It prevents eye strain.
(*d*) It provides a pleasant atmosphere.
(*e*) Sunlight prevents dampness.

Artificial light should be used only if natural light is not available. There are two ways of providing artificial lighting—by filament lamp or by fluorescent tube.

Filament lamps

These consist of coils of fine tungsten wire, supported in the centre of a glass bulb filled with an inert gas such as argon (the gas reduces the rate at which the tungsten evaporates). In order to produce light, electricity is fed through the wire until it glows white and a temperature of over 3,000 °C is obtained. The heat generated by filament lamps can cause damage to some paper, plastic or fabric fittings and so care should be taken to ensure the correct wattage bulb is used in each fitting.

Filament lamps have an average life of 1,000 hours (long-life bulbs last for up to 2,000 hours but cost correspondingly more). Certain areas require rough duty bulbs which will withstand vibration, e.g. lifts, but these are usually of low wattage.

Fluorescent tubes

These are filled with low pressure mercury vapour. When the electricity is passed through the tube, the mercury emits ultraviolet radiation which hits the fluorescent lining of the tube, making it glow. Each tube lasts between 5,000 and 7,000 hours but only if it remains on or off for a minimum of three hours. Fluorescent tubes are also three times more efficient than filament bulbs (i.e. one 40 watt tube equals one 120 watt filament). They are, however, more cumbersome to replace than filament bulbs and are frequently wired together in groups of two, four or six, so that if one begins to fail (flickering), the whole group has to be turned off to prevent irritation. As with filament bulbs, fluorescent tubes may be of varying wattage, but they may also be of different lengths and shapes (circular or linear). This can prove a problem when there is a request for a replacement as the exact size must be known as well as the colour (white, daylight, natural, etc) since they should preferably all be the same in one area. Considerable storage space is therefore necessary to allow for sufficient replacement tubes.

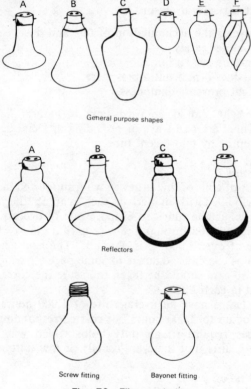

General purpose shapes

Reflectors

Screw fitting   Bayonet fitting

Fig. 70. *Filament bulbs.*

The effect of light fittings on the environment

The effect created by filament lamps depends on the type of bulb. General purpose bulbs may be clear, pearl or silica coated. Clear bulbs provide a very bright light and are used mainly with "sparkle" glass fittings and reflector systems. Pearl bulbs have a satin finish which obscures the filament to reduce glare and provide a soft lighting effect. A silica coating diffuses the light from the filament and provides a very uniform brightness. These three coatings can be applied to bulbs of varying shapes with either a bayonet or a screw fitting (*see* Fig. 70).

Most fluorescent tubes have a pearl finish. They provide good general lighting without any glare. However, the fittings used to cover the bare tube are less attractive than those used for filament lamps. As considerable thought is given to the lighting plan of a building it is important that the plan is adhered to, with housekeeping staff reporting any bulbs which do not work or fittings which are broken.

Maintenance

Replacement bulbs and tubes are usually provided by porters or maintenance staff. In large buildings the maintenance department may employ a full-time member of staff for the sole purpose of checking and replacing light bulbs and tubes.

The efficiency of artificial light, however, must be maintained by regular cleaning of the shades and covers which create the desired lighting effect and atmosphere. These may be made from a variety of materials—glass, plastic, parchment, textiles, metal, cane, paper, etc. The heat generated by the filament bulb or fluorescent tube attracts flies and moths and can cause discoloration. It also tends to attract dust and so wall lights and lamps should be dusted each day. Ceiling lights should be attended to during a periodic clean unless they can be lowered or are in areas where the presence of dust can be a danger such as hospital examination rooms. Operating theatres require very intense light from one or more large fittings. These may be coated with a thin film of oil so that any airborne dust will stick to the surface and can be removed easily with a damp cloth.

JOB PROCEDURE: CLEANING A LIGHT FITTING
Equipment: damp cloth;
              duster;
              detergent solution;
              spray polish;
              tea towel.

Method
1. Disconnect electricity and remove bulb/tube.
2. Remove shade or cover if possible and wash, rinse and dry it.
3. Wipe stand or suspension fittings if any.
4. Apply polish to metal/plastic areas to reduce static electricity.
5. Replace bulb after gently dusting it and reconnect to electricity.
6. Test that it works.
7. Wash, rinse and dry cloths. Replace cleaning agents.

Lighting requirements in accommodation establishments

These will vary with the activity pursued in each area (*see* Table XX). The type of lighting required may be direct, indirect, diffused or semi-indirect (*see* Fig. 71).

TABLE XX. LIGHTING REQUIREMENTS IN DIFFERENT AREAS.

Area	Type of activity	Key areas of lighting
Reception	Relaxing Writing Working Waiting	General and localised. Direct over reception desk.
Lounge	Relaxing Reading Watching TV	A variety to allow for varied activities. Dimmer switches should be considered.
Dining rooms	Regular eating Special occasions Banquets, etc.	Depends on type of establishment, type of service and time of day. Should be direct over service counters. Consider effect on food colour.
Corridors	Walking Reading notices Identifying room numbers Fire escape routes	Not necessarily bright but clear over door numbers and noticeboards. Provision of emergency lighting.
Bedrooms	Sleeping Dressing/shaving Writing Reading	Localised in certain areas, e.g. beside bed and above mirrors. Two-way switches should be provided.
Bathrooms	Washing Shaving, etc.	Localised above mirrors. Fittings must be vapourproof. Switches should be outside the room or be of a pull-cord type.

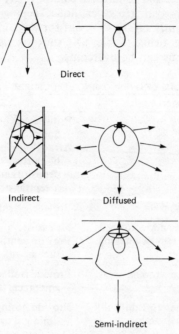

Fig. 71. *Lighting effects.*

Each room should have a switch near the entrance for safety and emergency lighting should illuminate stairs, corridors, exit signs and banqueting areas. This should be linked to an independent electricity supply. It is important that the system is maintained, and housekeeping staff should look out for any exit signs, etc. which are not illuminated.

REDUCING FATIGUE

Extremes of noise, temperature and light all contribute to the amount of energy expended by people working or trying to relax in a building. Two other factors influence their comfort and the speed and efficiency with which work is carried out:

(a) the layout of the building and its furniture and fittings,
(b) the design of tools and equipment

The layout of a building
There is usually very little that can be done to change the layout of a building. For example, stairs and steps cannot be removed, lifts

are costly to instal and room sizes cannot easily be altered without considerable upheaval. However, housekeeping staff of all grades should be constantly on the look out for ways in which their work can be made less tiring. Table XXI suggests ways in which some common problems can be overcome.

TABLE XXI. METHODS OF OVERCOMING STRUCTURAL PROBLEMS.

Problem	Remedy
No lifts.	Provide sets of equipment for each floor.
	Arrange for linen to be collected by porters or for residents to deposit their soiled bed linen at a central point.
Too few electric sockets.	Provide extension leads.
Rooms too small to allow for beds to be placed for easy bedmaking.	Fit castors to bed legs.
	Provide continental quilts (less tucking-in).
Too few service rooms/areas.	Provide trolleys on which to store equipment and linen.
No bucket sinks therefore difficulty in filling buckets, etc.	Provide hosing and if possible drain gulleys.
Corridors too narrow or uneven for trolleys.	Provide special boxes/buckets in which to carry equipment and arrange for daily issue and distribution of supplies.

The design of tools and equipment

All housekeeping equipment should be carefully assessed by the housekeeping manager before it is purchased. However, some items can be altered or adjusted to suit individual workers and supervisors should make sure that appropriate adjustments are made. A supervisor should also be aware of how staff use their equipment and investigate the reasons for equipment not being used or being used badly. Such reasons may include the following.

(*a*) Cloths too small for area to be wiped and for size of employee's hands.

(*b*) Floor machine handles too high or low.

(*c*) Storage cupboards too high, therefore failure to change dust bags, mop heads, etc.

(*d*) Disposable mop heads difficult to take off and put on.

(*e*) Cleaning agents too strong smelling or causing damage to skin.

(*f*) Vacuum cleaner too noisy because of a fault.

DÉCOR AND ITS EFFECT ON THE INTERNAL ENVIRONMENT

The décor of a building is made up from the colour, texture, pattern and design of:

(*a*) the wall and ceiling coverings;
(*b*) the floor coverings;
(*c*) the furniture and fittings;
(*d*) the window dressings;
(*e*) the incidental furnishings.

The materials used for the decoration of each of these have been discussed in previous chapters and the choice of designs and patterns are usually beyond the control of the housekeeping supervisor. However, housekeeping staff should be made aware of the reasons for keeping certain colours and textures in good condition.

Colour

Colour can play an important part in creating a certain atmosphere—white, for instance, indicates cleanliness. It can also make a small, oppressive area seem larger and more pleasant to be in.

If colour is used correctly, it can help to:

(*a*) increase safety;
(*b*) extend visibility;
(*c*) raise morale;
(*d*) promote cleanliness;
(*e*) encourage relaxation.

Colour has importance in the housekeeping department for the following reasons.

(*a*) It can be used to identify equipment for use in different areas, e.g. blue for toilets, yellow for kitchen areas, etc. (colour coding).

(*b*) Coloured linen can make stock control easier. Different colours can be allocated to each section of a building, e.g. blue towels for block A, green for block B, etc. So that a towel in the wrong place can easily be identified.

(*c*) Different coloured uniforms make identification of departmental staff easier and differentiation between grades of staff possible.

(*d*) Bed linen and bedding in hotels and hospitals is usually a pale colour as this makes it easier to judge the standard of cleanliness. Hostel blankets, however, may be darker or patterned as they are cleaned less frequently and will therefore show the dirt less. It also gives individuality to the rooms.

(*e*) Cleaning equipment should if possible be light and bright as this will assist morale and encourage staff to keep their equipment clean.

(*f*) Clerical work carried out in a housekeeping department can be greatly assisted by the use of coloured index cards. These help the housekeeping manager and supervisors to identify information relating to different floors, blocks or sections.

Colour plays an important part in maintaining a safe environment. Service pipes are identified by coloured tape or by being painted specific colours (BS1710):

(*a*) hot water supply — white/crimson/white;
(*b*) gas — yellow;
(*c*) steam — silver grey;
(*d*) fire installations — safety red;
(*e*) cold water down pipes — white/blue/white;
(*f*) electricity — orange;
(*g*) drinking water pipes — blue;
(*h*) furnace fuel oil (diesel) — brown;
(*i*) drainage pipes — black;
(*j*) central heating pipes — crimson/blue/crimson.

Signs may also be classified by colour as well as shape (*see* Fig. 72). Red and green, however, should not be used together for identification as these two colours are not easily distinguished by people who are colour blind.

Texture

Texture is often introduced to add interest to a décor scheme. Housekeeping staff should try to retain the texture of finishes applied to walls, floors, furniture, etc. when cleaning them:

(*a*) smooth surfaces such as ceramic tiles, veneered furniture and glass table tops must not be scratched by abrasive detergents or pads;

(*b*) rough textured wallpapers should not be scrubbed too hard and should be protected in areas where they may tear or rub.

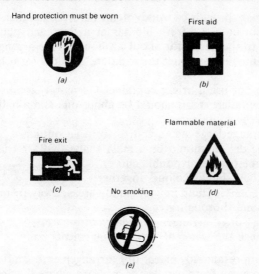

Fig. 72. *Use of colour in signs.*
(a) *Order signs, white on blue;* (b) *and* (c) *instruction signs, white on green;*
(d) *danger signs, black on yellow;* (e) *prohibitive signs, red on white.*

Incidental furnishings

These are added to a room to give interest or to provide the necessary atmosphere for a specific function or activity, e.g. flowers and festive decorations, or to add interest to a large entrance area or hall, e.g. foliage tubs and display stands.

The provision and maintenance of these items is frequently the responsibility of the housekeeping department. The preparation of floral arrangements takes considerable time and requires some knowledge of the principles of flower arranging. The housekeeper should be able to cope with this task although there is often a member of the department who enjoys flower arranging and is willing to assist. Where a regular supply of table decorations and displays is required contractors are usually employed to provide, maintain and replace the required number and type of arrangements.

Guidelines for arranging fresh or dried flowers

Basic equipment. Scissors, watering can or jug, wire mesh, pin holder, "Flora Pack" or similar, plasticine, string, sellotape, container, e.g. vase, plate, basket, pedestal or candlestick, beer mat, polystyrene tile, etc.

(*a*) Remove any leaves likely to be under water (fresh flowers).

(*b*) Crush the ends of woody stems before arranging, e.g. roses.

(*c*) Trim bases of fresh blooms at a slant and place in tepid water up to the necks for about an hour before arranging.

(*d*) Container must suit the location, e.g. low for use on dining tables.

(*e*) Do not use a bright container for pastel blooms.

(*f*) The tallest stems should be about one-and-a-half times the height of the container.

(*g*) Arrange large stems first to form an outline.

(*h*) The design should be a mass shape (ball or triangle) or a linear shape (single or double curve).

(*i*) Group similar colours together.

(*j*) If possible stand in cool, shady areas, away from radiators, draughts and thoroughfares.

(*k*) Dust dried arrangements daily with care.

(*l*) Check the water of fresh arrangements daily.

It is important to place dry arrangements and decorative trimmings away from candles or ashtrays where they could catch fire. Beware of superstitions regarding flowers, e.g. white signifies death to some people.

Plants
Pot plants, whether large or small, should be kept in watertight containers fitted with an irrigator which if kept full prevents over- or under-watering. The leaves must be kept dusted and occasionally polished, depending on the type of plant. Withered leaves and flowers should be removed. A "grow bulb" may be used to provide suitable growing conditions for plants placed in areas where there is no natural light. These should be kept clean and replaced when necessary. Plants in such areas should also be sprayed with water occasionally to counteract the dry atmosphere likely to prevail.

Other items
Murals, paintings, fire bells, CCTV equipment, "Muzak" speakers, etc. are all likely to be encountered by housekeeping staff while cleaning walls, etc. They should be kept dusted and free of sticky marks and stains, but must be handled with care to avoid damage. Display stands and notice-boards should be kept tidy as well as clean.

PEST CONTROL

Although standards of living have improved and hotels and residential establishments are more luxurious, higher room temperatures and lack of natural ventilation (chimneys, etc.) provide ideal conditions (warmth and moisture) for certain pests. Failure to remove dust, dirt, debris and food waste can encourage pests to remain in the building and breed. The pests which are most likely to be found in an accommodation establishment are:

(*a*) insects—moth larvae, bed bugs, lice, fleas, flies, cockroaches, beetles, silverfish, mites and spiders;
(*b*) rodents—rats and mice;
(*c*) Fungi—wet rot, dry rot and moulds.

Female cats are also considered pests when they find their way into basement areas or service ducts, and birds such as pigeons and starlings may cause problems on roofs and ledges. Housekeeping staff should report any sightings of pests or signs that they are in the building (e.g. damage from gnawing, droppings, unpleasant smells and small holes) so that their method of entry, food source and breeding sites can be investigated and blocked up or removed. Apart from the threat to standards of hygiene, the presence of pests can be upsetting to guests and staff who encounter them.

Insects

Moths
Those likely to be encountered are the clothes moth and the brown house moth (*see* Fig. 73), both of which are about 2 cm long.
Attraction. Soiled coloured wool (blankets, carpets, clothes), leather, dried fruit and cork.
Damage. Holes in textile fabrics or spoilage of dried fruit. The grubs eat wool, fur, hair or feathers.
Control.
(*a*) Keep clothes and bedding, leather furniture and luggage, cork tiles and mats, etc. clean.
(*b*) When in storage keep these items sealed in polythene bags or paper and place in cupboards or drawers in a cool area.
(*c*) Add naphthalene or paradichlorobenzene tablets to stored items.
(*d*) Clean carpets regularly and occasionally (about every six months) spray edges of fitted carpets and areas under furniture with a residual insecticide (mothproofer aerosol).
(*e*) Hang insecticidal vaporising strips in wardrobes, etc.
(*f*) Have carpets treated professionally with a mothproofer.

Bed bugs
The presence of bed bugs in a residence constitutes "verminous

Courtesy Rentokil

Fig. 73. *Brown house moth.*

conditions" which according to the Public Health Act empowers local authorities to disinfect the premises or to tell the proprietor to do so at his own expense. Bed bugs are only 3 mm long and resemble brown, flat discs (*see* Fig. 74). They usually enter a building in already infested bedroom furniture, luggage or clothing and live behind peeling wallpaper, in cracked plaster or woodwork, in bed frames, headboards and mattresses.

Attraction. Human blood; overcrowded, dirty rooms.

Courtesy Rentokil

Fig. 74. *Bed bug.*

Damage. Irritating bites to humans (small, hard, white swelling); unpleasant smell.

Control.

(*a*) Keep bedroom floors, walls, beds and bedding spotlessly clean.

(*b*) Spray with lindane spray or employ contractors to apply a fenitrothion or iodofenphos insecticide.

Lice

Lice which are attracted to humans are grey and measure 3 mm. The adult and its eggs, "nits", stick to hair or clothing fibres. They are easily passed on by the hand after scratching the infected area. The Public Health Act empowers local authorities to disinfect people within twenty-four hours of diagnosis.

Attraction. Human blood; hair, textile fibres.

Damage. Irritating bites, often on the scalp. Scratching can cause infection, e.g. impetigo. In the past, epidemics of typhus and trench fever resulted but this is rare today.

Control.

(*a*) Thorough personal cleanliness and hygienic use of combs, etc.

(*b*) Application of special shampoos and lotions containing carbaryl or malathion.

(*c*) Use of special combs.

(*d*) Regular cleaning of pillows, pillowcases and headboards.

(*e*) Use of head rests on chair backs which should be washed regularly.

Fleas

Human fleas and cat fleas measure 2–3 mm and are flat from side to side (*see* Fig. 75) with a reddish brown colour. Fleas are parasites which live off warm-blooded animals. They find their way on to human skin by jumping on to clothes or fur and working their way through them. The most frequently found flea in residences is the cat flea.

Attraction. Fur, feathers, clothing or sleeping places used by the host (where fleas lay their eggs, often several hundred); organic debris; fluff and dust under carpets and beds, etc.

Damage. Irritating bites leaving a small red spot. Cat and bird fleas may attack humans.

Control.

(*a*) Keep floors, beds, skirtings, etc. free of dust.

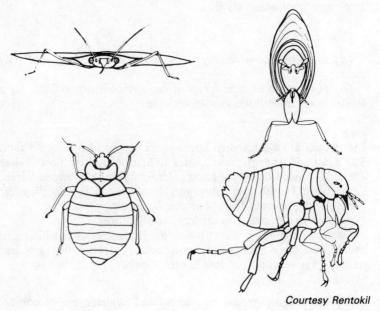

Courtesy Rentokil

Fig. 75. *Cat flea.*

(*b*) Burn infested bedding.

(*c*) Prevent the entry of cats, dogs, birds, etc. and check for birds' nests on or within the building.

(*d*) Spray bed frames and floors with insecticide.

Flies

The house fly measures 7–8 mm and is grey with black stripes (*see* Fig. 76).

Attraction. Decaying organic matter and refuse.

Damage. Gastro-enteritis; typhoid; diarrhoea; dysentery; diptheria and cholera may all be contracted by eating food contaminated by flies.

Control.

(*a*) Prompt disposal of food waste, tins and bottles.

(*b*) Regular, thorough cleaning of refuse bins and their storage areas.

(*c*) Tight fitting lids for refuse bins.

(*d*) Fly screens over windows that open.

Courtesy Rentokil

Fig. 76. *House fly.*

(*e*) Insecticide spray (permethrin or other pyrethroids).

(*f*) Electric ultraviolet fly traps.

(*g*) Automatic insecticide dispensers (unoccupied areas).

(*h*) Impregnated plastic strips giving off dichlorous vapour.

(*i*) Regular spraying of refuse areas and bins with insecticide in warm weather.

Cockroaches

These are approximately 2.5 cm long with flat brown/black bodies and long antennae. (*see* Fig. 77). They usually enter a building in boxes and packets of food, often as egg capsules which hatch later.

Courtesy Rentokil

Fig. 77. *Cockroach*

Attraction. Warm, moist atmospheres (bathrooms, kitchens, around hot pipes, central heating ducts); most types of food.

Damage. Food spoilage from vomit and excreta; unpleasant smell; transmission of food poisoning and other diseases.

Control.

(*a*) Spray infested floor cavities, pipe runs, sink areas, etc. with insecticide for crawling insects, ensuring penetration into all cracks and crevices.

(*b*) Employ contractors to spray or place powders and baits in strategic positions.

Beetles

There are very many types of beetle likely to enter a residential building but those which cause most damage to the structure or furnishings are the furniture beetle and the carpet beetle. Flour beetles

Courtesy Rentokil

Fig. 78. *Confused flour beetle.*

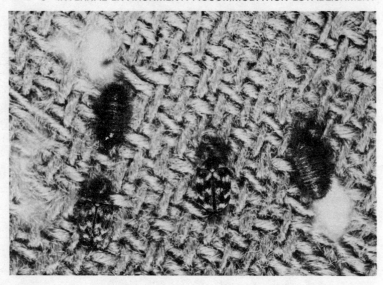

Courtesy Rentokil

Fig. 79. *Varied carpet beetle adults and "woolly bear" larvae.*

(*see* Fig. 78), spider beetles and others may turn up in the larder on cereals, pastas or dried fruit.

Carpet beetles. These are 2–4 mm long with an oval-shaped body and brown/cream mottled colouring (*see* fig. 79). They enter a building to lay their eggs in a birds' nest, accumulated wool, fur or feathers. The grubs may then travel along pipe lagging and into areas such as linen rooms which are kept warm.

Attraction. Feathers, fur, wool, skin flakes and hair.

Damage. Irregular holes on the seams of fabric, especially wool.

Control.

(*a*) Inspection of roof and eaves for dead birds.

(*b*) Inspection of pipe lagging.

(*c*) Regular dusting and vacuuming of shelves, floorboards, cupboards, carpets and upholstery.

(*d*) Spray infested areas with a proprietary mothproofer.

(*e*) Dust floorboards and under carpets and crevices with carbaryl or lindane insect powder or mothproofer.

(*f*) Place moth repellent crystals around stored clothes, carpets, blankets, etc.

Furniture beetles. These are about the size of the carpet beetle but are brown and their grubs are commonly known as the

Courtesy Rentokil

Fig. 80. *Woodworm: pupa of common furniture beetle.*

"woodworm" (*see* Fig. 80). They make clean round holes in wooden furniture, structural timber and wickerwork. They enter a building in packing cases, tea chests, wicker baskets, such as those used for linen, and second-hand furniture or just by flying, they then lay their eggs in the cracks or joints of rough, unpainted wood. From here the larvae bore into the wood leaving no sign of entry. The adults emerge after about three years leaving behind a labyrinth of tunnels which weakens the wood. The round holes through which they emerge to mate and lay more eggs are a sign of much more serious damage.

Attraction. Unprotected wood (not Cuban mahogany or teak).

Damage. Serious weakening and devaluing of wooden furniture, floorboards, rafters, joists, etc.

Control.

(*a*) Keep all wooden surfaces dusted, polished and protected with paint, varnish, oil, wax or plastic.

(*b*) Coat infested areas and surrounding areas including the base, back and insides of drawers and cupboards with a proprietary woodworm killer.

(*c*) Inject holes with woodworm killer prior to coating the surface.

(*d*) Occasional use of an insecticidal polish.

(*e*) Employ a specialist woodworm contractor for treatment of structural timber (preferably a member of the British Wood preserving Association).

Silverfish

These are 7 mm long with a silver grey, cigar-shaped body (*see* Fig. 81). They cause only minor damage to paper and similar material and are usually found in warm, moist areas such as bathrooms and kitchens. Their presence is usually a sign of a fault in the plumbing causing unwanted dampness, e.g. cracked water pipes, excessive condensation or rising damp.

Attraction. Carbohydrate material; moisture and warmth.

Damage. Minor damage to wallpaper (paste is made from a starch), books (adhesive may contain starch), etc.

Control.

(*a*) Inspect building for sources of damp.

(*b*) Spray cracks and crevices around plumbing fittings with carbaryl insect powder, or aerosol spray, or insecticide for crawling insects.

Mites and spiders

These are not strictly insects, but for convenience are considered with them.

Courtesy Rentokil

Fig. 81. *Silverfish.*

Mites. These are so small that they are rarely seen until their numbers are considerable. The furniture mite lives in damp, poorly ventilated areas and the house dust mite in upholstery and mattresses. The flour mite occurs in damp larders and the red spider mite occasionally invades from the garden.

Attraction. Food and dampness (furniture and house mites); human skin particles (dust mite).

Damage. Food spoilage and minor damage to upholstery. May cause an allergic reaction e.g. asthma, to occupants of beds or those who make them.

Control.

(*a*) Improve ventilation or heating.

(*b*) Dispose of unwanted food and tins, etc.

(*c*) Spray infested surfaces with insecticide.

(*d*) Remove dust regularly from mattresses and upholstered furniture.

Spiders. These are harmless, but their presence may indicate inefficiency on the part of housekeeping staff. They also cause revulsion in some people and may deter staff from working in areas where they have been seen. Spiders are advantageous in that they may destroy other insects which cause damage.

Attraction. Undisturbed areas, cracks or crevices neglected by routine cleaning.

Damage. Little or none; psychological disturbance in some people.

Control.

(*a*) Regular, thorough cleaning.

(*b*) General insecticide spray in areas where they have been seen.

Rodents

Rats and mice breed rapidly and so early detection and eradication are essential.

Rats

It is usually the brown rat (*see* Fig. 82) which is found in or around accommodation establishments. It nests in areas where there is loose soil, refuse, paper, straw or cartons and so a build-up of such items should be avoided. Signs of infestation are droppings (1.5 cm long), black smears and damage by gnawing.

Damage. Gnawing of materials such as woodwork, plastic, pipework (*see* Fig. 83) and electric wiring; spread of disease (salmonella food poisoning, Weil's disease, murine typhus, trichinosis and rat bite fever); food contamination.

Courtesy Rentokil

Fig. 82. *Brown rat.*

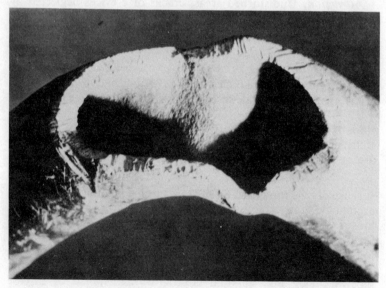

Courtesy Rentokil

Fig. 83. *Rat damage to lead pipe.*

Control.

(*a*) Block all possible entry holes, e.g. gaps around pipes.

(*b*) Remove possible nesting material, e.g. boxes, newspapers, patches of weed.

(*c*) Remove food sources e.g. cover waste bins, clear up spillages.

(*d*) Place bait near signs of infestation, e.g. difenacoum, brodifacoum or bromadiolone.

(*e*) Employ a contractor to apply rodenticides and provide follow-up inspections as necessary.

Mice

These are attracted by the warmth of a building, the shelter it provides and any food crumbs (*see* Fig. 84). Signs of infestation are similar to those for rats. They have a very acute sense of smell and are able to climb easily and squeeze through very small gaps. Like rats, they nest in deposits of paper and packaging and so a build-up of such items should be avoided.

Damage. Gnawing of packaging, woodwork, foodstuffs (particularly chocolate, nuts, seeds and cereals), electric wires (*see* Fig. 85) and pipework.

Courtesy Rentokil

Fig. 84. *House mouse.*

Courtesy Rentokil

Fig. 85. *Mouse gnawing power cable.*

Control.

(*a*) Block all possible entry points (holes around pipework, broken air-bricks).

(*b*) Place containers of rodenticide where there seem to be signs of infestation, e.g. alphachloralose, difenacoum, calciferol or bromadiolone. Traps may be used at wall/floor junctions.

(*c*) Cats are not recommended as a method of control as they can rarely reach the areas where mice breed or feed, and may themselves bring fleas into the building.

Pest control contractors

Accommodation establishments should employ a pest control contractor to visit their premises regularly. Such a contractor should be a member of the British Pest Control Association. Staff should also be informed of the necessity to report any signs of infestation, to co-operate with the contractor and to keep bait boxes in position.

Fungi

There is little that housekeeping staff can do to prevent the growth of fungi in a building as this often occurs as a result of faulty building construction and poor maintenance of the building fabric.

However, they can assist by reporting any signs of decay in woodwork.

Signs of fungal infestation

Dry rot. Cuboidal cracks in timber (*see* Fig. 86); matted, whitish strands on wood; plate-like, fruiting bodies (sporophores, *see* Fig. 87); rust-red spore dust.

Wet rot. Brittle timber, dark brown in colour; flaking paintwork (*see* Fig. 88); dark, fern-like strands on wood (*see* Fig. 89).

Mould. Green, black or pink discoloration on walls and woodwork. (Most likely to occur wherever condensation persists.)

Courtesy Rentokil

Fig. 86. *Typical cuboidal cracking of timbers caused by dry rot fungus,*

Courtesy Rentokil

Fig. 87. *The sporophore or fruiting body of the dry rot fungus.*

Signs of unwanted dampness

All fungi require water for survival and so any preventative measures should aim at identifying and removing sources of unwanted moisture, e.g.:

(*a*) peeling wallpaper;
(*b*) flaking plaster;
(*c*) discoloration of walls;
(*d*) condensation;
(*e*) leaking taps and overflow pipes;
(*f*) strong, unpleasant smells;
(*g*) the presence of certain insects, e.g. silverfish;
(*h*) warped skirtings;
(*i*) salt deposits on brick and plaster.

A dampproofing contractor may be employed to cope with serious and persistent problems of dampness.

Fig. 88. *Wet rot damage to paintwork.*

MAINTAINING A SAFE ENVIRONMENT

The general management of any accommodation establishment is legally bound to provide a hazard-free environment, at all times. To do this it must rely on employees to work safely and to report any damage to the building or to equipment and any situations which may prove hazardous.

In large establishments a fire and safety officer may be employed to work with departmental safety representatives. In smaller organisations a departmental manager such as the housekeeper may take on the responsibility for fire and accident prevention. This responsibility involves regular inspection of the building for structural damage and potential accident situations. He/she is also responsible for ensuring that all fire prevention equipment is kept in the correct positions and is always ready for use. Other duties

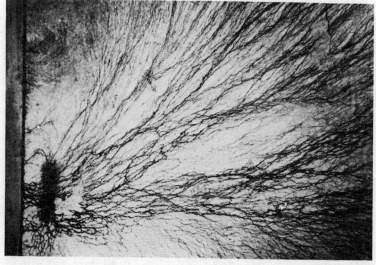

Courtesy Rentokil

Fig. 89. *Fern-like strands, indicating wet rot.*

include:

(*a*) arranging for regular testing of fire bells and fire drills;

(*b*) organisation of staff training sessions relating to safety in methods of work and knowledge of fire procedures;

(*c*) encouraging staff to become qualified in first aid;

(*d*) preparation and distribution of instructions for reference when using potentially dangerous equipment or procedures.

Housekeeping staff can play an important part in preventing accidents and fires as the nature of their work takes them to many parts of the building.

Housekeeping staff and accident prevention

Hazards
Unsafe and dangerous conditions should be reported to superiors immediately, e.g.:

(*a*) damaged floorings;

(*b*) loose stair treads;

(*c*) cracked or broken glass;

(*d*) chipped tiles;

(*e*) worn electrical insulation or fittings;

(*f*) dangerously slippery floors;

(*g*) obstructed staircases/corridors;

(*h*) spillages;

(*i*) inadequate lighting.

Methods of work

Regular inspection of work by supervisors should highlight any dangerous work methods, e.g.:

(*a*) trailing flexes;

(*b*) build-up of litter, linen or soiled cloths, especially those coated with solvent-based polish or strong smelling cleaning agents;

(*c*) fire doors propped open;

(*d*) equipment untidily stacked both during work and when stored;

(*e*) temporary storage of equipment in front of fire exits;

(*f*) smoking in non-smoking areas;

(*g*) failure to use warning signs when cleaning floors;

(*h*) cloths, clothes, etc. left drying over heaters;

(*i*) overloading of electric sockets.

Health and hygiene

Staff should be trained to work hygienically and safely and be encouraged to maintain a healthy constitution. Uniforms should always be worn and should be clean and in good condition, e.g. sleeves not rolled up, shoes in good repair so that they provide good support. They should be provided with the opportunity to eat a well-balanced diet in order to cope with the physical work required of the department and be made aware of the basic principles of personal hygiene as adherence to these will help to reduce the spread of infection among staff and consequently reduce absenteeism. The following rules should be observed.

(*a*) Keep fingernails short and clean.

(*b*) Wash hands after going to the toilet, sneezing or smoking.

(*c*) Use paper handkerchiefs and dispose of them immediately after use.

(*d*) Keep cuts and abrasions covered with a suitable dressing.

(*e*) Never smoke while working.

(*f*) Wear rubber gloves if skin is sensitive.

Posture

Maintenance of good posture when standing, sitting, reaching, lifting or carrying prevents body fatigue and strained muscles.

(*a*) Standing:
    (*i*)   shoulders back and down;
    (*ii*) stomach held in;
    (*iii*) legs straight;
    (*iv*) head upright;
    (*v*) hands at sides.

(*b*) Sitting:
    (*i*)   bottom must reach to the back of the seat;
    (*ii*) feet uncrossed and flat on floor;
    (*iii*) shoulders back;
    (*iv*) back resting against chair backrest;
    (*v*) head upright;
    (*vi*) hands on knee.

(*c*) Reaching:
    (*i*)   keep body balanced;
    (*ii*) keep reach as vertical as possible;
    (*iii*) find object, lift it up and lower it as close to the body as possible (arm muscles are stronger than back muscles).

(*d*) Lifting:
    (*i*)   place feet approximately 45 cm apart with one slightly in front of the other;
    (*ii*) stand near object;
    (*iii*) stoop, bending from the knees;
    (*iv*) grasp object keeping back straight;
    (*v*) lift object pushing up with the leg muscles;
    (*vi*) keep object close to body;
    (*vii*) seek assistance if object cannot be lifted in this way.

Safety rules

Housekeeping supervisors should make sure that:

(*a*) all cleaning agent containers are clearly labelled as to their contents and dilution ratios;

(*b*) stain removal agents are kept locked in a metal cupboard or box;

(*c*) electrical equipment is inspected regularly for worn or frayed flexes and damaged plugs, etc.;

(*d*) aerosol containers are stored away from heat and disposed of with care (not incinerated);

(*e*) cleaning materials stores are kept tidy, clean, well-ventilated and locked when not in use;

(*f*) staff are instructed in the use of any new equipment with which they are issued;

(*g*) all staff know the whereabouts of the nearest first aid box;

(*h*) every first aid box is kept supplied with waterproof adhesive tape, scissors, safety pins, antiseptic cream, eye bath, pain killers, cotton wool, gauze and roller bandage.

The action to be taken when an accident does occur depends on the type of accident and its seriousness.

What to do if somebody is injured

Minor accidents

Cuts and abrasions, etc. Bathe wound with cold water and convenient cloth, e.g. tissue or towel. Collect appropriate equipment from first aid box and deal with wound. Inform superior of accident and assist in the completion of an accident report form (*see* Fig. 90).

Falls. These must be reported to a superior as soon as possible so that an accident report form can be completed. This type of accident can cause damage which may not become apparent immediately and therefore a record must be available for reference before any industrial injury benefit can be claimed (staff). Residents or guests may also wish to claim damages from the establishment and so a record may prove useful in proving that the management was not negligent, i.e. it was the guest's fault that he fell.

Burns and scalds. Run cold water over the injured area to remove "heat". Leave exposed to the air if possible, but prevent contact with clothing. Inform superior and assist in the completion of an accident report form.

Serious accidents

(Electric shock, burns, scalds, fractures, sprains, deep cuts, etc.) These accidents require expert assistance but before this can be sought it is necessary for the victim to be calmed and reassured:

(*a*) sit him down (unless he is unconscious or on the floor);

(*b*) loosen any restricting clothes, e.g. tie, belt, shoe-laces;

(*c*) keep him warm but provide air.

If the victim has fainted or is unconscious, proceed as above but first lay him in the recovery position (*see* Fig. 91) and make sure his air passages are not blocked. As soon as possible, telephone for or fetch a first aider or a supervisor, and inform the housekeeper or manager immediately.

ACCIDENT REPORT FORM

Department: HouseKeepng

Date: 19/5/-7

Name of victim: B. Black

Name of witnesses: V. White

Exact location of accident: Backstairs floor 5

Injury/ies sustained: Sprained left ankle

Date injury occurred: 19/5/-7

Time injury occurred: 15.55

Further Information: Victim escorted to staff
room were seen to by myself.
Taken to hospital at 16.30 by
rs.White for X-ray where sprain
was confirmed. Sick note. for
2 weeks.

Signature: A. Green

Fig. 90. *Accident report form.*

Emergency first aid procedures

Fainting. Treat as for serious accident (*see* above).

Epileptic fit. Remove obstacles likely to cause harm during erratic movement. Place object which will not break e.g. item of clothing, in mouth to prevent tongue being bitten. Loosen collar if possible. Leave patient to run the course of the fit.

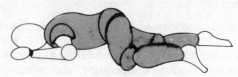

Fig. 91. *Recovery position.*

Asthma. Stay with sufferer and reassure.

Electric shock. Disconnect electricity supply. Apply artificial respiration. Place victim in recovery position (*see* Fig. 91). Treat burns as described above.

Nose bleed. Pinch top of nose. Refrain from blowing nose.

Foreign body or splash in eye. Bathe eyes in eye bath or with clean cloth and cold water. Blow nose. Try to remove object. Refrain from rubbing eye.

General comments

Accident prevention should be included in an induction programme, but the above procedures should be explained more fully during subsequent training sessions.

Whenever an accident has occurred, no matter how minor, the cause should be investigated and measures taken to ensure it does not recur.

All employers are required by the Department of Health and Social Security to keep an accident book in which every accident involving a member of staff should be recorded. The information entered is similar to that required by the accident report form.

Illness and death

There may be occasions when illness occurs to a guest or resident. If the sick person is too ill to travel home, or it is inconvenient for him to do so, as is often the case with overseas visitors or students and homeless people, he should be attended to by a local doctor and if necessary transferred to hospital, to a sick room or to an area where he can be looked after with the least inconvenience to staff caring for him. Students will usually have friends who can assist with their nursing, but hotel guests should be visited regularly by housekeeping staff. If the illness is contagious it is advisable for the local health authority to be informed but this is usually done by the doctor or hostel/hotel manager. All staff should also be informed. Housekeeping staff should be told about any guests/residents in their sections who are sick, and be given appropriate instructions.

Occasionally illness or accidents lead to death. Staff who encounter such a situation should not touch anything in the room which might be helpful in establishing the cause of death. They should lock the door or seal off the area and report the matter immediately to the housekeeper or manager. They should also be prepared to assist in any subsequent enquiry or investigation.

Housekeeping staff and fire prevention

Each type of accommodation establishment has its own specific problems with regard to fire prevention.

Hotels

All hotels and boarding houses except the very small are bound by the Fire Precautions Act 1971 to obtain a fire certificate. This requires the hotel to:

(*a*) provide and maintain suitable means of escape;
(*b*) train and instruct staff in fire drill procedures and fire prevention;
(*c*) limit the number of people using or entering the building at any one time;
(*d*) provide suitable fire warning systems;
(*e*) provide and maintain fire fighting equipment.

Hotels often contain large numbers of people who are generally unfamiliar with the layout of the building. It is essential therefore that instructions are clear and easily read and understood. Housekeeping staff should always check that these instructions are kept in a prominent position (often by the light switch just inside each room) and that they are not defaced or damaged.

The majority of hotel fires are discovered between 11.00 p.m. and 7.00 a.m. when people are normally asleep, and so a fire warning system must be efficient. However, many guests may require further encouragement to leave the building because they are heavy sleepers or are deaf or maybe they choose to ignore the warning. It is the responsibility of housekeeping staff particularly to make sure that all guests in their section leave the building via the designated route.

Hostels

Residents in hostels often surround themselves with electrical gadgets and appliances such as stereo equipment, heated hair rollers, etc. which if used simultaneously can overload the electric circuit. This is extremely dangerous and housekeeping staff should notify the housekeeper or supervisor of rooms where this occurs. Hostels often provide kitchen and laundry facilities to be shared by several residents. These areas contain equipment which unless treated with respect can become a fire hazard, e.g. irons left on, clothes left drying by electric fires, electric hot plates left on, etc. Housekeeping staff should be constantly on the look out for fire hazards in such areas.

There may be several television lounges in a hostel. It is important that someone is responsible for checking each night that the televisions are unplugged as failure to do this can cause a fire. (In student hostels, the warden on duty may be responsible for carrying out a late night patrol.) Unfortunately fire alarms in hostels are frequently set off for a prank so that a real fire warning may not be taken seriously. Residents must be informed of this danger as soon as they arrive.

Hospitals

Obviously the biggest problem in a hospital is the evacuation of patients. All hospital personnel including housekeeping staff are thoroughly trained in the recommended procedures to adopt.

A hospital also contains many chemicals and pressurised equipment which can create or exacerbate a fire. These should be treated with respect.

One of the main dangers in any fire is panic. Panic overcomes people and prevents them from thinking clearly. It is particularly important therefore that staff know what to do if a fire breaks out because if there is no need for original thought the right action is more likely to be taken quickly. This can only be achieved, however, by regular training and instruction, backed up by practical fire drills.

Causes of fire

A fire will only start if oxygen, heat and fuel come together in the correct proportions. Fire prevention is therefore aimed at ensuring this situation does not occur. If it does, fire fighting should aim at removing at least one of the three elements.

Heat
(*See* Table XXII.)

Fuel

The type of fuel likely to start a fire is classified according to the type of extinguishing equipment required to put out any fire it has created (*see* Table XXIII). All the fuels listed in Table XXIII should be used and stored in such a way that contact with heat and oxygen is avoided.

Cloth. Furnishings should be treated with a fire-retardant solution and kept away from heaters, radiators, televisions and areas where people may be smoking.

Paper/wood. Rubbish should be stored in metal bins and removed from temporary storage areas daily. A build-up should be avoided.

Liquids. These should be stored away from heat, e.g. not in a kitchen or near radiators and hot pipes. Spillages should be thoroughly removed as soon as they occur and kitchen ventilation

TABLE XXII. FIRE PREVENTION: HEAT ELEMENT.

Sources of heat	Methods of prevention
Matches and cigarettes	Provide designated smoking areas, ashtrays and metal waste bins.
Faulty wiring Incorrect earthing Incorrect use of fuses Worn insulation	Carry out regular maintenance of electrical equipment and installations. Immediately report to supervisor any damage to electrical equipment.
Faulty heating systems	Regular maintenance of heating systems. Immediate reporting of any unusual noises, leaks or inefficiencies.
Dangerous use of cooking equipment Spontaneous combustion	Thorough staff training and efficient supervision of staff especially in the catering department. Also of housekeeping staff who may be storing oily, greasy rags or failing to remove rubbish regularly.
Reflection of the sun	Position mirrors, etc. away from direct sunlight.
Direct ignition	Regular inspection of building by security staff to deter intruders with malicious intent.

TABLE XXIII. FIRE EXTINGUISHERS FOR DIFFERENT FUELS.

Wood, cloth, paper, etc.	Water (hose, bucket, extinguisher, sprinkler) Water/gas (extinguisher) Dry powder (extinguisher) Sand (bucket)
Liquids, e.g. fat, oil, petrol, paint	Dry powder (extinguisher) Carbon dioxide foam (extinguisher)
Electricity	Dry powder (extinguisher) Vaporising liquid, e.g. BCF (extinguisher)

hoods cleaned regularly. Flammable cleaning agents should be kept in a locked, metal cupboard.

Electricity. Electrical appliances should be unplugged after use and the supply turned off at the socket if this is possible. Electrical equipment and fittings should be kept dry and not overloaded. Any unusual noises should be reported immediately to superiors or maintenance staff. Filters in dry suction equipment, tumble dryers, etc. should be cleaned after use. Flexes should be stored neatly and not pulled tight when in use.

Oxygen

The amount of oxygen entering an area once a fire has started should be kept to a minimum and if possible removed completely. This can be done in several ways; as follows.

(*a*) Closing windows and doors immediately surrounding the fire and beyond if possible.

(*b*) Keeping fire doors closed at all times. (Housekeeping staff are often tempted to wedge them open to ease their passage along corridors when carrying or pushing equipment. This can be overcome, however, by magnetising the doors. The magnets are wired to the fire alarm warning system in such a way that when the alarm sounds the electric circuit will be broken and the doors will automatically close. It is important that their path is not obstructed by an uneven floor surface or by wedges.)

(*c*) Covering the flames completely with a fire blanket made from glass fibre.

(*d*) Switching off ventilation and air conditioning systems.

(*e*) Areas where spontaneous combustion might occur such as paint stores, cleaning materials stores, chemical stores, laboratories, etc., are often in out-of-the-way areas such as the basement. The doors to these areas must be kept closed when not in use, although some ventilation is necessary to prevent the fumes building up to a pitch when they may ignite.

Fire warning systems

The methods used to inform the occupants of a building that there is a fire vary with the size and type of building. Most accommodation establishments are fitted with either smoke detectors or sprinklers. These are situated on the ceiling of each room and automatically sound a bell and/or spray water when the room temperature rises above a certain level. Housekeeping staff should take care when cleaning these fittings as contact with hot water could set them off. They are also connected to the security office or reception area where the location of the fire can be identified immediately. Large buildings including hospitals may also have their fire warning systems linked directly to the nearest fire station to minimise any delay in obtaining help.

Old buildings and smaller establishments may find it uneconomical to have such sophisticated equipment installed. Instead they may use a system of buttons, sealed behind a glass plate. To sound the alarm the glass plate needs to be broken (there is usually a small hammer attached) and the button pressed. These buttons are linked to the fire bells and the switchboard.

What to do on discovering a fire

(*a*) Immediately operate the nearest fire alarm.

(*b*) If possible attack the fire with suitable equipment, remembering to direct extinguishers at the base of the flames. (Carbon dioxide foam should be directed towards the back of the flames first, to avoid dispersing them.) *Do not attempt to fight a fire if there is any danger of personal risk.*

(*c*) Close windows and switch off all electrical appliances including fans and lights.

(*d*) Close door and report to immediate superior for instructions.

(*e*) Carry out instructions, e.g. rouse guests in a designated area and direct or assist them to the nearest assembly point via the recommended route.

(*f*) Report to section or departmental fire representative for a roll call.

(*g*) The duty housekeeper should take out a list of the staff who are on duty, e.g. work rota, so that all those on duty can be accounted for.

(*h*) Remain at the assembly point until instructed to do otherwise.

(*i*) *Do not use lifts.*

(*j*) *Do not collect coats, bags, etc.*

The above procedure may be adapted slightly to cater for the threat of a bomb blast, e.g. collect personal belongings.

Fire practices

These should be held as often as is practical and should always be treated seriously. Fire practices not only make sure that staff are fully conversant with the escape routes in every part of the building (practices should occur at different times so that staff on all shifts can participate), but they also highlight any faults in the system, e.g. blocked escape routes, padlocked fire doors, fire doors which are left open, emergency lighting not working, exit signs not illuminated. A record should be kept of when fire practices have taken place together with comments on the performance of staff and equipment. Housekeeping supervisors should be responsible for informing contractors working in their department of the nearest fire points and assembly areas, as they are also expected to participate in fire practices.

Housekeeping staff and security

Everybody using a building whether for work or pleasure has a responsibility for security. Large organisations, however, may employ a security officer who in many cases is the same person as the fire and safety officer. Departmental heads may also be expected to be responsible for security on a rota basis, and this may involve the housekeeper.

There are four aspects to security in an accommodation establishment:

(*a*) loss of possessions;
(*b*) damage to the building and its furnishings;
(*c*) personal damage;
(*d*) fraudulent damage.

For each of these aspects there should be deterrents which are built into the establishment's organisational structure as well as its physical structure, e.g. burglar alarms and pressure pads. Tables XXIV–XXVII list the responsibilities of housekeeping staff in these four areas.

Key control

It is important that all housekeeping staff are made aware of the security risks created by a failure to adhere to the establishment's policy of key control. Most organisations use a four-key system of control, as follows.

Grand master key. This is usually kept by the duty or housekeeping manager. It will work on every door in the building both internal and external. It may also be able to double-lock doors, thus preventing a room from being entered by anyone without the manager's knowledge.

Master key. This may be known as a pass key. It is kept by the deputy or assistant housekeeper and will work on any internal door.

TABLE XXIV. PREVENTION OF THEFT.

Methods used	Responsibilities of housekeeping staff
Provision of safety deposit facilities.	Remind guests/residents/patients of facilities and encourage their use.
Scheduling of regular patrols around the building/department.	Housekeeping supervisors may have to undertake such patrols.
Limiting the number of unlocked entrances and exits.	Refrain from using fire exits as a quick way out. Report any forced door or window locks.
Provision of identification for all people entering the building including contractors.	Question anybody looking suspicious.
Strict adherence to lost property procedures.	Hand in any items left behind by guests, etc. to housekeeping supervisor as soon as they are found. They will record in a lost property book: (*a*) an exact description of the item including its condition; (*b*) who found it; (*c*) exact time it was found; (*d*) exact position it was found. The item should then be passed to the reception department, bursar or administrator together with the above information. They should attempt to trace the owner.
Efficient key control.	Never lend out room or master keys. Always ask to see identification before opening rooms for people. Sign for all keys when collecting them or handing them in.
Use of electronic locks.	
Fitting of window locks.	Make sure window locks are working and report any which fail to do so.
Employment of a hall porter or doorman.	

Table Continued

TABLE XXIV. (*Continued*).

Methods used	Responsibility of housekeeping staff
Application of anti-climb paint on pipework, etc.	
Provision of free gifts.	Keep free gifts in bedrooms, etc. replenished.
Limited window opening.	
Indestructible labelling of equipment.	
Non-detachable hangers.	
Closed-circuit television.	
Constant supervision of all staff during working hours.	Housekeeping supervisors should aim to remove any temptation to steal by guests or staff, i.e. keep stores locked, carry out spot checks of cupboards, etc., check stores requisitions thoroughly, challenge anybody seen to be stealing.

TABLE XXV. PREVENTION OF DAMAGE TO BUILDING (VANDALISM)

Methods used	Responsibilities of housekeeping staff
Blacklisting of all guests, etc. known to have caused damage.	Report any occurrences of vandalism immediately to superiors.
Scheduling of regular patrols around the building/department.	Housekeeping supervisors should patrol the department regularly especially during the evening.
Regular maintenance of fixtures, fittings and equipment so that damage is not caused through force, e.g. kicking doors which do not open readily.	Regular inspection of furniture, furnishings and services. Report any faults immediately to the maintenance department.
Request damage deposits from residents.	Report any damage to superior as soon as it is seen.
Regular inventory checks.	Carry out inventory checks regularly.

TABLE XXVI. PREVENTION OF PERSONAL DAMAGE (ASSAULT).

Methods used*	Responsibilities of housekeeping staff
Efficient key control.	Never lend out room or master keys
Use of electronic locks.	
Door chains.	Ensure door chains operate correctly.
Spy holes.	Keep them clean.
Regular room checks to ensure unoccupied rooms have not been disturbed.	Check unoccupied rooms daily.
Investigation of reports of "peeping toms", etc.	Report any occurrences of unwelcome guests.
Use a key card system or identification passes.	Carry identification passes all the time. Challenge any suspicious looking people.

*NOTE: These methods aim to prevent illegal entry into any part of the building.

TABLE XXVII. PREVENTION OF FRAUD (CRIMINAL DECEPTION).

Methods used	Responsibilities of housekeeping staff
Request payment in advance.	
Foolproof stock control system.	Adherence to and constant super-vision of stock control systems.
Membership of security associations (which notify all members of potential criminals).	
Thorough screening of staff before engagement.	Take up all staff references before engaging them.
Spot checks on employees and their areas of work.	Carry out spot checks in all areas of the department.

Sub-master key. This may be referred to as a floor key as it will work on any door on a particular floor or section. It is kept by the floor housekeeper or by the person responsible for the cleaning/servicing of a block of rooms, e.g. chambermaid.

Room key. This is given to the guest or resident when he registers or books in and is relinquished when he leaves. It is usually attached to a tag on which is written the room number and the address of the establishment so that it can be returned if it is lost or the guest forgets to hand it in on leaving.

All keys should be stored out of general view preferably in a locked key cupboard and a record made each time one is issued or returned.

Electronic door locks

Abuse of keys particularly in hotels has led to the development of key systems linked electronically to a computer, which is usually housed in the reception area. An electronic key looks like a piece of plastic-coated cardboard. However, imprinted on the key are a number of notches making it possible for a computer to alter the lock combination many thousands of times. This can be done as soon as a guest checks out so that he will not be able to regain admission to his room after this time.

Sub-master and master keys can also be provided with this system. Electronic keys are much lighter and less bulky for housekeeping staff to carry around.

SELF-ASSESSMENT QUESTIONS

1. What are the detrimental effects of excessive noise, heat and cold on an internal environment?

2. How can colour be used to assist the work of the house-keeping department?

3. Describe what is meant by "incidental furnishings". What responsibility does the housekeeping department have for their maintenance?

4. What part does the housekeeping department play in the prevention of pest infestation?

5. How can housekeeping staff assist in the prevention of accidents and fire?

6. How can a housekeeping supervisor help to prevent breaches of security by staff?

Appendix I
Stain Removal

Safety considerations when using stain removal chemicals
(*a*) Work in a well-ventilated area.
(*b*) Never work in an area where there is likely to be a naked flame such as a pilot light or a radiant heater.
(*c*) Never smoke while working with or near stain removal agents.
(*d*) Do not decant stain removal agents.
(*e*) Wear protective clothing including rubber gloves.
(*f*) Always have cold water and an eye bath close at hand in case any stain removal agent splashes into the eyes.

Safety considerations when storing stain removal chemicals
(*a*) Store chemicals in a locked cupboard, label the key and store it in a lockable key cabinet or drawer.
(*b*) Keep all containers clearly and correctly labelled.
(*c*) Only keep small quantities in stock to deter under-dilution or excessive applications and to reduce the risks of fire and accidents.

Guidelines for removing stains
(*a*) Treat a stain as soon as possible.
(*b*) Before attempting to remove a stain consider:
  (*i*) what caused the stain;
  (*ii*) the nature of the surface on which it has occurred including any special treatment it may have undergone, e.g. flameproofing.
(*c*) Always test the reaction of the surface to the stain removal agent before applying it to the stain.
(*d*) Several applications of a weak solution are preferable to one strong application.
(*e*) Apply stain removal agent around the edge of the stain and work towards the centre, to prevent it from spreading.
(*f*) Dab rather than rub to prevent damaging the surface.
(*g*) Apply stain removal agent with white absorbent fabric or cotton wool.
(*h*) If possible launder, shampoo or dry clean the entire surface as soon after removing the stain as possible.

(*i*) If professional help is required, inform them of any attempts which have already been made to remove the stain.

(*j*) If the cause of a stain is unknown proceed as follows.

(*i*)　Soak or sponge with cold salted water.

(*ii*)　If it still remains, soak or sponge with lukewarm water and leave for thirty minutes.

(*iii*) If it still remains, soak or sponge with warm biological detergent solution, leave for about thirty minutes then rinse.

(*iv*) If it still remains, if possible wash with a hot synthetic detergent solution as the high temperature activates the sodium perborate bleach. Rinse.

(*v*)　If it still remains, dry stain and apply solvent-based stain removal agent.

(*vi*) If it still remains, rinse and dry stain then apply an acid-based agent.

(*vii*) If it still remains, rinse and dry stain then apply an alkali-based agent.

(*k*) If a surface is known to have been specially treated in some way, it should be re-treated afterwards.

The main stain removal agents

Many proprietary stain removal agents can be obtained which deal with specific types of stain, e.g. tar removers, paint removers, grease removers, rust removers. They have the advantage of being ready to use and easy to apply. However, they are expensive and can be made more cheaply from the basic chemicals listed below.

Solvents
Benzene (petrol)
White spirit (turpentine substitute)
Amyl acetate (smells like pear drops)　⎫
Acetone (nail varnish remover)　　　　⎬　Flammable
Methylated spirit　　　　　　　　　　⎭

Perchlorethylene　　⎫　Non-flammable but
Trichlorethylene　　⎬　harmful if inhaled

(*a*) They will not harm fibres or dyes (except rubber and acetate rayon).

(*b*) Used to remove chewing gum (after freezing and scraping), grease, oil-based paint, lipstick, ballpoint ink and tar.

(*c*) Solvents are more efficient if these stains are first softened with glycerine.

Acids
Oxalic acid solution (30 g/570 ml water) ⎞
Potassium acid oxalate (salts of lemon)   ⎬ Poisonous
(10g/100 ml warm water)   ⎠
Acetic acid (vinegar)
Citric acid (lemon juice)

(*a*) Use on white or fast colours only.

(*b*) Always wash or sponge surface after use, with detergent solution or a weak alkaline solution such as borax, in order to neutralise the acid.

(*c*) Acid becomes more concentrated on drying.

(*d*) Acids can damage vegetable fibres.

(*e*) Used to remove alkali-based stains such as iron mould, rust and iron stains left after washing or sponging blood stains.

Alkalis
Washing soda (30 g/570 ml water)
Bicarbonate of soda
Borax
Ammonia
Bleach: Sodium hydrosulphite (reducing bleach)
       Sodium hypochlorite (household bleach) ⎞
       Hydrogen peroxide (will not harm animal ⎮ Oxidising
         fibres)   ⎬ bleaches
       Sodium perborate (present in most   ⎮ (strong)
         detergent powders)   ⎠
       Sodium thiosulphite ("hypo")

(*a*) Bleach should only be used as a last resort as it can weaken animal fibres and removes dyes easily.

(*b*) Used to remove acid-based stains, e.g. wine, tea, coffee.

(*c*) Sodium hydrosulphite is used on white surfaces. It may take up oxygen if left in the sun and therefore causes yellowing. It will remove iron mould.

(*d*) Sodium hypochlorite will tend to "fix" iron stains. Surfaces should be rinsed with a "hypo" solution to remove all traces of free chlorine.

Digesters
These are found in biological detergent powders, usually in the form of powdered pepsin. They do not remove stains but make them soluble in warm water. They are used to remove proteins (e.g. egg and gravy) and starches (e.g. sugar and potato). Digesters keep

indefinitely in powder form at room temperature but twenty-four hours only when in solution.

TABLE XXVIII. SUMMARY OF STAIN REMOVAL TECHNIQUES.

Surface	Stain	Methods of removal
Textiles	Blood	Wash. Soak in cold salt water (20 g/570 ml water) until loosened, e.g. overnight. Wash in warm detergent solution.
	Chewing gum	Rub with ice to harden. Scrape off with a blunt knife. Apply egg white to stiffen the remaining gum. Lift off. Shampoo with liquid detergent (10 g/200 ml water).
	Chocolate	Scrape with blunt knife and wash in hot detergent solution. If it still remains sponge with warm borax solution (30 g/570 ml water). Rinse and wash.
	Coffee	If possible stretch the stained area over a bowl and pour boiling water and borax over it.
	Fruit juice	Wash while still fresh. If possible stretch the stained area over a bowl and pour boiling water and borax over it.
	Grease	Iron with a warm iron placing brown paper or blotting paper over the stain. Sponge with a solvent cleaning agent followed by washing in a hot soap detergent solution.
	Ink	If fresh, blot immediately with blotting paper or absorbent powder such as talcum powder. Soak in milk or salt and lemon juice or salt followed by boiling water. Sponge with a solvent cleaning agent followed by rinsing.
	Lipstick	Wash in a synthetic detergent solution or sponge with cold water and apply glycerine or vaseline.
	Nail varnish	Sponge with acetone or nail varnish remover.

Table Continued

TABLE XXVIII. (*Continued*).

Surface	Stain	Methods of removal
	Paint	Treat as soon as possible. soften with glycerine then sponge with turpentine.
	Perspiration	Sponge with weak vinegar or ammonia before washing, or sponge with methylated spirits.
	Scorching	If fresh, soak in milk. If badly burnt brush, sponge with warm soap solution and borax. Rinse.
	Water marks	Sponge with warm water and dry with a soft towel.
	Liquid paper (Tippex)	Dab with an absorbent pad dipped in amyl acetate.
Leather and plastic	Grease	Scrape off as much as possible. Apply paste or absorbent powder and a solvent. Allow to dry, brush off and repeat. For leather dampen stain, apply oxalic acid solution (150 ml/1500 ml water). Rinse off.
	Ink	Sponge with methylated spirits, pure Dettol or trichlorethylene. Sponge with damp cloth. Repeat if necessary. *Or,* apply ink eradicator or oxalic acid as for grease. Test first for effect on colour.
	Paint	Apply water or turpentine, according to the type of paint. Scrape off softened paint, then shampoo with soap. Spirit paint removers may harm plastic surfaces.
Wallpaper	Crayon or lipstick	Scrape off with blunt knife. Sponge with grease solvent or apply proprietary spray dry cleaner. Treat remaining pigment stain with equal quantities of methylated spirits and ammonia.

Table Continued

TABLE XXVIII. (*Continued*).

Surface	Stain	Methods of removal
	Food	Wipe off lightly with damp cloth. If greasy, use grease solvent or spray dry cleaner. Treat remaining discoloration in the same way as for crayon or lipstick.
	Grease	Cover with soft paper and press with warm iron to absorb melted grease. Cover with dry powder such as talcum powder and a solvent. Allow to dry, then brush off and repeat if necessary or use proprietary spray dry cleaner.
	Ink	Blot up immediately. Sponge with warm water. Dab with clear methylated spirits. Use ink eradicator or sodium hypochlorite bleach.
	Paint	Fresh stains may be removed with the appropriate paint solvent, e.g. turpentine.
	Water marks	Apply a paste of fuller's earth and methylated spirits. Allow to dry thoroughly. Brush off surplus and sponge lightly with cold water.
Polished or sealed wood	Alcohol or perfume	Wipe up immediately. Rub with a little oil of peppermint or other light oil, e.g. lemon, almond, olive. For old or persistent stains, mix oil with finely powdered pumice or cigarette ash and rub in lightly with a circular motion. Sponge with oil, wipe dry and polish up. A mild application of metal polish may also be effective.
	Burns	If application of polish is unsuccessful, rub with raw boiled linseed oil and finely powdered pumice. Sponge with oil, wipe dry and rub up with a soft cloth. Metal polish may also be effective.

Table Continued

TABLE XXVIII. (*Continued*).

Surface	Stain	Methods of removal
	Candlewax or grease	Remove as much as possible with a blunt knife taking care not to damage the surface. Wash with warm soap solution. If it persists sponge with a solvent, rinse and polish.
	Dents	Slight dents may be raised by covering the area with damp blotting paper or paper tissues and pressing lightly with a warm iron. This will not work on wood veneers; in these cases use oil.
	Heat marks	Rub well with boiled linseed oil or a little turpentine. If mark persists dampen a soft cloth with oil of peppermint or spirits of camphor and rub. Polish up afterwards.
	Ink	Blot up immediately. Apply vinegar, leave for 2–3 minutes then wash off. If necessary bleach with ink eradicator or oxalic and (150 ml acid/ 200 ml warm water). Rinse well.
	Scratches	Apply wax polish or lightly sponge with methylated spirits or turpentine (for varnished surfaces) to soften the surface and therefore make the scratch disappear. Darken deep scratches with brown shoe or floor polish or apply wood stain then coat with varnish or wax polish.
	Water marks	If fresh rub vigorously with light oil. If it persists rub with a damp cloth dipped in ammonia or oil of peppermint. Rub dry and polish. For old stains, rub with metal polish or turpentine then repolish.
Sanitary fittings	Ring marks (hard water)	Sprinkle sponge with trisodium phosphate, Calgon or similar water softener. Rub then rinse well. For persistent stains fill fitting if possible with very hot water, add softener and leave until cool enough to scrub stain. Rinse well.

Table Continued

TABLE XXVIII. (*Continued*).

Surface	Stain	Methods of removal
	Green stains (copper pipes)	Rub carefully with abrasive pad and soap solution. If it persists, dip cloth into hot vinegar, sprinkle with salt and rub in. Rinse well. If it persists apply oxalic acid solution (150 ml/200 ml warm water). Rinse well.
	Rust stains	As for persistent green stains.
	Discoloration	Use sodium hypochlorite solution (150 ml/570 ml warm water). Do not use this solution if the fitting is cracked and made of cast iron as it will create rust. Alternatively apply a paste of cream of tartar and hydrogen peroxide, leave several hours then rinse well. Some soap detergent powders are also effective.
Ceramic tiles	Discoloration or rust	Dissolve one part sodium citrate crystals in six parts water then add an equal amount of glycerine and sufficient whiting to make a paste. Spread thickly over the stain and leave for about twelve hours. Wash and repeat if necessary.
	Discoloured grouting	Brush with sodium hypochlorite.
	Lime and soap scum	Scrub with a solution of vinegar and water (400 ml/4.5 litres). Rinse well.
Marble and terrazzo	Tea or coffee	Wipe with borax solution (150 ml/200 ml water). If stain persists wipe with a paste made from hydrogen peroxide and whiting. Rinse well.
	Scratches	Rub gently with fine sandpaper. Polish with jewellers' rouge or similar on a damp cloth, rub up then repolish.
	Ink	Apply equal quantities of methylated spirits and ammonia with a soft cloth. Leave for about six hours covered with plastic and repeat if necessary.

Table Continued

TABLE XXVIII. (*Continued*).

Surface	Stain	Methods of removal
	Ring marks	Scrub with mild abrasive detergent powder containing bleach. Rinse well.
Linoleum, etc.	Black marks	Sponge with paraffin, rinse and repolish.
	Heat marks	Apply a light oil and rub well.
	General staining	Rub lightly with fine steel wool then repolish.
	Tar	Soften with a solvent and lift off

Appendix II
Example Job Descriptions

Domestic Bursar   **(Managerial)**

Tenby Hall is a social welfare settlement which is involved in a variety of social work projects which benefit the community around it. These projects are run by organisers with paid assistants and volunteers. In addition, there are a number of elderly people living independently in sheltered housing in the complex. There is also a resident community of fifty, largely composed of young people who either work or study full time and have a commitment to voluntary social work in their spare time.

The Domestic Bursar will be required to supervise all aspects of the domestic efficiency of the settlement. This will include:

1. the appointment and supervision of the domestic staff who clean the various buildings in the complex; ordering and costing of cleaning materials, etc.;
2. the supervision of the laundry and soft furnishings and the maintenance of the stock in a reasonable condition;
3. the calculation and payment of wages for staff under his/her control;
4. calculation and collection of residents' payments for lodging;
5. the maintenance of a petty cash book and other paying-in books as may be required by the accountant.

Domestic Services Manager, Grade 1   **(Managerial)**

Area of function To participate in multidisciplinary type management in the following units which the appointment covers:

Aston Court Hospital
The Meadows Hospital
St Jude's Hospital
Undercliffe Grange
Willow Bank Hospital
Oakwood House
Mental Handicap Hostels

Accountable to Unit administrator.

Responsible for The maintenance of an acceptable standard of cleanliness throughout the units together with appropriate housekeeping services; welfare and administration of domestic and housekeeping staff at the above named units; maintenance of acceptable levels of personalised clothing and hospital linen.

Specific duties

1. Organisation of domestic and housekeeping services, drawing up of appropriate work schedules in consultation with senior nursing and other officers.
2. Monitoring of service contracts, arranged by area domestic manager in conjunction with area supplies, i.e. window cleaning, dispensers, machine maintenance, etc.
3. Liaison with unit administrator on agreed level of service.
4. Support of supervisory grades in the following functions.
   (*a*) Recruitment of staff within the financial establishment.
   (*b*) Organisation of in-service training, induction, supply of relevant up-to-date information, allocation of staff.
   (*c*) Maintenance of official records, staff details, wages information, lost labour due to absence, sickness, annual leave, as required by personnel and finance departments.
   (*d*) Control and issue of cleaning materials, equipment. Control and issue of sewing room materials, crockery and cutlery and personalised clothing where a housekeeping service is provided. Maintenance of records and issue of same. Ensuring secure and safe storage of same.
   (*e*) Frequent inspection of domestic machinery, dispensers, etc. Requisitioning of service to maintain machines and equipment in a safe and efficient condition. Maintenance of records of machinery.
   (*f*) Requisitioning of structural and fabric repairs in an interdisciplinary working relationship with planned maintenance, nursing officers and unit administrator.
   (*g*) Compiling of staff duty rotas, annual leave programmes, etc.
   (*h*) Issue of protective clothing, barrier creams, etc. to ensure the safety, health and welfare of staff.
   (*i*) Checking of facilities for staff, ensuring safe and hygienic environment within the unit.
5. Discussion of proposed policies and priorities with unit administrator.

Executive Housekeeper   (Managerial)
Purpose To manage the housekeeping department so that set standards and procedures are achieved and maintained.
Responsible to Manager
Subordinates directly supervised Assistant housekeeper, laundry supervisor, floor supervisors, public area cleaners.

Working in liaison with Food and beverage manager, front office manager, chief engineer, security officer, personnel manager, banqueting manager/supervisor, restaurant manager, head office specialists.

Main duties

1. To plan and organise the staffing and recording of all housekeeping activities.
2. To ensure house and room inspections are carried out.
3. To achieve and maintain group standards.
4. To organise regular departmental inventories.
5. To assist in the preparation of the annual budget and to control costs within the department.
6. To provide services for guests, i.e. laundry, lost property, first aid, etc.
7. To ensure security within the department is maintained.
8. To control the laundry operation.
9. To provide uniforms for all staff.
10. To roster staff according to work-load and to provide back-up documentation regarding the above.
11. To co-ordinate or carry out any training of new staff.
12. To fulfil any other duties as designated by the manager or his deputy.

Head Housekeeper   **(Managerial)**
(60 bedroom hotel)

Job title Head Housekeeper.

Responsible for Maids.

Responsible to General manager.

Place of work Accommodation block and public areas of the hotel.

Scope and general purpose of job To be responsible for the housekeeping operation of the hotel according to the guidelines and standards laid down in the Standards of Performance Manual.

Main duties

1. To arrive for work on time as dictated by the rota, dressed to the standard of uniform provided.
2. To compile weekly rotas for housekeeping, ensuring that all rooms are serviced according to the business forecast. Rotas to be approved by the general manager.
3. To compile time-sheets for housekeeping to be submitted to the general manager every Thursday for approval.
4. To liaise with reception with regard to the daily arrivals and departure list, weekly forecasts and any other special requirements.

5. To be aware of any current hotel, brand or company promotion and actively to encourage all others in your department to do the same.
6. To be aware of the company training policy and the use of Standards of Performance Manuals.
7. To be aware of the main provisions of the Fire Precautions Act 1971 and the action to take in the event of fire.
8. To be aware of the main provisions of the Health and Safety at Work Act 1974.
9. To recognise the importance of the customer comment forms and to know how to use them.
10. To be aware of the company's children's policy.
11. To report all maintenance defects within your department.
12. To be responsible for the daily cleaning of the ladies' powder room and public areas as directed by the general manager.
13. To be aware of the procedure to deal with lost property as laid down in the Standards of Performance Manual.
14. To ensure the correct receiving of soiled linen and issuing of clean linen to the maids as laid down in the Standards of Performance Manual.
15. To ensure the security of the linen room to minimise stock loss to the standard laid down in the Standards of Performance Manual.
16. To ensure all linen sent for laundering is accounted for.
17. To ensure the linen room is kept clean and tidy to the standard in the Standards of Performance Manual, ensuring all legal aspects are adhered to.
18. To service bedrooms daily to the standards laid down in the Standards of Performance Manual.
19. To ensure key security is adhered to at all times.
20. To be responsible for the requisitioning and issuing of all private bar stocks to maids on a daily basis.

Deputy Head Housekeeper   **(Managerial)**
(910 bedroom hotel)
Title Deputy Head Housekeeper.
Department Housekeeping.
Unit/Location Kimber Hotel.
Responsible to Head Housekeeper.
Purpose and scope of post Efficiently and economically to manage the department in the absence of the head housekeeper.
Duties and responsibilities
1. Aim to achieve satisfactory customer and staff relationships.

2. To have effective communications with the staff at all times.
3. To train the staff to the standard of work laid down in the training manual.
4. To be responsible for floors six to eight, the house porters and the front stair cleaner.
5. To check standards on these floors daily.
6. On the days the office assistant is off duty to run the office and deal with all work relevant to the day.
7. To have full knowledge of the computer and ensure all housekeepers are trained likewise.
8. To liaise with all departments relevant to housekeeping.
9. To ensure all master keys are kept under strict supervision.
10. To ensure all staff are dressed in correct uniform.
11. To have full knowledge of fire and evacuation procedures concerning the department.
12. To be conversant with all laundry and dry cleaning systems used.
13. To be conversant with the cloakrooms and duties of the cloakroom attendant.

Scope of authority
1. Payment of wages within stated scale.
2. Appointment of staff up to housekeeper level.
3. Transfer of staff up to housekeeper level.
4. Leave of absence up to two weeks.

Relationships (Titles and number of subordinates) 2 assistants, 8 floor housekeepers, 6 relief housekeepers, 70 resident maids, 20 non-resident maids, 4 part-time maids, 1 net curtain lady, 1 front stair cleaner, 4 house porters, 1 carpet cleaner, 1 floor cleaner, 5 cloakroom attendants, 8 evening maids, 1 linen porter.

Specialist departments to whom the job holder needs to relate to fulfil the purpose of the job Head housekeeper, personnel department, works department, front hall manager, reception, training department, security, annexe housekeeper, essential services.

Areas on which performance is judged because they are critical to the achievement of its purpose
1. Domestic standard and hygiene standards judged by guests' complaints and compliments and efforts made to ensure continuity of standards.
2. Communications, judged by seriousness and frequency in breakdown in communications.
3. Staff competence and morale, judged by observation of staff turnover, complaints, and staff evidence of team spirit.
4. Training of staff, judged by how effectively the staff operate.

5. Efficiency of department, judged by efforts made to anticipate business needs, efforts made to ensure sufficient staff attendance to meet the needs of the business and any innovations achieved which lead to more efficient working methods.

Domestic Supervisor   (Supervisory)

Job title Domestic Supervisor.
Responsible to Domestic services manager.
Role To control on a day-to-day basis a unit within the hospital, which may comprise either several wards, several departments, various residences or a cross-section of each.
Liaise with Unit nursing officer.
Responsibilities
1. *Domestic*
   (*a*) Visit all wards, departments or residences within the defined unit at least three times per day (twice for evening supervisors).
   (*b*) Ward sister, charge nurse or head of department to be informed of any changes in staffing, e.g. absences.
   (*c*) Check in person that work is being carried out satisfactorily and in accordance with work schedules.
   (*d*) Ensure that any specialised team is working according to planned programmes.
   (*e*) Check and record stores required weekly, issue clean dust control mops, mats, etc.
   (*f*) Check all electrical equipment, ensuring that it is cleaned regularly and is in good working order. Report any defects to works department and ensure that faulty equipment is taken out of use immediately.
   (*g*) Ensure that manual cleaning equipment is regularly cleaned and properly stored.
   (*h*) Physically check all window cleaning completed by contractors.
   (*i*) Deal with any cleaning task that may arise in an emergency and assist with the work as and when the necessity arises.
2. *Administrative*
   (*a*) Staff to be checked on duty and allocated to the required areas.
   (*b*) Complete check sheets in respect of work performed and submit these to domestic services manager weekly.
   (*c*) Observe and report on the need for repairs and maintenance to buildings, furniture and fittings.
   (*d*) Clerical duties as required, e.g. attendance book, stores changes, etc.

(e) All supervisors will report daily to domestic services manager for discussion on daily arrangements.

(f) A regular monthly meeting will be held with the domestic services manager to discuss general problems, changes in policy and procedures and any other business.

3. *Personnel*

(a) Induction of new staff into the department.

(b) Physical training of new and existing staff in all designated cleaning procedures and in the correct use of mechanical and manual equipment.

(c) Report any accidents to domestic services manager and ensure that an accident form is completed and sent to domestic services manager—this is a statutory requirement.

(d) Welfare of staff under control, solving on-the-job problems whenever possible and reporting any problems which cannot be handled adequately at the time.

(e) Take part in participative department groups in order to solve problems.

(f) Report to domestic services manager any complaints as to the standard of work or behaviour of any employee necessitating disciplinary action.

(g) Ensure the observance of safe working methods and routines and guard against and if necessary report any possible dangers, in the interests of both staff and the general public (Health and Safety at Work etc. Act 1974).

Assistant Housekeeper   **(Supervisory)**

Job title Assistant Housekeeper.

Department Housekeeping.

Responsible to Head housekeeper.

Responsible for Linen keeper, chambermaids, cleaner.

Place of work Accommodation and public areas (except banqueting suite).

Purpose of position To assist the head housekeeper in maintaining an efficient department and to deputise for her in her absence.

Detailed duties

1. To maintain a high standard of cleanliness in bedrooms by training the chambermaids, linen keeper and cleaner in room cleaning procedure and special departmental functions (according to the Standards of Performance Manual).

2. To assist the head housekeeper in maintaining a high level of staff discipline and morale.

3. To control issue of keys to maids and additionally to control

the issue of stores to the maids. To ensure that store areas are kept clean and tidy.

4. To supervise the linen keeper and/or assist as necessary, ensuring that systems for control are always adhered to.
5. To check the public areas to ensure no outstanding cleaning has been left unattended.
6. To carry out daily checks of all bedrooms to ensure the highest standard of guest comfort, hygiene and facilities and report any anomalies in the normal way to maintenance engineer.
7. To report as necessary any anomalies in room status to reception and assist the head housekeeper in fulfilling special guest requirements.
8. To be aware of all current company promotional literature, etc. and to ensure that the department adheres to policy decisions regarding the same, paying particular emphasis to "Bedroom Information Folders".
9. To report all accidents to the duty manager.
10. To record all lost property found in the hotel according to the departmental system.
11. To assist where necessary in the cleaning of the staff block with regard to corridors, public rooms, bathrooms, etc. and arrange for spring cleaning of vacant rooms for new staff arriving at the hotel.
12. To carry out under direction of head housekeeper the cleaning of all blankets/bedspreads/pillows/and other soft furnishings on a rota basis.
13. To service a section if the situation arises.
14. To recognise and comply with company policy with regard to health and safety and fire procedure.

Occasional duties

1. To assume total responsibility for the department in the absence of the head housekeeper and carry out items 2, 3, 4, 5, 9, 11, 14, 19, 22, 23, 24—Detailed Duties.
2. To carry out any reasonable request that may be made by management relating to the housekeeping department.

Floor Supervisor   **(Supervisory)**

Job title Floor Supervisor.

Purpose To ensure that all guest rooms and sundry areas for which she is responsible are maintained to company standard and to achieve maximum efficiency and guest satisfaction.

Responsible to Executive housekeeper.

Shifts 07.00–15.30
         08.00–16.30
         09.00–17.30

Subordinates directly supervised Maids working on her floor.
Working in liaison with Other supervisors, executive housekeeper, laundry supervisor, reception and maintenance staff.
Basic duties
1. Checking that all guest rooms and sundry areas are cleaned and maintained to company standards.
2. Making out housekeeping, reception and maintenance reports and liasing with these departments.
3. Daily work allocation.
4. Supervision of maids on own floor.
5. Supplying guest and cleaning supplies to own maids.
6. Carrying out and administering special requests for guests, e.g. irons, hairdryers, laundry and dry cleaning and generally assisting guests promptly and politely.
7. Checking rooms for VIP guests.
8. Maintaining security procedures with regard to keys, fire drill, etc.
9. General administration work.
10. Fulfilling any other duties as designated by the general manager or his deputy.
Additional duties
1. Cleaning rooms, when staff shortage.
2. Laundry work, if required.
3. Evening duty, if required.
4. Induction and training of new staff.
5. On-going training with existing staff.
6. Taking of regular meetings with own maids.
7. Stocktaking.
8. Stock control and purchasing.
9. Rotas.
10. Uniform, issue, control and inventories.

Head House Porter   **(Supervisory)**
(910 bedroom hotel)
Title Head House porter.
Department Housekeeping.
Unit/location Kimber Hotel.
Responsible to Head housekeeper.
Responsible for Four house porters.
Purpose and scope of post To collect and deliver all laundry and dry cleaning from guests' rooms, working on floors 1–8. To supervise the house porters' work and duties.
Duties and responsibilities
1. To collect and deliver all guests' laundry and dry cleaning.

2. To make sure ansaphone is functioning correctly so that guests' calls are recorded.
3. To supervise and help with all guest removals.
4. To supervise and help with taking of transformers, Z-beds, cots, bed boards, irons, ironing boards, hairdryers, etc. on request.
5. To change bed bases and mattresses on request.
6. Pressing of guests' clothes on the Hoffman presser on request.
7. Any light sewing that a guest may require.
8. To supervise cleaning of all shoe machines on floors 1–8.

Scope of authority
1. Granting of holidays in agreement with head housekeeper.
2. Making out weekly rotas.

Specialist departments to whom the job holder needs to relate to fulfil the purpose of the job Housekeeping, linen room, reception, works department.

Key areas
1. Laundry and dry cleaning.
2. Supply of specific items to guest on request.
3. Providing a pressing service.
4. Carrying out all removals.
5. Changing beds.

Room Maid   **(Unskilled)**
Hotel Queens.
Position Room Maid.
Purpose To clean the rooms to the company standard.
Responsible to Floor supervisor.
Duties
1. To report to housekeeper's office at 07.15, sign in (in uniform) and collect floor list and keys and bucket.
2. To clean bathrooms.
3. To strip, inspect and make beds.
4. To clean and polish furniture.
5. To clean bathroom fixtures and fittings.
6. To replenish all guest supplies.
7. To clean floors, walls and fittings.
8. To clean carpets, upholstery and soft furnishings.
9. To handle linen.
10. To report all maintenance requirements to floor housekeeper.
11. To replenish and tidy maids' trolley.
12. To mark and hand in all lost property to head housekeeper.
13. To hand in keys and list before leaving hotel.
14. To work with colleagues.
15. To know fire evacuation procedure.

Occasional duties To supply incidental requirements.

Evening Room Maid   (Unskilled)

Title Evening Room Maid.
Department Housekeeping.
Unit/location Kimber Hotel.
Responsible to Head housekeeper.
Responsible for —
Purpose of post To service guest rooms in the evening working on floors 1–8.
Duties and responsibilities
1. To carry out late departures as instructed by the housekeeper.
2. To service rooms that require a late service.
3. To service all let suites and turn down beds.
4. To clean sitting rooms.
5. To turn down guest rooms as requested by housekeeper.
6. To give guests any additional item they may require for their room.
7. If allocated a bleep, to take all messages and act on them.
8. To clean marble on the floor as requested by housekeeper.
9. To clean front stair areas as requested by housekeeper.
Scope of authority No authority; no limitations.
Subordinates None.
Specialist departments to whom job holder needs to relate Housekeeping.
Key areas
1. Cleanliness of departure rooms.
2. Cleanliness of let rooms.
3. Cleanliness of suites.

Linen Maid/Linen Porter   (Unskilled)

Position Linen Maid/Linen Porter.
Purpose. To provide clean, well-laundered linen and uniforms.
Responsible to Head linen keeper.
Duties
1. Receiving, sorting and checking clean and dirty linen.
2. Washing and drying of all linen, uniforms and other items according to established procedures.
3. Folding of all laundered items according to hotel standards and design.
4. Delivery to and stacking of adequate quantities of linen in linen storage areas.
5. Maintaining the cleanliness of laundry area and equipment.
6. Reporting of maintenance defects and sub-standard linen to linen keeper.
7. Handling and issue of staff and guest laundry and uniforms, according to procedure.

8. Maintaining personal hygiene and appearance.
9. Mending and sewing.
10. Relieving and assisting on floors if needed.

Public Area Cleaner   (Unskilled)

Job title Public Area Cleaner (1) 07.00–15.30.
Purpose To clean and maintain all designated areas to group standards.
Responsible to Executive housekeeper.
Subordinates None.
Working in liaison with Housekeeping.
Main duties

1. To clean back office and reception areas (before 08.30).
2. To clean ladies' and gents' saunas and areas outside each.
3. To clean all areas of pool, e.g. gym and tonic, chairs, walls/ledges, floor, gulleys and tracks.
4. To clean female staff toilets/changing room and housekeeping area on four days per week.
5. To clean both fire stairs one day per week.
6. To deal with deliveries and goods as required.
7. To be security conscious.
8. Prompt reporting of lost and found property to housekeeper or duty manager.
9. To maintain personal hygiene and neat appearance.
10. To carry out special job assignments on request of housekeeper in charge.
11. To be friendly and helpful to guests.
12. To fulfil any other duties as designated by the manager or his deputy.

Appendix III
Case Studies

MACHINE FAILURE

One Friday morning Mr Medway was buffing his section of corridor in the teaching block of St Matthews Training Centre for the Physically Handicapped, when he noticed a friend of his just about to leave the building. He stopped what he was doing and called to his friend. Being of a curious nature, Mr Medway went to ask him why he was leaving so early and after a very long and involved explanation, he returned to his machine to find that it would not start. (It had been temperamental of late.) After several unsuccessful attempts to restart it he went to check that the plug was still in its socket. (There was a shortage of sockets along his corridor and this one was round a corner.) He discovered that the plug was in its socket but that the wires had come free from the plug.

At that moment he noticed that further along the corridor one of the students was entering the tutorial room and he concluded that her wheelchair had run over the flex causing it to pull away from the plug.

Mr Medway completed his work with the scissor mop and took the machine back to his cupboard promising himself he would fix the plug next week.

The next week, however, Mr Medway was transferred to the residential wing and Miss Cox, one of the part-time cleaners employed at holiday times, took over the care of this corridor. Miss Cox did not like using the big polishing machine and so instead she proceeded to use the scissor mop along the tutorial room corridors.

When Mrs West, the senior training instructor, returned from her two-week vacation she noted immediately that there was a drop in the standard of cleaning in the tutorial room section of the building, and brought the matter to the attention of the cleaning supervisor at the staff meeting that week.

Suggested discussion topics
1. How many things did Mr Medway do wrong?
2. How could this incident have been avoided?

3. What special considerations should be given to a school like this with regard to its cleaning and maintenance?

4. What type of flooring and related machinery would you choose for such a building?

SOFT FURNISHINGS

The Radbury Infirmary is a 500-bed general hospital in the Midlands. The domestic services manager is responsible for maintaining the twelve-year-old main block and the thirty-year-old, fifty-bed nurses home which also houses a lecture block.

During the past year the domestic department has had to cope with several periods of industrial action, resulting in the temporary closure of the laundry on three occasions. On two of these occasions hospital bed linen was sent to the local commercial laundry and domestic staff were asked to wash their own uniforms, but the regular washing programme for soft furnishings in the nurses' home was delayed by six months. It was decided that use of a commercial laundry for such items was too costly and so the cleaning supervisor at the nurses' home delegated two of her staff to the washing of the nurses' home curtains (cotton) and those from the offices in the main block (nets). The equipment used consisted of two domestic automatic washers, two domestic tumble driers and two ironing boards, with the result that the task took five days to complete.

The first batch were very acceptable but those processed in the last two days were most unsatisfactory. These happened to be office curtains and were returned to the main block looking rather creased and having shrunk slightly. The office staff had to manage but the set from the boardroom had to be replaced.

Suggested discussion topics

1. What fabric would you replace the boardroom curtains with?
2. What might have caused the creasing and shrinking?
3. Who was to blame for the mishap?
4. How could it have been avoided?
5. What procedure should be adopted for the maintenance of such curtains?
6. Would it be feasible to install an OPL (own premises laundry) as a result of this situation?
7. What equipment would you install if an OPL was installed in the nurses' home?
8. What problems do you think this type of hospital might have with regard to the normal provision and maintenance of soft furnishing, if any?

CONTROL OF LINEN

On Monday 7th May, Mrs Freeman began working at the Devonshire Hotel as executive housekeeper. This five-star hotel has been in existence for eighty years and with its 150 bedroom/bathrooms attempts to offer its guests a high standard of service. This is very costly in labour and so strict control must be kept on all items of expenditure over and above that of labour.

On taking up her post Mrs Freeman had been informed that Mr Clarke, a representative from the Clean Quick Laundry, wished to speak to the person in charge of linen, regarding the loss of a considerable number of items in recent months. The hotel hires all its linen from this laundry and has received what appears to be good service over the last three years.

Mrs Freeman contacted Mr Clarke and made an appointment to see him on Monday 14th May at 10.00 a.m. Meanwhile she felt it necessary to speak to certain members of her staff about the matter.

On May 14th Mr Clarke arrived. He was pleased to meet Mrs Freeman and hoped she would remain with the hotel longer than her two predecessors who had left during the past year. He expressed his concern over the way in which the hotel was making it increasingly difficult for the laundry to keep to the terms of the contract. In broad terms this was:

"to provide each week a maximum of 650 clean white cotton sheets, 650 hand towels, 650 face cloths, 50 bath robes, 1,300 pillowslips, 100 cotton damask table cloths, 100 red cotton damask slip cloths, and a supply of waiters' cloths, kitchen linen and uniforms as specified, all in good condition and for the price quoted. They would also undertake to replace worn or damaged items ...."

Mr Clarke explained that the laundry were having difficulty in keeping within the price quoted, owing to the extra work which had to go into the cleaning of many of the items they received and because they had had to replace many items which had been mislaid.

Mr Clarke then presented Mrs Freeman with a list of particular areas of complaint:

(*a*) sheets torn at the hem edges;
(*b*) tablecloths with mildew stains;
(*c*) tea towels with scorch marks or holes;
(*d*) chef uniforms disappearing;
(*e*) the necessity constantly to replace face cloths.

Mrs Freeman showed concern at these facts and said she had already instigated some new linen control procedures which should reduce the loss of linen. She suggested that they meet again in one month to discuss any improvement and possibly any alteration in procedures which could be adopted to improve standards of cleanliness.

Mr Clarke agreed to this and suggested Mrs Freeman visit the laundry to see the work that goes on there. This arrangement was agreed and they parted after a meeting of forty-five minutes.

Suggested discussion topics

1. Which staff should Mrs Freeman speak to prior to Mr Clarke's visit?

2. What information would Mrs Freeman need to have before meeting Mr Clarke?

3. Was there sufficient or too much linen being supplied by the laundry?

4. What specification would you draw up for the laundry to be used by a hotel such as this?

5. What kind of extra work do you think the laundry had to carry out?

6. Suggest causes of the specific complaints.

7. What system of control do you think might have been in existence in this hotel prior to Mrs Freeman's arrival?

8. What measures should Mrs Freeman adopt to improve standards?

SECURITY

At a meeting between the domestic bursar and the three student wardens of Hilton Hall of Residence the following points were discussed:

(a) the increase in the number of thefts from student bedrooms;

(b) regular sightings of a "peeping tom";

(c) the use of fire exits as thoroughfares.

Suggested discussion topics

1. What measures should be taken to reduce thieving from student bedrooms?

2. How would you prevent the entry of unwelcome guests and intruders?

3. How would you cope with the security problem imposed by the misuse of fire doors?

HOSPITAL FLOORING

Storham Hospital has 500 beds for both long and short-term psychiatric patients. Whenever possible patients are allowed to walk around the hospital usually in their own clothes and in slippers. The hospital was built just after the Second World War and stands on a hillside two kilometres from the local town centre.

Like many hospitals it has many corridors leading to wards of up to thirty beds and also to the various subsidiary areas of the hospital—occupational and physiotherapy rooms, a chapel, canteens, offices, consultants' rooms, etc. In this hospital there is one main corridor on three storeys, with the wards leading off from it. It runs down a gradual slope of approximately 18°.

Recently, one of the many voluntary organisations associated with Storham Hospital managed to open up a bar for patients in what used to be a small dining room for visiting doctors and consultants. This room has a wood block floor which when sealed and polished formed a very attractive surface.

Mrs Fenton was the domestic assistant assigned to spray clean the floor in the bar once a week; for the remainder of the week, the volunteers maintained it by sweeping and mopping. However, as might be expected the floor area around the bar counter soon became marked and scratched and so Mrs Fenton applied polish twice a week instead of only once.

Six weeks after its opening a patient slipped and fell in the bar damaging his ankle. The accident had occurred as the patient entered the bar and so there was no evidence to suggest he was under the influence of alcohol. It was not until this incident that Miss Craven the domestic services manager became aware of the condition of the bar floor, as her monthly maintenance check was due to occur during the following week—slightly later than scheduled as she had been coping with the result of industrial action in her department. On inspecting the bar floor, Miss Craven was surprised at how slippery it was. She was always very careful to use non-slip products and procedures, knowing that patients in slippers could easily fall, especially on the main sloping corridor.

She spoke to Miss Green, the supervisor in charge of the bar, shop and main corridor, Mrs Fenton and Mrs Worsethorne, representing the voluntary organisation running the bar.

It transpired that Miss Green was aware that Mrs Fenton was using more polish than expected but as this was the only wooden floor in the hospital, she assumed it must need more polish than was first anticipated. Mrs Fenton explained her reasons for spray cleaning twice a week and Mrs Worsethorne described how her assistants gave the floor a "good scrub" every day with a disinfectant, after sweeping. Miss Craven returned to her office with Miss Green to discuss the situation. She then visited the injured patient.

Suggested discussion topics

1. What extra precautions if any should a cleaning supervisor take in a hospital like this where patients are walking around corridors?

2. What special cleaning problems, if any, is the age of this hospital likely to create?

3. What floor surface would you suggest for the main corridor?

4. What is the correct procedure for the renovation of a wood block floor such as this and what type of cleaning agent and equipment would you use?

5. Was the cleaning routine adequate and correct?

6. Do you think the arrangement of the cleaning routine was satisfactory?

7. What causes floor damage in a bar area such as this? How can it be reduced?

8. How had this particular situation arisen and who was to blame?

9. How would you improve the situation and ensure the accident is not repeated?

10. What implications would there have been if Mrs Fenton had slipped and fallen?

11. How would you cope with any possible criticism from nursing staff over what happened?

12. What type of floor would you consider appropriate for this area if money had been found to build a new bar?

A MAINTENANCE PROBLEM

Oakam Hall is a hostel built specially for foreign students visiting England from underdeveloped countries to attend courses on forward planning and management. Many of these students are mature, some have families and they come from parts of the world where the climate is much warmer than that in England. The hall has forty rooms with private bathrooms, ten shared kitchen/utility/leisure areas, and ten small flats (bedroom, bathroom, living room, kitchen). The students, who are sponsored by their own governments, pay £36 per week for a room and £50 for a flat. Meals are included on both rates as well as the cost of electricity, heat, television rental and bedding. The bed linen is also supplied and laundered.

At the end of the academic year the domestic bursar had one month in which to thoroughly clean the Hall and its soft furnishings, etc. before the start of a week-long conference. She also took the opportunity to make a thorough inspection of the building as the University were planning to build another such Hall and wished to have her opinion on the way in which Oakam Hall had withstood the general wear and tear of a year's occupation so that any structural problems could be eradicated during the design stage. The following points were noted.

(*a*) Discoloration of white emulsioned walls around window frames.

(*b*) The white emulsioned corridor walls were badly scuffed and the plaster had chipped in several places.

(*c*) Cleaners' cupboards had had to be used for the storage of trunks and cases with the result that kitchen areas were used for storing cleaners' equipment.

(*d*) Electric sockets were inconveniently positioned for cleaners using electric equipment in corridors.

(*e*) With no lift, staff found it tiring having to carry linen and equipment up and down staircases.

(*f*) There was a rather strong, musty smell pervading the building.

Suggested discussion topics

1. Do you consider the accommodation adequate for such students?

2. What equipment and furnishings would you provide in each area?

3. What colour scheme would you choose for each area?

4. What type of bedding would you provide and why?

5. Would it be practical to provide a laundry to give these mature students greater independence?

6. What proportion of the room/flat charge would go towards cleaning and maintenance?

7. Suggest suitable staffing and compile a rota for them.

8. Suggest possible reasons and remedies for the points noted by the domestic bursar.

9. What equipment would be needed by cleaning staff?

Index